TEACH ALL, REACH ALL

Instructional
Design & Delivery
With TGIF

SUSAN L. MULKEY & *KAREN A. KEMP*

Published in the United States by
Pacific Northwest Publishing
2451 Willamette St.
Eugene, Oregon 97405
www.pacificnwpublish.com

12 11 10 09   5 4 3 2 1

ISBN: 978-1-59909-029-0

Cover and book design: Hannah Bontrager
Illustrations: Tom Zillis
Editors: Natalie Conaway and Sara Ferris

Much of the material in this book was originally published in 1995 as *TGIF: But What Will I Do on Monday?* This version has been revised and updated.

ABOUT THE AUTHORS

SUSAN L. MULKEY

Susan L. Mulkey is an author and trainer in social skills, behavior management, effective instructional practices, reading strategies, classroom coaching, and collaborative teaching. Susan has more than 30 years of experience across several educational settings, including elementary, middle school, and high school. She conducts over 50 workshops and staff development sessions each year in Utah and across the United States. She spent six years conducting training for the Department of Defense schools in Germany, Japan, and Korea. She is a former project coordinator for a statewide staff development center, university instructor, consulting teacher, and special/general education teacher. She continues to consult independently for schools and school teams participating in Positive Behavior Supports. She is currently involved in a variety of classroom coaching activities and demonstration teaching related to the use of effective instructional strategies, pre-referral interventions related to RTI, schoolwide social skills, and behavior management. Susan has co-authored *TGIF: But What Will I Do on Monday?*; *TGIF: Making It Work on Monday*; *Cool Kids: A Proactive Approach to Social Responsibility*; *One-Minute Skill Builder*; *TRIP: Translating Research Into Practice*; *Working Together: Tools for Collaborative Teaching*; and a video, *Working Together: What Collaborative Teaching Can Look Like*.

KAREN A. KEMP

Karen Kemp is a 30-year public school teaching veteran who has held a number of leadership and administrative positions, including director of special education, assistant principal, pupil services coordinator, adjunct faculty, program specialist, and, of course, classroom teacher. She has authored and co-authored more than 30 publications, including the books *Cool Kids: A Proactive Approach to Social Responsibility*; *RTI: The Classroom Connection for Literacy*; *RTI & Math: The Classroom Connection*; *One-Minute Skill Builder*; *TRIP: Translating Research Into Practice*; and the DVDs *RTI Tackles the LD Explosion* and *RTI Tackles Reading*. Karen has presented workshops and professional development seminars in the United States and Europe. Karen is currently Director of Special Programs in Cohoes City Schools in New York. Her areas of expertise include instructional support teams, Response to Intervention, Positive Behavior Supports/social responsibility, reading strategies, effective instruction for inclusive classrooms, and progress monitoring techniques.

ACKNOWLEDGMENTS

We want to thank the many people who have helped bring this book into being. We are convinced that no book or important piece of work is ever the result of the efforts of just one person. This product reflects not only our own experiences in teaching, but contributions from many of the expert teachers, just like you, who are making efforts to improve the quality of classroom instruction for all students. We are especially grateful to our own children—Erica Bruen, Corey Kemp, and Curtis Kemp—for their ideas and support while continuing to teach us about the important things in life. We also wish to thank Duane Webb, and also Stuart Horsfall and Ray Beck for introducing us to a range of opportunities.

We dedicate this book to all the students who have improved our teaching and the voices of wisdom who have whispered to us along the way. Some of those voices include:

Janet Freston
Box Elder School District
Brigham City, UT

Cyrus Freston
Honeyville, UT

Anita DeBoer
Salt Lake City, UT

Denise Conrad
Great Falls Public Schools
Great Falls, MT

Candy Barela
Santa Ana Unified School District
Santa Ana, CA

Carol Massanari
Mountain Plains Regional Resource Center
Logan, UT

Tricia Wells
Longmont, CO

Carol Hvidston
Sweetwater County School District
Rock Springs, WY

Thomas Lovitt
University of Washington
Seattle, WA

Siegfried Engelmann
Engelmann-Becker Corporation
Eugene, OR

Michael Maloney
Quinte Learning Center
Bellville, Ontario, Canada

Randy Sprick
Educational Consultant
Eugene, OR

We would also like to acknowledge the late Ogden Lindsley and Ken Reavis.

TESTIMONIALS

"Our teachers follow the TGIF model to plan effective, engaging instruction for students and love the easy-to-remember TGIF as it guides their instruction daily. The easy-to-use materials help teachers find an intervention to support students academically or behaviorally, and the ready-made materials can be used immediately. TGIF is a fantastic tool for the experienced as well as novice teacher. It is the must-have handbook for every teacher's personal professional library!"

—Jan Whimpey, Principal, Syracuse Arts Academy
Charter School, Syracuse, UT

"All educators would likely agree that 'teaching is easy if you don't know how, but it is very difficult if you do.' This book takes the mystery out of teaching and fills in the science so that teachers get the result they need to enjoy their profession. As a former university professor and experienced educator, I would have loved to have had this book available to assist in my efforts to help both novice and experienced teachers build their toolkit as they learned the skills and strategies to become effective, competent teachers. This book is chock-full of easy-to-use, proven strategies as well as several that take a little more effort but may produce significantly better results. All educators need this information to guide their lesson design and delivery. It makes the difference between struggling with and enjoying teaching because educators have the confidence of 'doing it right' and getting the results teachers and students need and deserve from their efforts."

—Anita DeBoer, author, teacher trainer,
and independent consultant, Salt Lake City, UT

"*Teach All, Reach All* is an excellent resource to help you get the most out of Tier 1 core instruction. It provides an array of effective strategies to differentiate each essential component of lesson design and delivery. The strategies can be used quickly and easily in any learning environment. Our building intervention teams and co-teaching teams successfully use this resource to assist in designing lessons that meet the needs of all learners. This is an excellent resource for all educators."

—Carol Ness Hvidston, Director of Special Services,
Sweetwater County School District #1, Rock Springs, WY

QUESTIONS AT A GLANCE

T • Teacher-Directed Instruction

WHAT CAN I DO ABOUT THE STUDENTS WHO . . .

T1	do not achieve the classroom goals and objectives?
T2	do not respond to my instructions?
T3	do not participate during my instruction?
T4	disrupt during my instruction?
T5	forget information that I presented yesterday, or a few hours ago?
T6	fail to see the relevance of my instruction?
T7	following my instruction, do not understand or misgeneralize the concept?
T8	do not volunteer during my instruction?
T9	make hesitant responses or frequent errors during my instruction?
T10	have difficulty taking notes during my instruction?
T11	have a difficult time determining the critical information from my instruction?
T12	do not respond to my questions?

G • Guided Practice Activities
WHAT CAN I DO ABOUT THE STUDENTS WHO . . .

G1	do not begin or complete practice/seatwork activities?
G2	make careless errors when completing practice/seatwork activities?
G3	do not comprehend and/or respond to written material during practice/seatwork activities?
G4	do not work cooperatively, or rely on others to do the practice/seatwork activities?
G5	do not contribute to class discussions during practice activities?

I • Independent Practice Activities
WHAT CAN I DO ABOUT THE STUDENTS WHO . . .

I1	do not organize or manage assignments, materials, and/or time?
I2	do not complete or submit assignments?
I3	do not understand the independent assignment?
I4	do not check work for accuracy and/or completeness?
I5	do not know how to prepare for and/or study for a test?

F • Final Measurement
WHAT CAN I DO ABOUT THE STUDENTS WHO . . .

F1	do not perform well with traditional test formats?
F2	do not use strategies for taking a test?
F3	do not monitor work performance?
F4	do not respond to traditional grading procedures?

TABLE OF CONTENTS

About the Authors i
Acknowledgments ii
Testimonials iii
Questions at a Glance iv

Introduction 1

What Is This Book About? 1
Why a Book on Instructional Interventions? 2
Who Can Use This Book? 3
What Is TGIF? 4
How Can I Use This Book? 6
How Long Should I Spend on Each Component of TGIF? 7
What Are Some Assumptions Underlying TGIF? 8
How Can I Design Instruction According to TGIF? 8
Instructional Organizer (Sample) 10
Instructional Organizer (Blank) 15

Lesson Delivery 21

What is Lesson Delivery? 22
    Active Student Response/Participation 22
    Correcting Student Errors/Appropriate Feedback 24
Strategies to Enhance Lesson Delivery 25
    Six Steps to Increase Opportunities to Respond 26
    Affirming/Echoing Individual Responses 26
    The "Get Ready" Cue 27
    Correcting an Incorrect Answer 28
    Think-Ink-Link-Ink 29
    Effective Acknowledgment/Descriptive Praise 30
    Three-Minute Timed Review 31

Teacher-Directed Instruction 33

T1: What can I do about the students who do not achieve the classroom goals and objectives? 34

Prep Time	Number	Technique	Page	Forms on CD?	Grade Levels	Intervention Type
⚡	T1.1	Essential Questions	34		**K–8**	Academic—All
	T1.2	Condition Shift	35		**K–8**	
	T1.3	Proficiency Shift	35		**K–8**	
	T1.4	Product Shift	36		**K–8**	
	T1.5	Ticket Out the Door	36		**K–8**	Academic—All; Behavior—Motivation
🕐	T1.6	What Will I Do? Log	38	📄	**3–8**	Academic—All
	T1.7	Minimal/Advanced Competencies	39	📄	**4–8**	

T2: What can I do about the students who do not respond to my instructions? 40

Prep Time	Number	Technique	Page	Forms on CD?	Grade Levels	Intervention Type
⚡	T2.1	Get Ready	40		**K–8**	Academic—All; Behavior—Motivation
	T2.2	Listening Cues	41		**K–6**	
	T2.3	You-Me Game	41		**K–6**	
	T2.4	I Can Say It	41		**K–8**	
🕐	T2.5	Following Instructions	42	📄	**K–8**	
	T2.6	Buddy Nose (Knows)	43	📄	**K–6**	
	T2.7	Behavior Bingo	43		**3–8**	
	T2.8	Yes/No Game	44		**3–8**	
	T2.9	Tracking Directions	44	📄	**3–8**	

T3: What can I do about the students who do not participate during my instruction? 46

Prep Time	Number	Technique	Page	Forms on CD?	Grade Levels	Intervention Type
⚡	T3.1	Participation Board	46		**K–8**	Behavior—Motivation
	T3.2	Participation Buddies	47	📄	**K–8**	
🕐	T3.3	Participation Jigsaw	48		**K–8**	
	T3.4	Wild Card Spinner	48		**K–8**	
	T3.5	Participation Dots	49	📄	**K–6**	
	T3.6	Mystery Motivators	50		**K–8**	
	T3.7	Participation Points	50	📄	**3–8**	

T4: What can I do about the students who disrupt during my instruction? 52

Prep Time	Number	Technique	Page	Forms on CD?	Grade Levels	Intervention Type
⚡	T4.1	Everybody Say	52		**K–8**	Academic—All
	T4.2	Frequent Questions	53		**K–8**	
	T4.3	On-Task Chart	53	📄	**3–8**	Behavior—Motivation
	T4.4	Name's Up Listening Board	54		**K–6**	
🕐	T4.5	Following Instructions	54		**K–8**	Behavior—Social
	T4.6	Keeping the Numbers Low	55		**K–8**	Behavior—Motivation
	T4.7	Getting the Teacher's Attention	55	📄	**K–8**	Behavior—Social
	T4.8	Responsibility Roles	56	📄	**K–8**	
	T4.9	Countoon	57	📄	**K–8**	Behavior—Motivation

Icons

 = Little preparation time

 = Reproducible Form on CD

🕐 = More preparation (time and/or materials)

T5: What can I do about the students who forget information that I presented yesterday, or a few hours ago? 58

Prep Time	Number	Technique	Page	Forms on CD?	Grade Levels	Intervention Type
	T5.1	Highlighting	58		**4–8**	
	T5.2	Recycling	59		**K–8**	
	T5.3	Mnemonics	59		**K–8**	
	T5.4	Note Stacks	60		**3–8**	Academic—All
	T5.5	Memory Log	61		**3–8**	
	T5.6	Study Guides (Standard)	62		**4–8**	
	T5.7	Graphic Organizers (Top Down)	63		**K–8**	

T6: What can I do about the students who fail to see the relevance of my instruction? 64

Prep Time	Number	Technique	Page	Forms on CD?	Grade Levels	Intervention Type
	T6.1	Rationale Questions	64		**K–8**	
	T6.2	Think and Say Why	64		**K–8**	
	T6.3	Share Your Reasons	65		**K–8**	Academic—All
	T6.4	What, Where/When, and Why Strategy	65		**4–8**	
	T6.5	Futures Map	67		**4–8**	

T7: What can I do about the students who, following my instruction, do not understand or misgeneralize the concept? . . . 68

Prep Time	Number	Technique	Page	Forms on CD?	Grade Levels	Intervention Type
	T7.1	Positive and Negative Examples	68		**K–8**	Academic—All
	T7.2	Strategies and Rules	71		**K–8**	
	T7.3	Corrective Feedback	72		**K–8**	Behavior—Social
	T7.4	Concept Angles	73		**K–8**	
	T7.5	Plus, Minus, Interesting (PMI)	73		**K–8**	
	T7.6	I Question That!	74		**3–8**	
	T7.7	Know/Want to Know/Learned (KWL)	74		**K–8**	
	T7.8	Learning Logs	75		**3–8**	Academic—All
	T7.9	Study Guides (Margins)	76		**3–8**	
	T7.10	Graphic Organizers (Sequence)	77		**3–8**	
	T7.11	Attribute Maps	78		**3–8**	

T8: What can I do about the students who do not volunteer during my instruction? 80

Prep Time	Number	Technique	Page	Forms on CD?	Grade Levels	Intervention Type
⚡	T8.1	Group/Individual Questioning	80		K–8	
	T8.2	Responses Without Talking	80		K–8	
	T8.3	I Am Ready	81		K–8	
	T8.4	Please Come Back	81		K–8	
	T8.5	Name's Up Volunteer Board	81		K–6	Academic—All
🕐	T8.6	Heads Together	82		K–8	
	T8.7	Folded Corners	83		K–8	
	T8.8	Draw-a-Name	83		K–8	

T9: What can I do about the students who make hesitant responses or frequent errors during my instruction? 84

Prep Time	Number	Technique	Page	Forms on CD?	Grade Levels	Intervention Type
⚡	T9.1	Think About That	84		K–8	
	T9.2	All Talk Together	84		K–8	
	T9.3	Think, Pair, Share	85		K–8	
	T9.4	Formulate, Share, Listen, Create	85		3–8	
	T9.5	Prompts	85		K–8	Academic—All
	T9.6	Prequestioning	86		K–8	
	T9.7	Please Come Back	86		K–8	
	T9.8	Rapid-Fire Questions	86		K–8	
	T9.9	Think and Say Ideas	87		K–8	
🕐	T9.10	Up the Numbers	87		K–8	Behavior—Motivation
	T9.11	Corrective Feedback	87		K–8	Behavior—Social
	T9.12	Question Challenge	88		K–8	

T10: What can I do about the students who have difficulty taking notes during my instruction? 90

Prep Time	Number	Technique	Page	Forms on CD?	Grade Levels	Intervention Type
	T10.1	Buddy Notes	90		**4–8**	
	T10.2	Four-Fold	90		**4–8**	
	T10.3	Index Cards	91		**4–8**	
	T10.4	Slotted Outline	92		**3–8**	
	T10.5	LITES	92		**4–8**	Academic—All
	T10.6	Note Checks	93		**4–8**	
	T10.7	Cooperative Notes	94		**4–8**	
	T10.8	Graphic Organizers (Partial)	95		**K–8**	

T11: What can I do about the students who have a difficult time determining the critical information from my instruction? . . . 96

Prep Time	Number	Technique	Page	Forms on CD?	Grade Levels	Intervention Type
	T11.1	Defend Your Position	96		**3–8**	
	T11.2	Five-Minute Reviews	97		**3–8**	
	T11.3	Advance Organizers	97		**3–8**	Academic—All
	T11.4	Think and Write Questions	98		**4–8**	
	T11.5	Presentation Cues	99		**4–8**	

T12: What can I do about the students who do not respond to my questions? 100

Prep Time	Number	Technique	Page	Forms on CD?	Grade Levels	Intervention Type
	T12.1	Ask, Pause, Call	100		**K–8**	
	T12.2	Restate	101		**K–8**	
	T12.3	Pass for Now	101		**K–8**	
	T12.4	Consult	101		**3–8**	
	T12.5	All Together	102		**K–8**	Academic—All
	T12.6	No Surprises	102		**3–8**	
	T12.7	Answer, Pair, Spotlight	103		**K–8**	
	T12.8	Clarification	103		**K–8**	Behavior—Social
	T12.9	Draw-a-Name	104		**K–8**	Academic—All
	T12.10	Counting Responses	104		**K–8**	Behavior—Motivation

Guided Practice Activities 105

G1: What can I do about the students who do not begin or complete practice/seatwork activities? 106

Prep Time	Number	Technique	Page	Forms on CD?	Grade Levels	Intervention Type
⚡	G1.1	Effective Praise/Acknowledgment	106		K–8	Behavior—Social
	G1.2	Think Out Loud	107		K–8	Academic—All
	G1.3	Rationale Statements	107		K–8	
	G1.4	Alternating Buddies	108		3–8	
	G1.5	Strategic Skills	108		3–8	
	G1.6	Beat the Clock	108		K–8	Behavior—Motivation
	G1.7	Assignment Questions	109		4–8	Academic—All
	G1.8	Star Stickers	109		K–6	Academic—All Behavior—Motivation
	G1.9	Cut-Up	110		K–6	
	G1.10	Colored Pencils	110		3–8	
🕐	G1.11	Split the Assignment	111		3–8	Behavior—Motivation
	G1.12	Change the Channel	111		K–8	Academic—All
	G1.13	Slice Back	112		K–8	
	G1.14	Behavior Bingo	112		K–8	Behavior—Motivation
	G1.15	Design Your Own Assignment	113	📄	4–8	Academic—All
	G1.16	Assignment Aims	113	📄	3–8	Behavior—Motivation
	G1.17	Completion Dots	114		K–8	
	G1.18	Ask for Help	114	📄	K–8	Behavior—Social
	G1.19	Start/Stop Time	115		K–8	Behavior—Motivation
	G1.20	Monitoring Seatwork	116	📄	K–8	

G2: What can I do about the students who make careless errors when completing practice/seatwork activities?   118

Prep Time	Number	Technique	Page	Forms on CD?	Grade Levels	Intervention Type
⚡	G2.1	Color Coding	118		K–8	Academic—Reading
	G2.2	Oral Reading Points	118	📄	K–8	
🕐	G2.3	Stop and Switch	119		3–8	Academic—Reading, Math
	G2.4	Self-Check and Count	120	📄	3–8	Academic, Behavior—Motivation
	G2.5	Magic Pens	121		K–8	

G3: What can I do about the students who do not comprehend and/or respond to written material during practice/seatwork activities? 122

Prep Time	Number	Technique	Page	Forms on CD?	Grade Levels	Intervention Type
	G3.1	Change the Channel	122		**K–8**	
	G3.2	Page Numbers	123		**3–8**	
	G3.3	Questions First	123		**3–8**	
	G3.4	Question/Instruction Repeat	123		**K–8**	
	G3.5	Listen, Write, Listen, Say	124		**3–8**	Academic—All
	G3.6	Key Words	124		**3–8**	
	G3.7	I Am Ready to Find Out	126	✓	**4–8**	
	G3.8	What Is the Main Idea?	126		**K–8**	
	G3.9	Mark and Say Main Idea	127		**4–8**	
	G3.10	Answer Experts	127	✓	**4–8**	
	G3.11	Add It Up	128	✓	**3–8**	Academic—ELA
	G3.12	Step-by-Step	128	✓	**3–8**	
	G3.13	Overlapping Circles	129	✓	**3–8**	
	G3.14	Cause/Effect	129	✓	**3–8**	
	G3.15	Star Book Report	130	✓	**3–8**	
	G3.16	Herringbone	130	✓	**3–8**	
	G3.17	Comprehension Wheels	131	✓	**3–8**	
	G3.18	Story Charts	132	✓	**3–8**	
	G3.19	Know/Do Not Know	132	✓	**3–8**	
	G3.20	Comprehension Outlines	133	✓	**K–8**	Academic—All
	G3.21	Practice Sheets/Cards	133	✓	**K–8**	
	G3.22	Stop and Think	135	✓	**4–8**	
	G3.23	Students Ask Questions	135	✓	**4–8**	
	G3.24	Study Guides (Prompts)	136		**4–8**	
	G3.25	Graphic Organizers	137		**3–8**	
	G3.26	SR.I.SRV (Scanning)	138	✓	**4–8**	
	G3.27	SQ3R Worksheets	139	✓	**4–8**	

G4: What can I do about the students who do not work cooperatively, or rely on others to do the practice/seatwork activities? 140

Prep Time	Number	Technique	Page	Forms on CD?	Grade Levels	Intervention Type
⚡	G4.1	Cooperation Keys	140		K–8	Behavior—Social Development
	G4.2	Partner Board	140		K–6	Behavior—Social
	G4.3	Step Out	141		K–8	Behavior—Social, Motivation
🕐	G4.4	Team Skills	141		3–8	Behavior—Social Development
	G4.5	Role Cards	142		K–8	Academic—All; Behavior—Social
	G4.6	Reflection Cards	144	📄	3–8	Behavior—Social
	G4.7	Assignment Co-Op	144		3–8	Academic—All Behavior—Social
	G4.8	Processing	145		K–8	Behavior—Social
	G4.9	Classwide Peer Tutoring	146		K–8	Academic—All Behavior—Social
	G4.10	Team-Building Exercises	148		K–8	Behavior—Social Development

G5: What can I do about the students who do not contribute to class discussions during practice activities? 150

Prep Time	Number	Technique	Page	Forms on CD?	Grade Levels	Intervention Type
⚡	G5.1	Huddle	150		3–8	Academic, Behavior
	G5.2	Write and Speak	150		4–8	Academic—All
	G5.3	Signals	151		K–8	
	G5.4	Contribution Points	151		K–8	Academic; Behavior—Motivation
	G5.5	Contribution Chips	151		K–8	
	G5.6	Pens in the Jar	152		K–8	
🕐	G5.7	Corners	152		K–8	Academic—All
	G5.8	Graffiti Papers	153		3–8	
	G5.9	Inside/Outside Circle	153		3–8	
	G5.10	Making a Contribution	154	📄	3–8	Academic; Behavior
	G5.11	Pair Interviews	154		3–8	Academic
	G5.12	Contribution Aims	155	📄	K–8	Behavior—Motivation
	G5.13	S.M.A.R.T.S. Review	156	📄	4–8	Academic

Independent Practice Activities 157

I1: What can I do about the students who do not organize or manage assignments, materials, and/or time?   158

Prep Time	*Number*	*Technique*	*Page*	*Forms on CD?*	*Grade Levels*	*Intervention Type*
	I1.1	Assignment Buddies	158		**3–8**	Academic; Behavior—Motivation
	I1.2	Think Out Loud	158		**K–8**	Academic—All
	I1.3	Mystery Motivators	159		**K–8**	Behavior—Motivation
	I1.4	Am I Working?	159		**K–8**	
	I1.5	Make the GRADE	160		**3–8**	Academic—All; Behavior—Motivation
	I1.6	Assignment Initials	160		**3–8**	Behavior—Motivation
	I1.7	Assignment Banking	161		**3–8**	
	I1.8	Organization Cards	162		**4–8**	
	I1.9	Assignment Log	162		**4–8**	
	I1.10	Time Management Charts	163		**4–8**	Behavior—Social, Motivation
	I1.11	Self-Management	163		**K–8**	Behavior—Motivation
	I1.12	Parent Partners	164		**K–8**	
	I1.13	Assignment Notebooks	165		**4–8**	

Icons

= Little preparation time

= More preparation (time and/or materials)

= Reproducible Form on CD

I2: What can I do about the students who do not complete or submit assignments? 166

Prep Time	Number	Technique	Page	Forms on CD?	Grade Levels	Intervention Type
⚡	I2.1	Daily Checkout	166		**3–8**	
	I2.2	Stop/Go Folders	167		**K–8**	
🕐	I2.3	Home/School Talk	167	📄	**K–8**	
	I2.4	Home/School Folders	168	📄	**K–8**	
	I2.5	Homework Tracking Charts	168	📄	**3–8**	
	I2.6	Hit the Homework Target	169	📄	**3–8**	
	I2.7	Homework Teams	170		**3–8**	
	I2.8	Self-Graphing Charts	172	📄	**3–8**	Behavior—Motivation
	I2.9	Assignment Contracts	172	📄	**4–8**	
	I2.10	Fill in the Dots	173	📄	**K–6**	
	I2.11	Assignment Champion Notebook	173	📄	**3–8**	
	I2.12	How Do I Rate?	174	📄	**K–8**	

I3: What can I do about the students who do not understand the independent assignment? 176

Prep Time	Number	Technique	Page	Forms on CD?	Grade Levels	Intervention Type
⚡	I3.1	I Am Working/I Need Help Sign	176	📄	**K–6**	Behavior—Motivation
	I3.2	Ask Three Before Me	177		**K–8**	Behavior—Social
	I3.3	The Fooler Game	177		**K–8**	Behavior—Motivation
	I3.4	Emphasize Instructions	178		**3–8**	
	I3.5	Highlight Key Words	179		**4–8**	Academic—All
🕐	I3.6	Key Words Mean	179	📄	**4–8**	
	I3.7	Getting the Help I Need	181		**K–8**	Behavior—Social
	I3.8	Map the Instructions	181	📄	**4–8**	Academic—All
	I3.9	Instruction Cards	182	📄	**4–8**	
	I3.10	Group Roles	182	📄	**4–8**	Behavior—Social
	I3.11	Independent Work Buddies	183	📄	**4–8**	Behavior—Motivation

I4: What can I do about the students who do not check work for accuracy and/or completeness? 184

Prep Time	Number	Technique	Page	Forms on CD?	Grade Levels	Intervention Type
	I4.1	Checking Station	184		**3–8**	
	I4.2	Write the Steps	184		**3–8**	
	I4.3	Checking and Completing	185		**3–8**	
	I4.4	Proofing Skills	185		**3–8**	Academic—All
	I4.5	Count Corrects and Errors	187		**3–8**	
	I4.6	Accuracy Aims	188		**3–8**	
	I4.7	Challenge the Time	188		**K–8**	
	I4.8	Check-Off List	188		**4–8**	Behavior—Motivation
	I4.9	Partners Plus	189	(forms)	**3–8**	Academic—All

I5: What can I do about the students who do not know how to prepare for and/or study for a test? 190

Prep Time	Number	Technique	Page	Forms on CD?	Grade Levels	Intervention Type
	I5.1	Test Study Sheet	190	(forms)	**4–8**	
	I5.2	TERM	191		**4–8**	
	I5.3	Study Scheduling	191		**3–8**	
	I5.4	Review Guides	192		**3–8**	
	I5.5	Study Checklists	193	(forms)	**3–8**	
	I5.6	Active Reading	194		**3–8**	Academic—All
	I5.7	PREPARE	194		**4–8**	
	I5.8	Write About	195		**3–8**	
	I5.9	Information Coding	195		**4–8**	
	I5.10	Map It Out	196		**3–8**	
	I5.11	Practice Sheets	197		**3–8**	

Final Measurement 199

F1: What can I do about the students who do not perform well with traditional test formats? 200

Prep Time	Number	Technique	Page	Forms on CD?	Grade Levels	Intervention Type
🕐	F1.1	70/30 Splits	200		**K–8**	
	F1.2	Word Probes	202	📄	**K–6**	
	F1.3	Oral Passage Probes	204		**3–8**	
	F1.4	Comprehension Probes	206	📄	**3–8**	
	F1.5	Written Expression Probes	207		**4–8**	Academic—All
	F1.6	Math Probes	208		**3–8**	
	F1.7	Social Skills Probes	210	📄	**K–8**	
	F1.8	Content Area/Functional Skills Probes	212		**K–8**	

F2: What can I do about the students who do not use strategies for taking a test? 214

Prep Time	Number	Technique	Page	Forms on CD?	Grade Levels	Intervention Type
⚡	F2.1	Confidence Building	214		**3–8**	
🕐	F2.2	Test-Taking Awareness	215		**3–8**	
	F2.3	Knowing the Question	215		**3–8**	Academic—All
	F2.4	Post-Test Checklist	217	📄	**4–8**	
	F2.5	Math Problem Solving	217		**3–8**	
	F2.6	RIDGES	218		**4–8**	Academic—Math
	F2.7	PIRATES	219		**4–8**	Academic—All

F3: What can I do about the students who do not monitor work performance? 220

Prep Time	*Number*	*Technique*	*Page*	*Forms on CD?*	*Grade Levels*	*Intervention Type*
	F3.1	Performance Tracking Sheets	220		**3–8**	
	F3.2	Performance Conference	221		**3–8**	
	F3.3	Performance Checkouts	221		**3–8**	
	F3.4	Performance Journal	222		**4–8**	Academic—All
	F3.5	Charting	222		**3–8**	
	F3.6	Goal Setting	223		**3–8**	
	F3.7	Performance Choices	224		**4–8**	

F4: What can I do about the students who do not respond to traditional grading procedures? 226

Prep Time	*Number*	*Technique*	*Page*	*Forms on CD?*	*Grade Levels*	*Intervention Type*
	F4.1	Formative Assessment	226		**K–8**	
	F4.2	Coded Grading	227		**3–8**	
	F4.3	Asterisk Grading	227		**K–8**	
	F4.4	A/B/C/Not Yet	228		**4–8**	Academic—All
	F4.5	Double Grading	228		**3–8**	
	F4.6	Challenge Grading	229		**4–8**	
	F4.7	Contract Grading	230		**4–8**	

Quick Reference Guide 231

References 238

INTRODUCTION

What Is This Book About?

This is a resource book of "smart" instructional techniques that will contribute to student achievement and success. The techniques and interventions included in this book are supported by evidence-based research surrounding two critical elements of good teaching:

1. The design of good lessons

2. Effective delivery and presentation of the information

Lesson Design

Designing good lessons and instruction is not an easy task. Therefore an acronym has been used to assist teachers in remembering the "nonnegotiable" elements of what must occur in good lesson design. The acronym goes like this: "GROW I.Q. with TGIF" (in other words, make kids smarter—grow I.Q. with TGIF.) Each letter in TGIF represents one of the four essential parts of every lesson:

Teacher-Directed Instruction

Guided Practice Activities (structured and monitored to eliminate student errors)

Independent Practice Activities (on your own)

Final Measurement (How will we know if the objectives were achieved?)

GROW I.Q. represents subcomponents of the lesson that generally occur during Teacher-Directed Instruction but can occur throughout all four lesson parts (TGIF). The diagram below illustrates what each letter in the acronym stands for.

Gain and maintain student attention.

Review before, during, and after the lesson.

Objectives communicated in student-friendly language.

Why is this lesson important to the student?

Input and modeling on new skills, concepts, and critical information.

Questioning to check for understanding and extending thinking.

Lesson Delivery

Effective delivery and presentation of the lesson that you've designed is an equally difficult task. One can design a gorgeous-looking lesson on paper; however, presenting that information to students effectively and efficiently while maintaining attention and active student participation is another matter! The essential elements of lesson delivery are summarized in the four questions below.

1. What can I do to ensure that I am providing frequent opportunities for all students to respond?

2. What can I do to ensure that I am using strategies for and cues to evoke active student participation while maintaining a brisk pace?

3. What can I do to ensure that I am correcting student errors appropriately?

4. What can I do to ensure that I am providing appropriate feedback for correct student responses?

Why a Book on Instructional Interventions?

Most educators that we encounter in classrooms are always genuinely searching for more ideas, tips, techniques, and strategies to support and enhance high-quality instruction. Most of us are eager to continue to fill our bag of tricks with additional ideas. This book will do just that—it provides more than 175 techniques to improve instructional design and delivery. Furthermore, it is organized around typical concerns and questions that we as teachers are often dealing with, such as:

- What can I do about the students who do not participate during my instruction?

- What can I do about the students who forget information that I presented yesterday or a few hours ago?

- What can I do about the students who do not work cooperatively, or rely on others to do the practice activities?

- What can I do about the students who do not complete or submit assignments?

- What can I do about the students who do not perform well with traditional test formats?

This book offers a variety of options for addressing these and 20 other common questions related to TGIF.

Additionally, it is not uncommon in our schools to see more students with challenging academic and social behaviors being included in general education settings. This means that many students who had previously been served in district self-contained programs or separate schools are now attending neighborhood schools in their respective grade-level classroom. The success or failure of these students is often determined by the ability of the teacher to accommodate diverse needs and differentiate instruction accordingly.

Many educators and researchers consider effective lesson design and delivery to be the "first line of defense" as well as a key aspect of student success in the classroom (Hall, 2004; Bost & Riccomini, 2006; Mastropieri & Scruggs, 2004).

Instructional design and delivery become even more critical as schools implement Response to Intervention (RTI). The fundamental concept of RTI is that students receive high-quality instruction and intervention that enable them to be successful. In order for this to occur, RTI involves frequent and ongoing classroom-based assessment of a student's progress in specific academic and behavioral areas. As soon as it is determined that a student begins to fall behind his or her peers in any academic or behavioral area, that student receives more strategic instruction in that area. If the student continues to underachieve after a specified time period, in spite of strategic instruction, he or she is provided with an even more intensive instructional intervention. RTI is designed to catch underachievement early and to address the problem in individualized ways.

RTI has the advantage of broad application that can potentially benefit *all* students. Likewise, this book is about high-quality instruction and interventions that are literally available for *all* students. *Teach All, Reach All* complements the fundamental premise of RTI.

Who Can Use This Book?

Anyone interested in improving the quality of instruction can use this book. The ideas can be used with all students, students who are not encountering success, or students who are falling between the cracks in the existing instructional process. Unfortunately, this book does not offer all of the possible solutions to the myriad of instructional challenges we face in today's classrooms. It will hopefully trigger your own thinking and assist you in generating many more instructional interventions!

This book is designed to assist:

- Teachers who are working alone in a classroom setting
- Teachers who are collaborating with other staff
- Instructional Support Teams
- Support service providers (e.g., psychologists, diagnosticians, therapists, special education teachers, reading coaches, etc.)
- Tutors
- Paraprofessionals
- Parents
- Others who are looking for interventions to use within the instructional process

What Is TGIF?

INSTRUCTIONAL COMPONENTS

T — Teacher-Directed Instruction

G — Guided Practice Activities

I — Independent Practice Activities

F — Final Measurement

T: Teacher-Directed Instruction

Throughout T, the teacher orchestrates the teaching process by gaining and maintaining the attention of the learner, reviewing pertinent information, communicating goals and outcomes, and teaching why the information is important. The teacher presents new information, skills, concepts, and vocabulary. He or she models and demonstrates examples of new concepts, strategies, and rules, and asks appropriate questions to check for initial student understanding. High rates of active student involvement, brisk-paced lessons, immediate positive feedback, and correction procedures for student errors are evident during the course of teacher-directed instruction.

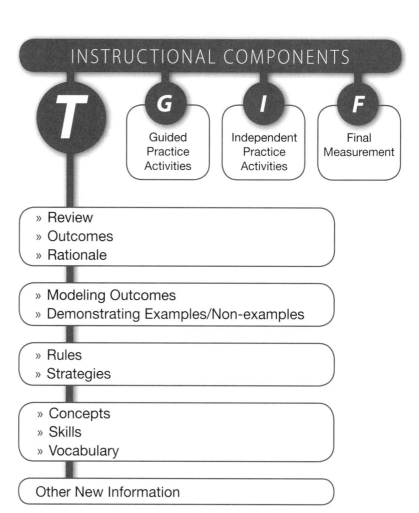

INSTRUCTIONAL COMPONENTS

T

G — Guided Practice Activities

I — Independent Practice Activities

F — Final Measurement

» Review
» Outcomes
» Rationale

» Modeling Outcomes
» Demonstrating Examples/Non-examples

» Rules
» Strategies

» Concepts
» Skills
» Vocabulary

Other New Information

G: Guided Practice Activities

Throughout G, the teacher leads and prompts students through structured activities designed to provide frequent opportunities for students to practice new skills and eliminate errors. Practice can be arranged individually with support or through a variety of peer-mediated structures such as partner activities, cooperative learning, and classwide peer tutoring structures. These practice opportunities are directly related to the outcomes and assist students in reducing errors as they master new information. A suggested guideline for mastery after completing guided practice activities involves high levels of accurate performance, ranging from 85% to 95% correct. If students have not achieved high levels of mastery,

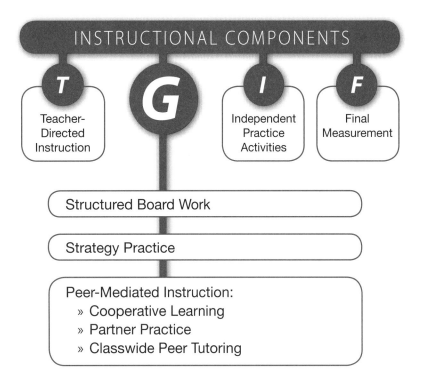

then re-teaching must occur, accompanied by additional appropriate practice activities. The consequences of not re-teaching will result in unwarranted academic failure.

I: Independent Practice Activities

Throughout I, the teacher facilitates activities that provide continued or extended practice opportunities. These activities involve fewer prompts and less guidance from the teacher, as students are now building fluency and generalizing the information related to the instructional outcomes. Successful completion of independent work involves continued high levels of accuracy as well as appropriate speed of response. If students are not able to perform the skill independently, it may be necessary to provide more guided practice or teacher-directed instruction.

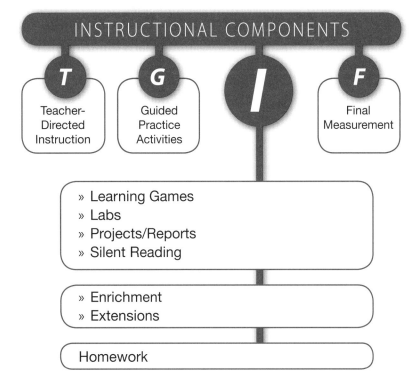

F: Final Measurement

F is defined as an end-of-unit measurement rather than the checking for understanding that occurs during the lesson. This type of measurement, which may be included in a student portfolio, is valued as an integral and legitimate component of the overall instructional process. Appropriate measurement can also serve as a powerful instructional tool. Throughout F, the teacher designs one or more end-of-unit performance assessments that adequately reflect the objectives identified in a unit of curriculum. The measurement instrument/tool is administered repeatedly (on the first day of instruction and as often as possible throughout the instructional unit) to determine whether the students are

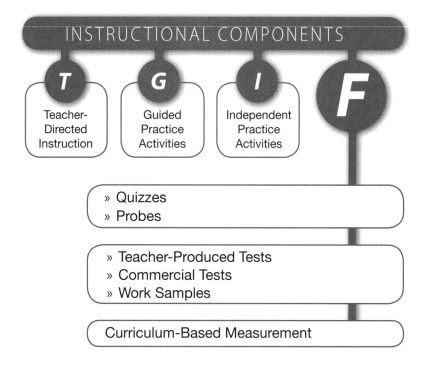

progressing toward the end-of-unit objectives. In other words, one might think of the pretest and the post-test being administered as many times as possible throughout the unit. Without ongoing measurement, it is difficult to determine whether or not student performance is improving, staying the same, or getting worse. Furthermore, powerful instructional effects are lost. To effectively manage final measurement and ensure immediate feedback to the learner, it is important that students learn to keep track of their own performance. Ongoing decisions can then be made regarding possible instructional changes needed throughout the T, G, I, and F process.

How Can I Use This Book?

1. Reflect on your own design and delivery of instruction using the Lesson Delivery section starting on p. 21.

2. Determine if you need an instructional accommodation for T, G, I, or F.

3. Refer to the Table of Contents and read through the questions.

4. Identify the TGIF question(s) that best represents the challenge you are facing.

5. Locate the section and page number for that question in the Table of Contents.

6. Read the suggested techniques for that question and choose one that fits your situation. You can also modify, adapt, or create a new one based on the techniques presented.

7. Refer to the Quick Reference Guide, starting on p. 231, for an alphabetical listing of all instructional interventions under each area of TGIF, with page numbers and information about implementation time, appropriate grade levels, and type of intervention.

The following codes have been provided to assist you in selecting and implementing the techniques.

Can be implemented with little preparation time.

Requires a bit more preparation and time or materials, but is well worth the effort!

A full-size reproducible version of the form is included on the CD that accompanies this book. The CD contains blackline masters that are ready to print, copy, and use in the classroom.

MATERIALS PREP ✂ Be sure you have required materials ready before implementing this technique.

The grade-level column indicates appropriate grade levels for each technique. Note that you can modify virtually all of the techniques covered in this book based on the needs and abilities of your students.

Intervention type indicates whether the technique addresses academic or behavioral challenges. See the Quick Reference Guide at the end of the book to find techniques based on grade level, preparation time, and intervention type.

How Long Should I Spend on Each Component of TGIF?

The circle graph at right illustrates approximate percentages of time that could ideally be devoted to each of the instructional components. The time allotments should be viewed in terms of a daily lesson, weekly instruction, or a unit of instruction. In most instances, teacher-directed instruction precedes guided and independent practice activities.

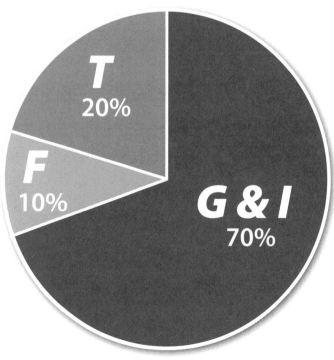

What Are Some Assumptions Underlying TGIF?

1. Schools, classrooms, and educational personnel are caring and nurturing. They treat students with dignity and respect, and promote the concept that all students belong and all students can succeed.

2. Fairness does not mean that everyone gets the same treatment. Fairness means that everyone gets what he or she needs.

3. Appropriate outcomes/curriculum have been well articulated and communicated for all students.

4. Carefully planned lessons are used that incorporate validated elements of effective lesson design and delivery.

5. When students do not learn, they need to be re-taught, not blamed, ignored, or left to fall behind.

How Can I Design Instruction According to TGIF?

Use the TGIF Instructional Organizer (pp. 15–19) and the sample lesson (pp. 10–14) as planning tools for promoting effective instruction as well as for recording interventions that may be made during T, G, I, and F. The organizer can be used by an individual teacher, collaborating teachers, or grade-level teams as they plan for instruction. The organizer also lends itself well to planning integrated and thematic units of instruction.

The Instructional Organizer defines components of effective instruction. Following are some points to consider as you develop lessons using TGIF. The Instructional Organizer is useful for planning daily instruction, weekly instruction, and longer units of instruction. Following the example organizer, a blank Instructional Organizer is included on pp. 15–19 and on the companion CD for duplication.

Gain Attention

Gain the attention of every student at the beginning and throughout instruction. Use the following procedure:

- Give a verbal or nonverbal prompt.
- Pause and wait for student compliance.
- Scan the classroom visually and by physically moving about.
- Give feedback to students by describing their appropriate behavior.

Review

Active review, rather than passive, is conducted prior to, during, and after the introduction of new topics. Students are continuously recycling important information that relates to both current and past topics. Active review can include asking content questions from previous lessons, asking questions related to the lesson objective and rationale, correcting homework, incorporating review questions from previous units on current tests, and cumulative review during a lesson. Active review involves eliciting high rates of group and individual responses. Remind students of the Essential Questions (T1.1, p. 34) they are focusing on throughout the unit.

Outcome

The lesson outcome is clearly communicated in terms of what the student will be able to do as a result of the instruction, such as: "You will be able to write, list, compare, demonstrate, analyze, or critique." The verb that is used in the outcome should match the level of cognition that is the focus of instruction and measurement. The outcome is verified with students by asking a question such as: "What will you be able to do at the end of the lesson?" The outcome is stated in student-friendly language. It is specific, measurable, and directly connected with the end-of-unit objectives and the test or measurement that will be used to assess mastery.

Why? Rationale

The rationale for the lesson is clearly communicated in terms of how mastery of the objective will personally benefit the student both in and out of the classroom. Examples are provided that are relevant to the developmental level of the learner and related to past and future instruction. The rationale is verified with students by directing questions and eliciting student responses that address the important benefits. An example of this is: "It is important to be able to define the words because you will understand what the author means and then you will be able to talk about it with your friends."

Another example might be: "It is important to be able to follow instructions and accept feedback so that you will get your work done the correct way. Your future boss will also view you as a good worker, and you'll have a better chance of getting a raise."

Input and Questioning

Explicit teacher modeling and multiple demonstrations of the new skill and/or concept are followed by teacher questions to check for comprehension. The questions are first directed to the examples that were modeled. If students are correct, ask questions about similar examples that were not modeled to determine whether students can begin to generalize the information. The underlying format for this phase of instruction is "I Do It" (modeling), "We Do It" (prompted), and "You Do It" (unprompted). During this component, the teacher is overt, not covert. The teacher articulates the process by using several pairs of examples and non-examples. These examples represent a wide range and highlight the critical attributes of the concept. The teacher maintains a sequential and consistent presentation format. Questions to students following the model may require more or fewer teacher cues, depending on the student responses. Eliciting frequent group responses (verbal and nonverbal) during prompted and unprompted questioning gives the teacher feedback regarding the need to re-teach.

Instructional Organizer

Unit: _____ Date: _____ Teacher(s): _____

Objective: _____ Subject/Period: _____

TEACHER-DIRECTED INSTRUCTION

G Gain Attention

1. Say: "Give me 5" in an upbeat, expressive voice as you hold up five fingers and smile.
2. Instruct the students to say back to you: 1, 2, 3-4-5. They should pause slightly after saying 1,2 and then quickly say 3-4-5 while you put up your thumb, index finger, etc. The students' response must be in unison, in a peppy voice, not shouting. Repeat step 1 if the students are not 100%.
3. Pause, visually scan the group, and WAIT until you get complete silence with student eyes focused on the speaker.
4. Say: "Thank you" or "Good job! Your eyes are on the speaker. You are quiet and ready for the next instruction."
5. Repeat the process as often as necessary during instruction until students are clear about the relationship between the instruction and their behavior.

R Review

1. Say: "Get ready to think about your own thinking. You will think on your own for 30 seconds. When you think on your own, it is silent. Your task is to think about what you already know about the vocabulary word *ecstatic*. Please begin." (So that they are not threatened by this activity, tell the students that you hope that no one knows what ecstatic means.)
2. At the end of 30 seconds, say: "Thank you. Get ready to tell your partner what you were thinking if you had an idea. Tell your partner things you think you might know about the vocabulary word *ecstatic*. Partner A, tell Partner B for 30 seconds."
3. At the end of 30 seconds say: "Thank you. Partner B, now get ready to tell Partner A in 30 seconds the ideas that you think you might know about the vocabulary word *ecstatic*." (Repeats of partner's responses are acceptable.)
4. On subsequent timed reviews, alternate which partner goes first.

O Outcome

Say: "Get ready for your ticket out the door. At the end of this lesson, you will be able to correctly define 5 to 7 new vocabulary words. You will be able to tell if the new word is used correctly or incorrectly in a sentence. The words will be in our next story." After telling the students the ticket out the door, say: "Now get ready to tell me what you will be able to do at the end of this lesson (your ticket out the door)." Call for a group response or several individual responses to check understanding.

W Why?/Rationale

Say: "One reason it is important to be able to use juicy/cool vocabulary words (in your speaking and writing) is because oftentimes other people may see you as looking and acting really smart. When people hear you use these smart, intelligent words, you may put yourself in a position to receive some other cool choices and/or privileges that are important to you. For example, you could be selected as a leader in charge of a special writing project! Another reason is that if other people use the vocabulary words that you know, you will know what they are talking about and so you will understand the conversation! When we read the next story, you will understand what is happening because you will know the new vocabulary words."

Instructional Organizer

TEACHER-DIRECTED INSTRUCTION *(continued)*

I & **Q** Input and Questioning

Sequence:

"I Do It" (Modeling)

1. Say: "Get ready to look and listen. The first new word is *ecstatic*."

"We Do It" (Prompted)

2. Say: "Please say the new word with me." (Signal for students to say the word in unison.) "Say it again." (If needed, have students clap the syllables with you, then tell how many.)

3. Give the meaning of the word. Make sure you use a familiar (accessible) synonym or brief explanation appropriate for the students' level: "The word *ecstatic* means extremely happy."

4. Use the word in a sentence: "I was *ecstatic* when I got my new puppy." Then have students repeat the sentence with you.

"You Do It" (Unprompted)

5. Rephrase the explanation, asking students to complete the statement (in a unison group response) by substituting the new word. Say: "So another way of saying that I was extremely happy when I got my new puppy is to say I was . . . (Students should say the word *ecstatic*.)

6. Repeat step 5 with at least two more examples. For example, say: "So another way of saying that I was extremely happy when our team won the state championship is to say I was . . ." (Again, students should say the word *ecstatic*.)

7. Provide a showing sentence or image that can logically represent or be associated with the new word. For example, you might use an exclamation point as a showing image to visually represent the word *ecstatic*. If you are putting the word on a word wall, you could put an exclamation point under the word. Explain why the exclamation point might be a visual association for the word *ecstatic* (e.g., exclamation point shows excitement or enthusiasm).

8. Ask several focused questions like the following: "Get ready to answer yes or no and be ready to tell why. Would you be ecstatic if your friend was seriously hurt in an accident? Yes or no?" Then ask why. "Would you be ecstatic if you won a new car? Yes or no?" Then ask why. Continue with additional sentences until students are firm.

Concepts, Skills, Vocabulary

9. Ask students to generate their own example using the new word. For example, say: "Think of a time when you were ecstatic." Pause for thinking time. Instruct students to tell their partner. Then call for several individual responses. Tell the students to say the whole sentence (e.g., I was ecstatic when . . .).

Examples/Non-examples

10. Repeat the Review activity and the above Input/Questioning procedure for 5 or 6 more vocabulary words.

Rules/Strategies

Questions:
Prompted
Unprompted

GUIDED PRACTICE

❑ **Content Practice**   ❑ **Strategy Practice**
❑ **Structured Boardwork**   ❑ **Peer-Mediated Instruction**

Explanations/Directions to Students	Monitoring/ Feedback
Demonstrate how to make a vocabulary index card for each of the new words. These cards will be added to the stack of vocabulary cards that each student has already developed. (This is similar to Key Words Mean (I3.6, p. 179) Students write the vocabulary word in large, clear print on the front side of the index card. On the reverse side, they print the exact student-friendly definition provided for the word. Students can also include the visual image under the definition (exclamation point). Repeat for the remaining new vocabulary words. Instruct students to use their one-minute partner practice strategy. (Model the strategy if this is the first day of practicing vocabulary cards with a partner.) Each student shuffles his or her stack of cards, being careful to keep the cards in the correct position. (A corner can be cut off the top left side of each card to keep them in the correct position.) Say: "Please begin." The first student shows the partner the definition side of the first card in the pile. The partner reads the definition and says the vocabulary word out loud. If the student makes an error or hesitates, the partner supplies the correct answer immediately (the partner is looking at the side of the card that has the correct answer). Students move through the cards as quickly as possible for one minute. At the end of one minute, students switch roles and repeat for another minute.	

Teach All, Reach All

INDEPENDENT PRACTICE

❏ **In-Class** ❏ **Homework** ❏ **Extensions**

❏ **Out-of-Class**

Monitoring/Feedback

Explanations/Directions to Students

Repeat the procedure described in Guided Practice, but this time each student will do the timing independently. Show students how to shuffle the cards before beginning. Demonstrate how each student will hold the stack of cards, look at the definition side, and then quickly say the vocabulary word and move on to the next card. The completed card is placed at the bottom of the pile. When students don't know a word, they should turn the card over, look at the correct answer, and say it correctly before moving on to the next card. The student should go through the stack of cards as many times as possible during the one-minute timing.

[Following the Independent Practice, say: "Get ready to tell me what you can now do as a result of this lesson!" Call for several individual responses to check for understanding.]

Instructional Organizer

FINAL MEASUREMENT

	Monitoring/ Feedback
❑ **Quizzes** ❑ **Probes** ❑ **Curriculum-Based Assessment** ❑ **Portfolio** ❑ **Teacher-Produced Test**	

Explanations/Directions to Students

Procedures for: ❑ *Counting* ❑ *Recording*
  ❑ *Charting* ❑ *Training Period*

Develop a student handout with several (8-10) sentences that use the new vocabulary words correctly and incorrectly. (Previously taught vocabulary words can also be included.) Make sure that any other vocabulary words included are known to the students. For example:

Yes/No 1. The new bride was ecstatic when she got married.

Why? Because_____

Yes/No 2. Grandfather was ecstatic after he was in the car
  accident.

Why? Because_____

Yes/No 3. The team was ecstatic after losing the soccer game.

Why? Because_____

Provide the following instructions to students: "Read each sentence. Then decide whether the underlined word is used correctly or incorrectly. If it's used correctly, circle Yes. If it's used incorrectly, circle No. Then tell why in the blank under the sentence, starting with the word *Because*."

Instructional Organizer

Unit: _____   Date: _____   Teacher(s): _____

Objective: _____   Subject/Period: _____

TEACHER-DIRECTED INSTRUCTION

G **Gain Attention**

R **Review**

O **Outcome**

W **Why?/Rationale**

Instructional Organizer

TEACHER-DIRECTED INSTRUCTION *(continued)*

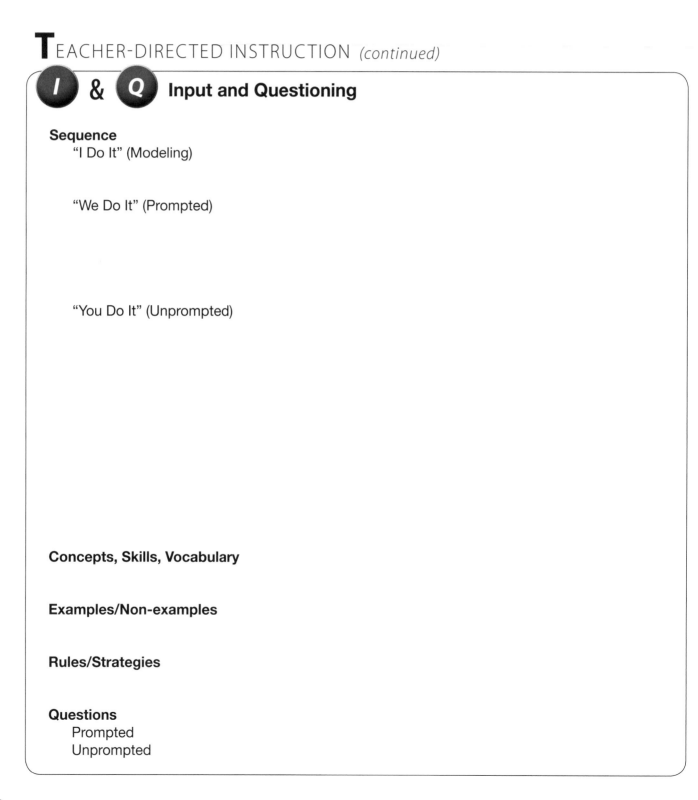

I & **Q** **Input and Questioning**

Sequence
"I Do It" (Modeling)

"We Do It" (Prompted)

"You Do It" (Unprompted)

Concepts, Skills, Vocabulary

Examples/Non-examples

Rules/Strategies

Questions
Prompted
Unprompted

Instructional Organizer

GUIDED PRACTICE

❑ Content Practice ❑ Structured Boardwork ❑ Strategy Practice ❑ Peer-Mediated Instruction	Monitoring/ Feedback
Explanations/Directions to Students	

17

Instructional Organizer

INDEPENDENT PRACTICE

❑ In-Class ❑ Homework ❑ Extensions ❑ Out-of-Class	Monitoring/ Feedback
Explanations/Directions to Students	

Instructional Organizer

FINAL MEASUREMENT

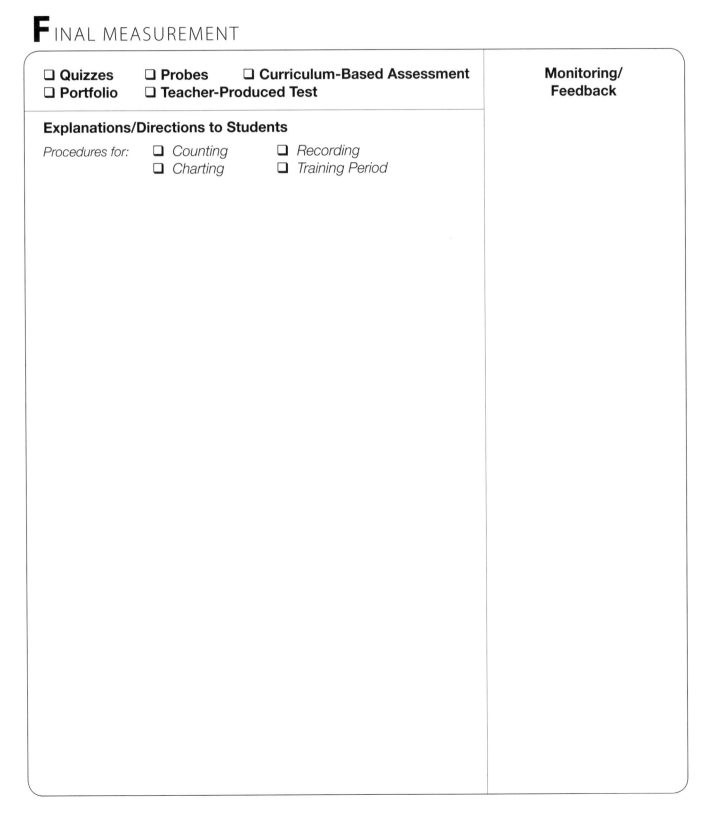

❑ **Quizzes**   ❑ **Probes**   ❑ **Curriculum-Based Assessment**
❑ **Portfolio**   ❑ **Teacher-Produced Test**

Explanations/Directions to Students

Procedures for: ❑ *Counting*   ❑ *Recording*
                      ❑ *Charting*   ❑ *Training Period*

Monitoring/ Feedback

Lesson Delivery refers to how an instructional lesson is presented to students, generally during teacher-guided instruction and practice sessions. Lesson delivery includes the strategies and techniques that a teacher plans for and addresses before and during any lesson.

LESSON DELIVERY

LESSON DELIVERY

What is Lesson Delivery?

Lesson delivery refers to **how** an instructional lesson is presented to students, generally during teacher-guided instruction and practice sessions. Lesson delivery includes the strategies and techniques that a teacher plans for and addresses before and during any lesson. Such strategies require the teacher to address the following questions:

- How will I provide frequent **opportunities for all students to respond?**

- How will I use strategies for and cues to evoke **active student participation** while maintaining a **brisk pace** throughout the lesson?

- How will I **correct student errors** appropriately?

- How will I provide **appropriate feedback** for correct student responses?

Active Student Response/Participation

Historically, the process of learning has been largely viewed as a passive experience in which knowledge is received and stored for future use. However, during the last 20 years, research into the human brain has led to theories that indicate a far more active model of acquiring knowledge. According to this model, teachers need to provide frequent opportunities for all students to respond along with appropriate and brisk pacing throughout the lesson. These factors are all associated with higher achievement and greater academic performance for students.

Active student engagement also requires students to use multiple learning skills and higher-order thinking to construct meaning and knowledge. Additionally, while delivering a lesson, the teacher needs to appropriately address student errors that may occur as well as use effective procedures for reinforcing correct student responses and behaviors.

Active student responding refers to the use of strategies that provide opportunities for learners to make frequent responses to the lesson content. An active student response is defined as a detectable reply to a lesson-related antecedent such as a prompt or a question by the teacher. Research has shown that students who are actively engaged in their instruction will retain more information on both short- and long-term assessments.

More specifically, the research shows that students assessed for information after being on-task (listening, paying attention, etc.) and engaged through active involvement will retain more information. Studies conducted by Taylor, Pearson, Peterson, and Rodriguez (2003) examined 792 students in 88 classrooms in grades 1–5 in nine high-poverty schools. They found significant positive correlations between active learning environments and growth in reading comprehension, with negative correlations in passive learning environments.

It is clear that providing students with multiple opportunities to respond increases student responses and engagement in a learning activity and will increase student performances. Observational studies of what students actually do in the classroom are somewhat disturbing. Less than half of a seven-hour school day is spent doing the real work of learning (Harmin, 1995). One study of six inner-city elementary classrooms found that students spent the largest portion of the day passively attending to the teacher and less than 1% of the day actively responding. Again, there is a strong relationship between increased student engagement and academic achievement.

Much of the debate surrounding the use of lecture-based classes as a method for lesson delivery has focused on the passive role assumed by students. The communication channel is primarily instructor-to-student. Numerous studies have shown that student performance in science classes improves with increasing levels of active participation by students in classroom discussions. Methods designed to improve not only instructor-to-student communication but also student-to-instructor and student-to-student communication include:

- Cooperative learning techniques
- Classroom discussion
- "Turn-to-your-neighbor" activities

> *Students who are actively engaged in their instruction will retain more information on both short- and long-term assessments.*

A common strategy used by teachers to engage students during group instruction is to present a question to the entire class and then call on one student to respond. The student who responds is generally the only student who has an active learning opportunity. Further, the students who generally respond are more often the higher-achieving students than the lower-achieving ones. The result can be that the students who need the most practice get the least, and those who need the least practice get the most.

Clearly, there is no question that active student responding techniques increase student engagement and produce more learning. Increasing student responses is an important goal for teachers of any grade level or subject area. Active student responses can be verbal or nonverbal, covert or overt. They can occur with individual students, partners, and small or large groups. Active student responding strategies can include:

- Choral responses with individuals or groups
- Use of response cards or boards
- Use of guided notes
- A variety of partner activities

Correcting Student Errors/Appropriate Feedback

Obviously, when teachers employ strategies for active responding and increasing opportunities to respond, students make more responses. Those responses are generally partially correct, correct, and/or constitute some type of an error. Therefore, lesson delivery must also include the use of appropriate and effective feedback procedures for error correction, and appropriate and effective procedures for providing praise and positive feedback when correct responses are given. These two additional aspects of lesson delivery are powerful and essential.

Although the planning of how and when to use praise rests with the teacher, this is a strategy any teacher (or para-educator) can learn to use effectively. Several elements should be carefully considered when praise is given:

- Praise should include defining the appropriate behavior.
- Praise should be given as immediately as possible after the appropriate behavior has occurred.
- Praise statements should be varied.
- Praise should not be given continuously or without reason.

Praise should be given as immediately as possible after the appropriate behavior has occurred.

- Praise must be delivered sincerely.

- Praise should be consistently delivered with the target behaviors.

- Praise should be developmentally appropriate.

It is also essential to minimize student errors by carefully sequencing instruction. When errors do occur, careful error correction procedures (model, lead, test, and retest) should be delivered. Teachers must be alert to student error responses. When students have begun to acquire a skill but need opportunities to practice it, teacher oversight and feedback is especially important to prevent students new to the skill from practicing it incorrectly (Marchand-Martella, Slocum, & Martella, 2004).

Strategies to Enhance Lesson Delivery

The strategies described on the next pages are provided to assist teachers in improving their skills in lesson delivery. Specifically, the strategies address the following four critical questions:

1. What can I do to ensure that I am providing **frequent opportunities for all students to respond**?

2. What can I do to ensure that I am using strategies for and cues to evoke **active student participation** while maintaining a **brisk pace**?

3. What can I do to ensure that I am **correcting student errors appropriately**?

4. What can I do to ensure that I am providing **appropriate feedback** for correct student responses?

It is also essential to minimize student errors by carefully sequencing instruction.

Six Steps to Increase Opportunities to Respond

> - What can I do to ensure that I am providing frequent opportunities for all students to respond?
> - What can I do to ensure that I am using strategies for and cues to evoke active student participation while maintaining a brisk pace?

WHEN: After the teacher presents information to the students (e.g., teacher has given one important fact about mammals).

Step 1. Tell students they will repeat what you just said. Say: "Everybody, think and get ready to tell me/us what I just said . . ." (e.g., one important thing we know about mammals).

Step 2. Provide time for all students to develop responses. Say: "Keep it a secret. When you have an idea, signal by touching your forehead (holding up your green card, etc.)."

Step 3. Have students share responses with each other. Say: "Now, whisper/share your idea with your learning partner. Partner A, tell Partner B. Partner B, tell A."

Step 4. Have students share responses with the class. Call for the response: "Everybody, say it."
> or
"When I call/pull your name, say your idea or your partner's idea."

Step 5. If it's an individual response, always reaffirm the response with the group. Say:
"Everybody, what did [*student's name*] say?"

Step 6. If you didn't get 100% of the class responding, repeat and say: "I need to hear everybody. Everybody, say it again."

Affirming/Echoing Individual Responses

> - What can I do to ensure that I am providing frequent opportunities for all students to respond?
> - What can I do to ensure that I am using strategies for and cues to evoke active student participation while maintaining a brisk pace?
> - What can I do to ensure that I am providing appropriate feedback for correct student responses?

WHEN: After a student gives a correct response to a question or offers an important idea, call for a group choral response to echo, affirm, validate, and reinforce that student's response. Say:

"Everybody, what did he/she just say?"
> or

"That was an important idea! Everybody, please say it again."
> or

"Everybody, that's worth repeating. Let me hear everybody say it again."

The "Get Ready" Cue

- What can I do to ensure that I am providing frequent opportunities for all students to respond?

- What can I do to ensure that I am using strategies for and cues to evoke active student participation while maintaining a brisk pace?

WHEN: Immediately before the teacher gives information, begins instruction, gives a direction, starts an activity, etc., in order to prevent errors from occurring (e.g., the teacher requests that the students put their materials away, take notes, transition, listen, etc.).

Step 1. Say "Get ready to use your skills for . . ." and then describe what is coming next. Examples of where students might apply skills include:
- Looking and listening
- Following an instruction
- Listening to a speaker
- Taking notes
- Working with a partner
- Working with a group
- Taking a test
- Working independently
- Choral responding
- Transitioning
- Lining up
- Reading out loud
- Timed reading
- Learning center

Step 2. If the students do not know the steps for the activity, say: "Let's review the steps to use." For example, if the "Get Ready" cue is for following instructions, say:

"The steps for following instructions are to:
- Look and listen to the speaker.
- Acknowledge the instruction by saying OK (if necessary).
- Just do it right away."

Step 3. Have students repeat the steps after you. Say:
"Everybody, please repeat those steps."
(It may be helpful to have the steps written on a chart or white board so the students can read back the steps in unison.)

Step 4. Give students the "Get Ready" cue.

Step 5. If all students comply, provide praise. If not, repeat steps 2 through 4.

Correcting an Incorrect Answer

- What can I do to ensure that I am correcting student errors appropriately?

- What can I do to ensure that I am providing appropriate feedback for correct student responses?

WHEN: Immediately after a student gives an incorrect response to a teacher's question (e.g., student replies that the vocabulary word "ecstatic" means sorrowful or pitiful).

Dignify the error by saying:
"[*Student's name*], I bet you are thinking about our vocabulary word *pathetic*. Pathetic means sorrowful or pitiful."

Correct the error by saying:
"I'm talking about the word *ecstatic*. Ecstatic means extremely happy!"

Validate the correct response with the student by saying:
"Say *ecstatic*." [*Student repeats the word.*]
"So, another word for extremely happy is . . ." [*Student supplies the word* ecstatic.]

Validate the correct response with the group by saying:

"Everybody—another way of saying that the girl was extremely happy with her new puppy is to say that she was . . . "

Validate the error response with the group by saying:

"Everybody—another way of saying that the homeless man was sorrowful or pitiful is to say that he was . . . "

Validate the correct response with the student who made the error by saying:

"So, another way of saying that the homeless man was sorrowful or pitiful is to say that he was . . . "

Praise the student and group, and note that everybody knows the difference between pathetic and ecstatic. For example:

"Great! I think you all know the difference between pathetic and ecstatic."

Think–Ink–Link–Ink

- What can I do to ensure that I am providing frequent opportunities for all students to respond?

- What can I do to ensure that I am using strategies for and cues to evoke active student participation while maintaining a brisk pace?

WHEN: Before, during, or after teacher-directed instruction to review and firm students on skills or concepts.

THINK

Say: "Get ready to think on your own for one minute. When you think on your own, it is silent. Your task is to think about what you already or now know about our topic. Please begin."

(The topic is whatever you have been teaching, such as the weather, causes of the war, steps for solving a problem, life stages of a butterfly, etc.)

INK

At the end of one minute, say: "Thank you. Now get ready to write your ideas (or facts) about the topic. Write as many as you can in one minute. Please begin." (Correct spelling is not necessary.)

LINK

At the end of another minute, say: "Thank you. Now get ready to read your ideas to your partner. Partner A, tell Partner B for one minute. Please begin."

At the end of one minute, instruct the partners to reverse roles. (Partner B reads ideas to Partner A.)

INK

Say: "Thank you. Now get ready to combine and refine your ideas into one list, with no ideas repeated." Call on partners to share ideas from their list. Don't allow repeats—only new or different ideas from those previously shared.

Effective Acknowledgment/Descriptive Praise

> • What can I do to ensure that I am providing appropriate feedback for correct student responses?

WHEN: Immediately following a correct answer or correct social behavior to affirm, validate, and reinforce the student's response.

Express regard by making eye contact with the student, saying the student's name, moving closer to the student (around 21 inches), using a pleasant tone of voice and facial expression, and using touch if appropriate (e.g., on the wrist or shoulder).

If you are using this strategy with a group of students, make eye contact with as many students as possible, try to mention several students' names, express regard within close proximity to the group, and if appropriate, touch one or two students on the shoulder.

Acknowledge the student's responsible behavior by making an enthusiastic statement such as:

- Nice job!
- Wow, that was great!
- How nice!
- You can be proud of yourself.

Describe the student's behavior in specific behavioral terms, telling the student exactly what he or she did that was correct or appropriate. You might say:

"You remembered to _____ by doing _____."

or

"That time you did _____, _____, _____, and _____."

Here are some examples of specific descriptions of student behavior:

You remembered to follow instructions the first time they were given by looking, listening, and then getting started within five seconds.

That time you read smoothly and quickly with lots of expression in your voice.

If you are using this strategy with a group, highlight as many different student behaviors as possible.

Provide a reason (if possible). You might say:

"It's important to behave that way because _____."

or

"It's important to do it that way because _____."

Examples of reasons include:

It's important to behave that way because then you will be more likely to get your work done on time and avoid giving up some of your valued time.

It's important to do it that way because you will stop making the same mistakes over and over again and you will better understand what you are reading.

NOTE: This strategy is similar to G1.1, Effective Praise, found on p. 106.

Three–Minute Timed Review

- What can I do to ensure that I am providing frequent opportunities for all students to respond?

- What can I do to ensure that I am using strategies for and cues to evoke active student participation while maintaining a brisk pace?

WHEN: Before, during, or after teacher-directed/guided instruction to review and firm students on skills or concepts.

Say:

"Get ready to think about your own thinking. You will think on your own for one minute. When you think on your own, it is silent. Your task is to think about what you already know or now know about our topic. Please begin."

(The topic is whatever you have been teaching—for example, new vocabulary, steps for solving a problem, prime numbers, steps for finding lowest common denominator, steps for writing a paragraph, etc.)

At the end of one minute, say:

"Thank you. Get ready to tell your partner what you were thinking. Tell your partner as many things as you know about our topic. Partner A, tell Partner B for one minute."

At the end of another minute, say:

"Thank you. Now, Partner B, get ready to tell Partner A as many ideas as you can in one minute." (Repeats of partner's responses are acceptable.)

On subsequent Three-Minute Timed Reviews, alternate which partner starts first.

OPTIONAL: Partners can count and record the number of ideas said by their partner.

Throughout **T**, the teacher orchestrates the teaching process by gaining and maintaining attention of the learner, reviewing pertinent information, communicating goals and objectives, and teaching why the information is important.

TEACHER-*DIRECTED* **INSTRUCTION**

T₁

TEACHER-DIRECTED INSTRUCTION

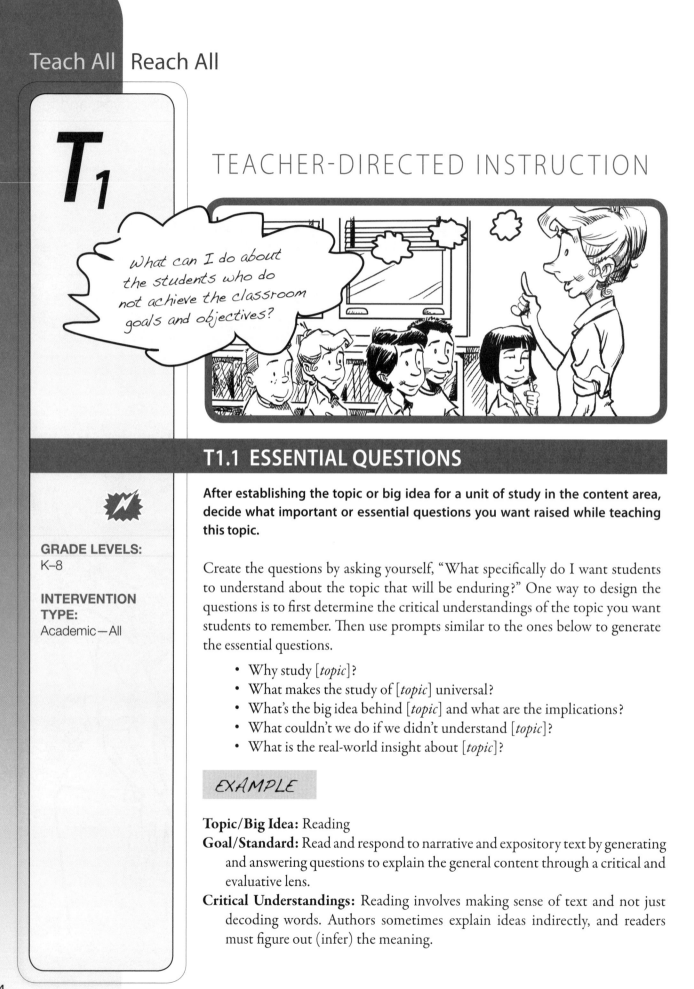

What can I do about the students who do not achieve the classroom goals and objectives?

T1.1 ESSENTIAL QUESTIONS

GRADE LEVELS:
K–8

INTERVENTION TYPE:
Academic — All

After establishing the topic or big idea for a unit of study in the content area, decide what important or essential questions you want raised while teaching this topic.

Create the questions by asking yourself, "What specifically do I want students to understand about the topic that will be enduring?" One way to design the questions is to first determine the critical understandings of the topic you want students to remember. Then use prompts similar to the ones below to generate the essential questions.

- Why study [*topic*]?
- What makes the study of [*topic*] universal?
- What's the big idea behind [*topic*] and what are the implications?
- What couldn't we do if we didn't understand [*topic*]?
- What is the real-world insight about [*topic*]?

EXAMPLE

Topic/Big Idea: Reading

Goal/Standard: Read and respond to narrative and expository text by generating and answering questions to explain the general content through a critical and evaluative lens.

Critical Understandings: Reading involves making sense of text and not just decoding words. Authors sometimes explain ideas indirectly, and readers must figure out (infer) the meaning.

Essential Questions:
- What do good readers do?
- Why do writers sometimes confuse readers by writing things that mean something different?
- How do we read between the lines?

The important understandings and essential questions provide students with outcomes that go beyond skill development and provide a rationale for engaging in new learning.

> *Source: McTighe & Wiggins,* Understanding by Design, *2004.*

T **G** **I** **F**

T1.2 CONDITION SHIFT

Narrow or broaden the amount of time, the setting, or the circumstances in which the student is to perform the desired behavior.

EXAMPLE

- **Reduce the duration of time for performance of the behavior.**
  Instead of expecting the student to follow instructions throughout a six-hour school day, the student could be expected to follow instructions during a 30-minute reading activity.

- **Change the circumstances in which the student is expected to demonstrate the behavior.**
  Instead of expecting the student to transition from one activity to another independently, the student could make the transition with the assistance of a peer buddy.

GRADE LEVELS:
K–8

INTERVENTION TYPE:
Academic—All

T1.3 PROFICIENCY SHIFT

Change the way in which student proficiency is measured.

The following terms represent three hierarchical levels of proficiency:

- **Accuracy:** The number of items correct.

- **Mastery:** The number of items correct in a specified amount of time.

- **Automaticity:** The number of items correct in a specified amount of time with distractors present.

GRADE LEVELS:
K–8

INTERVENTION TYPE:
Academic—All

When you modify these levels, automaticity should be strongly considered for objectives that represent high-priority or functional skills.

EXAMPLES

- An objective that requires **accuracy** might read: Write/spell ten words 100% correctly.

- An objective that requires **mastery** would involve performing the behavior accurately and quickly, such as: Write/spell ten words correctly at a rate of 40 letters per minute in sequence.

- An objective that requires **automaticity** involves completing the task accurately and quickly in the presence of relevant distractors. For instance, write/spell words correctly in a 15-minute book report.

T1.4 PRODUCT SHIFT

GRADE LEVELS:
K–8

INTERVENTION TYPE:
Academic—All

Change the way in which the student is expected to demonstrate understanding of the concept.

EXAMPLE

If the outcome for the class is to indicate comprehension of a story topic by writing a book report, the target student could use alternate techniques to demonstrate the concept. Alternative methods might include:

- An oral book report
- Pictures to represent characters, setting, or events in the story
- A play or skit
- A story board
- A collage

T1.5 TICKET OUT THE DOOR

GRADE LEVELS:
K–8

INTERVENTION TYPE:
Academic—All
Behavior—Motivation

Use this intervention before each lesson to tell students what they will be able to do at the end of the lesson that they can't do now.

Step 1. Say, "At the end of this lesson, you will be able to _____ _____."

Fill in the first blank with an appropriate action verb from one of the categories in the box on the next page. Then insert the skill you are teaching in the next blank. This is the "Ticket Out the Door."

T1: What can I do about the students who do not achieve the classroom goals and objectives?

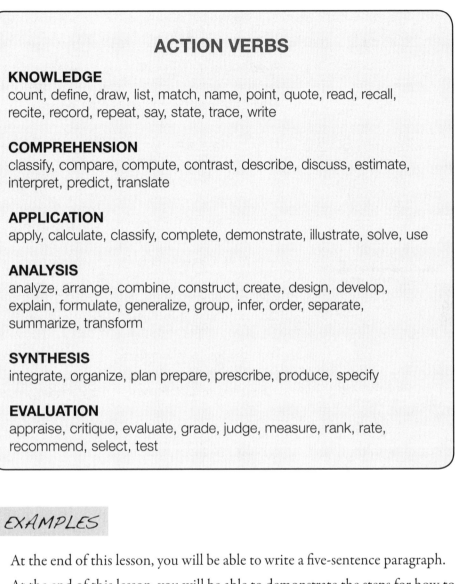

ACTION VERBS

KNOWLEDGE
count, define, draw, list, match, name, point, quote, read, recall, recite, record, repeat, say, state, trace, write

COMPREHENSION
classify, compare, compute, contrast, describe, discuss, estimate, interpret, predict, translate

APPLICATION
apply, calculate, classify, complete, demonstrate, illustrate, solve, use

ANALYSIS
analyze, arrange, combine, construct, create, design, develop, explain, formulate, generalize, group, infer, order, separate, summarize, transform

SYNTHESIS
integrate, organize, plan prepare, prescribe, produce, specify

EVALUATION
appraise, critique, evaluate, grade, judge, measure, rank, rate, recommend, select, test

EXAMPLES

At the end of this lesson, you will be able to write a five-sentence paragraph.

At the end of this lesson, you will be able to demonstrate the steps for how to accept feedback.

Step 2. After telling the students their "Ticket out the Door," say:
"Get ready to tell me what you will be able to do at the end of this lesson (or your ticket out the door)."
Call for a group response or several individual responses to check for understanding.

Step 3. At the end of the lesson, say:
"Get ready to tell me what you can now do as a result of this lesson!"
Call for a group response or several individual responses to check for understanding.

T1.6 WHAT WILL I DO? LOG

MATERIALS PREP ✂

GRADE LEVELS:
3–8

INTERVENTION TYPE:
Academic—All

REPRODUCIBLE on CD

NOTE:
A similar technique called the What, Where/When, and Why Strategy (T6.4, p. 65) can be used for the same purpose.

Provide the student with a log to record what he or she will be able to do as a result of the lesson. Communicate the objective in terms of what the student will be able to do at the end of the lesson.

Have students write the objective in their log exactly as you have stated it or in their own words. Next, check for comprehension by having the students as a group read aloud what they have written as a group, state the objective to each other, or show a partner what they have written in the log.

Add objectives to the log each time new information is presented. Have students keep the log in a notebook or folder to refer to throughout the lesson and the unit.

Teach All, Reach All

What Will I Do? Log

Name: _Benny_   Subject: _Language Arts_

TOPIC/LESSON	DATE	OBJECTIVE/OUTCOME
Punctuation	11/2	Write sentences correctly.

REPRODUCIBLE T1.6

EXAMPLES

- At the end of this lesson, you will be able to pronounce and define five words.

- You will be able to compare and contrast democracy and socialism.

- You will be able to identify the problems that require regrouping.

T1: What can I do about the students who do not achieve the classroom goals and objectives?

MATERIALS PREP

GRADE LEVELS:
4–8

INTERVENTION TYPE:
Academic—All

REPRODUCIBLE on CD

T1.7 MINIMAL/ADVANCED COMPETENCIES

Determine which outcomes in the unit of instruction are minimal competencies and which are considered advanced.

Provide students with a list of all the competencies at the beginning of the unit. Explain which competencies are required and have students choose which advanced competencies they will achieve based on teacher guidelines.

EXAMPLE

In a science unit on rocks and minerals, the following objectives would be presented in a competency contract to the students. Each objective is labeled with an (**m**) for **minimal** or an (**a**) for **advanced**.

- Define vocabulary (**m**)

- List three types of rocks (**m**)

- Identify the characteristics of each rock type (**m**)

- Translate the scientific rock and mineral names to common names (**a**)

- Compare and contrast the three rock types (**m**)

- Evaluate the geographical area around your neighborhood and write a paper explaining your conclusions (**a**)

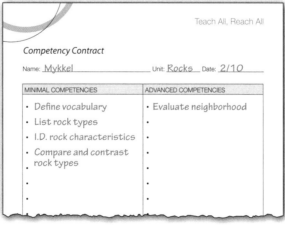

REPRODUCIBLE T1.7

All students are responsible for the minimal competencies and may choose which advanced competencies they would like to complete based on the teacher's guidelines.

T_2

TEACHER-DIRECTED INSTRUCTION

What can I do about the students who do not respond to my instructions?

T2.1 GET READY

GRADE LEVELS:
K–8

INTERVENTION TYPE:
Academic—All
Behavior—Motivation

Tell the students that you will provide a "get ready" signal prior to giving directions.

Signal the students that a direction is about to be given.

EXAMPLES

- Say something like, "Get ready for an instruction."
- Switch a light globe on.
- Turn over a red card on the chalk board.

If the students comply, acknowledge the response immediately. Reinforce them with verbal praise, show of a green card, a star next to their name, etc.

T2.2 LISTENING CUES

GRADE LEVELS:
K–6

INTERVENTION TYPE:
Academic — All
Behavior — Motivation

Teach students that a particular sound or signal (e.g., a clapping rhythm, quiet hand raise, etc.) represents "eyes up here" or "stop, look, listen, and freeze."

An electronic noisemaker that produces a variety of different sounds can be used for this purpose. After giving the signal, pause, scan the classroom, and provide descriptive feedback to the students who are responding to the direction/signal. Frequent comments, like "Good for Stuart—he stopped talking and looked at me when I gave the signal," should be given to students who respond to the signal.

T2.3 YOU-ME GAME

GRADE LEVELS:
K–6

INTERVENTION TYPE:
Academic — All
Behavior — Motivation

Encourage students to follow instructions.

Set up a YOU-ME Chart on the chalk board. Each time the students use the predetermined steps (see T2.5) for following instructions, a point is quickly marked for the students under the YOU side. The teacher can say something like, "You got me!" If the students do not use the strategy for following instructions, the teacher quickly marks a point under the ME side of the chart and says something like, "I got you!" The daily counts under YOU and ME can also be recorded on a class chart that can serve as a challenge for the following day.

YOU	ME
III	I

T2.4 I CAN SAY IT

GRADE LEVELS:
K–8

INTERVENTION TYPE:
Academic — All
Behavior — Motivation

Give the direction to the class and ask the students to repeat the direction as a group or call on an individual.

EXAMPLES

Say: "Everybody, what are you supposed to do?"

Say: "Raise your hand if you can repeat the instruction." Then call on individual students. After one student has repeated an instruction, call on another student to repeat what the first student just stated.

MATERIALS PREP

GRADE LEVELS:
K–8

INTERVENTION TYPE:
Academic—All
Behavior—Motivation

REPRODUCIBLE on CD

T2.5 FOLLOWING INSTRUCTIONS

Teach students to follow instructions by modeling.

Model each of the following steps for students. It is important to demonstrate several examples of what each of the behaviors/steps looks and sounds like. Also, demonstrate several examples of what the behaviors do not look or sound like.

Step 1. Look at the person giving the instruction when he or she says your name.

Step 2. Acknowledge the person who has given you the instruction by saying "yes," "OK," "all right," or another acceptable acknowledgment.

Step 3. Do the instruction immediately.

Step 4. Check back with the teacher if appropriate.

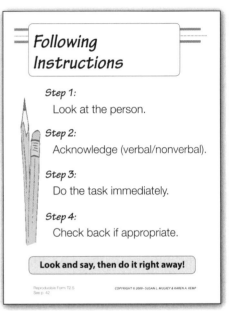

Following Instructions

Step 1:
Look at the person.

Step 2:
Acknowledge (verbal/nonverbal).

Step 3:
Do the task immediately.

Step 4:
Check back if appropriate.

Look and say, then do it right away!

Reproducible Form T2.5
See p. 42   COPYRIGHT © 2009 · SUSAN L. MULKEY & KAREN A. KEMP

REPRODUCIBLE T2.5

To suit different grade levels, each of the steps can be modified to use fewer words or pictures. Another option is to use rhymes or short phrases such as:

When given an instruction, look alive!
Say "OK," and do it in five.

A T-chart such as the one below can clarify for students what the appropriate behaviors look and sound like.

Looks Like	Sounds Like
In seat	No noises from hands, mouth, or body
Looking at person	No whining, pouting, or arguing while talking
Pleasant face	Saying "OK," "all right," or "yes"
Starting the task quickly	Pleasant voice

Source: *Fister & Kemp, 1994.*

T2.6 BUDDY NOSE (KNOWS)

MATERIALS PREP ✂

GRADE LEVELS:
K–6

INTERVENTION TYPE:
Academic—All
Behavior—Motivation

REPRODUCIBLE on CD

After an instruction has been given, ask the students to tell the direction to the person sitting next to them.

If correct, buddies (partners) award their dyad a point on their "Buddy Nose" card.

Marks can be tallied at the end of the day or week. Recognition is given to the students who followed the most directions.

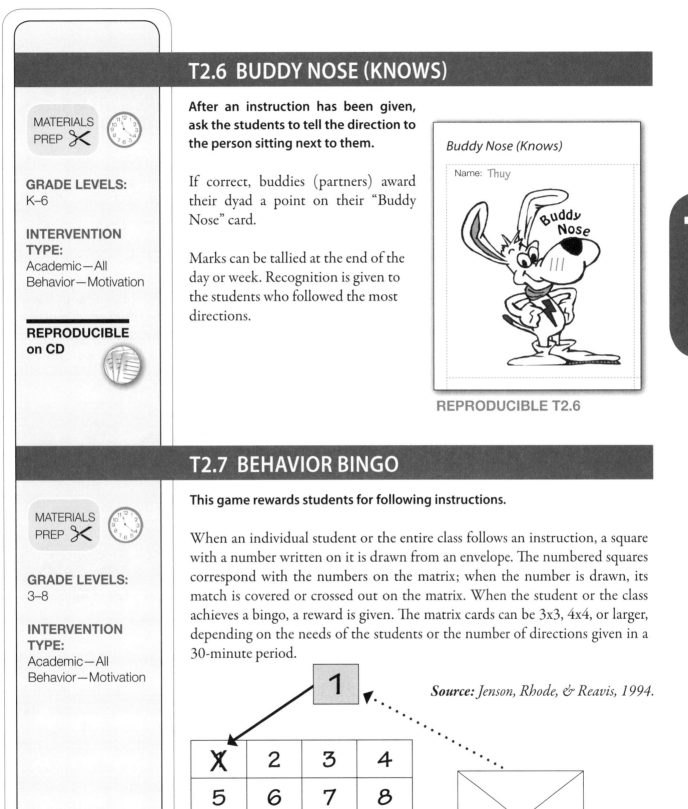

Buddy Nose (Knows)

Name: Thuy

REPRODUCIBLE T2.6

T2.7 BEHAVIOR BINGO

MATERIALS PREP ✂

GRADE LEVELS:
3–8

INTERVENTION TYPE:
Academic—All
Behavior—Motivation

This game rewards students for following instructions.

When an individual student or the entire class follows an instruction, a square with a number written on it is drawn from an envelope. The numbered squares correspond with the numbers on the matrix; when the number is drawn, its match is covered or crossed out on the matrix. When the student or the class achieves a bingo, a reward is given. The matrix cards can be 3x3, 4x4, or larger, depending on the needs of the students or the number of directions given in a 30-minute period.

Source: *Jenson, Rhode, & Reavis, 1994.*

1			
X	2	3	4
5	6	7	8
9	10	11	12
13	14	15	16

T2.8 YES/NO GAME

MATERIALS
PREP ✂

GRADE LEVELS:
3–8

INTERVENTION TYPE:
Academic—All
Behavior—Motivation

To encourage students to follow instructions, make a stack of Yes and No cards or slips of paper that are two different colors.

When students comply with a direction, describe the behavior and place a Yes card into an opaque jar or bag. If students do not comply with an instruction, place a No card into the jar. If it is necessary to deliver a No card, keep your comments brief and businesslike, such as, "When I give an instruction, you need to look and do. A No card goes in the container." It is important to remember to use verbal praise and encouragement when the class earns Yes cards.

Students earn Yes cards and No cards continually throughout a class period based upon their ability to follow directions. At the end of the time period, pull one card from the container. If it is a Yes card, the class earns a prearranged reward such as minutes of free time, buddy time, or other privileges. If a No card is pulled, no reward is given.

Source: Jenson, 1994.

T2.9 TRACKING DIRECTIONS

GRADE LEVELS:
3–8

INTERVENTION TYPE:
Academic—All
Behavior—Motivation

**REPRODUCIBLE
on CD**

To focus attention on following directions, all students or a target student can be given a tracker card like the one in the illustration.

The student is taught to circle a number (1) on the card when you give the first direction. Prompt students initially by saying something like, "Get ready for the first direction." Students circle the number and then decide if they followed the direction. If yes, they put a mark through the circled number. The card in the illustration shows that the student recorded the teacher giving nine instructions, eight of which the student followed during the recording period. You may find it useful to keep a tracker card to determine the total number of instructions given. This also provides a way to check the students' accuracy at recording marks.

T2: What can I do about the students who do not respond to my instructions?

At the end of the marking period, the student can count, record, and chart the number of directions followed and not followed or the percentage of directions followed. The students can punch a hole in the card each time they follow a direction. They can also paste their own photos on the card to personalize and add meaning to the procedure.

Source: Fister & Kemp, 1994.

Tracker Cards

Name   Jim

Beginning Date   5/21   1:00–1:30

Target Behavior   Following Directions

1	64											35	34
2	63											36	33
3	62											37	32
4	61											38	31
5	60											39	30
6	59											40	29
7	58											41	28
8	57											42	27
9	56											43	26
10	55	54	53	52	51	50	49	48	47	46	45	44	25
11	12	13	14	15	16	17	18	19	20	21	22	23	24

REPRODUCIBLE T2.9

T
G
I
F

T₃

TEACHER-DIRECTED INSTRUCTION

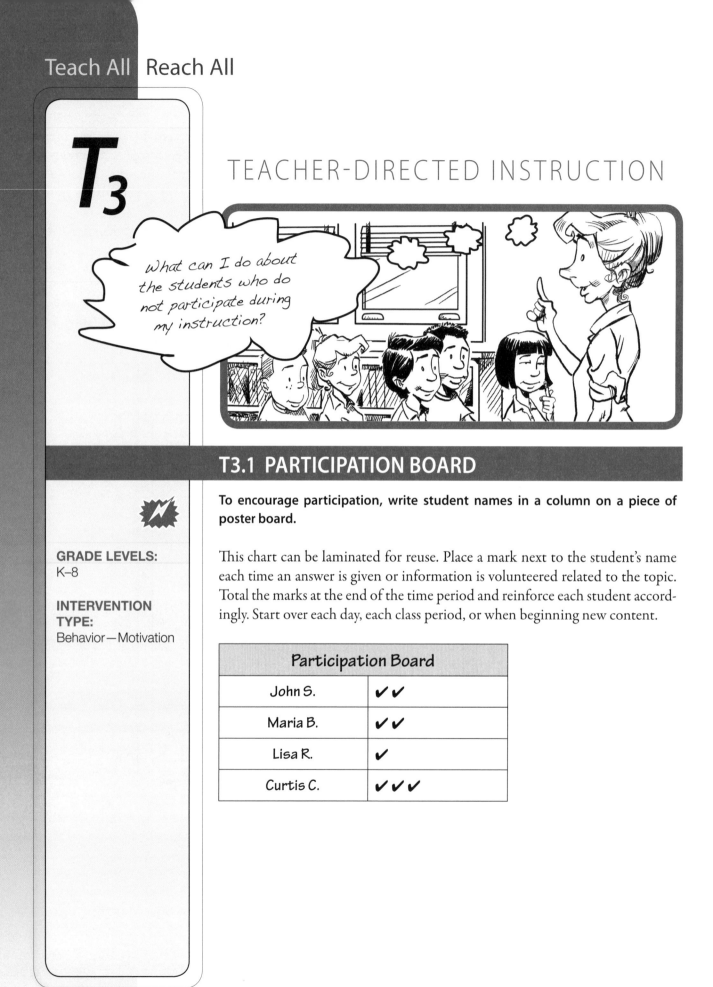

T3.1 PARTICIPATION BOARD

GRADE LEVELS:
K–8

INTERVENTION TYPE:
Behavior—Motivation

To encourage participation, write student names in a column on a piece of poster board.

This chart can be laminated for reuse. Place a mark next to the student's name each time an answer is given or information is volunteered related to the topic. Total the marks at the end of the time period and reinforce each student accordingly. Start over each day, each class period, or when beginning new content.

Participation Board	
John S.	✔✔
Maria B.	✔✔
Lisa R.	✔
Curtis C.	✔✔✔

T3: What can I do about the students who do not participate during my instruction?

T3.2 PARTICIPATION BUDDIES

MATERIALS
PREP ✂

GRADE LEVELS:
K–8

**INTERVENTION
TYPE:**
Behavior—Motivation

**REPRODUCIBLES
on CD**
(2 versions)

Involve more students by pairing them up to discuss certain questions.

Allow students to choose partners, or determine partners ahead of time by using one of the following formats:

- **Clock:** the face of a clock with the numbers 12, 3, 6, and 9 in their respective places.

- **Baseball Diamond:** an outline of a baseball diamond with first, second, and third base and home plate identified.

- **Map:** An outline of a state, country, or the world with designated cities or travel sites.

Students find classmates to pair up with and write the names of the other students next to each of the times, bases, or locations on their partner sheet.

When you pose a question to the class, have everyone think about the response and then find their "3 o'clock" partner to discuss the question or reflection statement with for one minute.

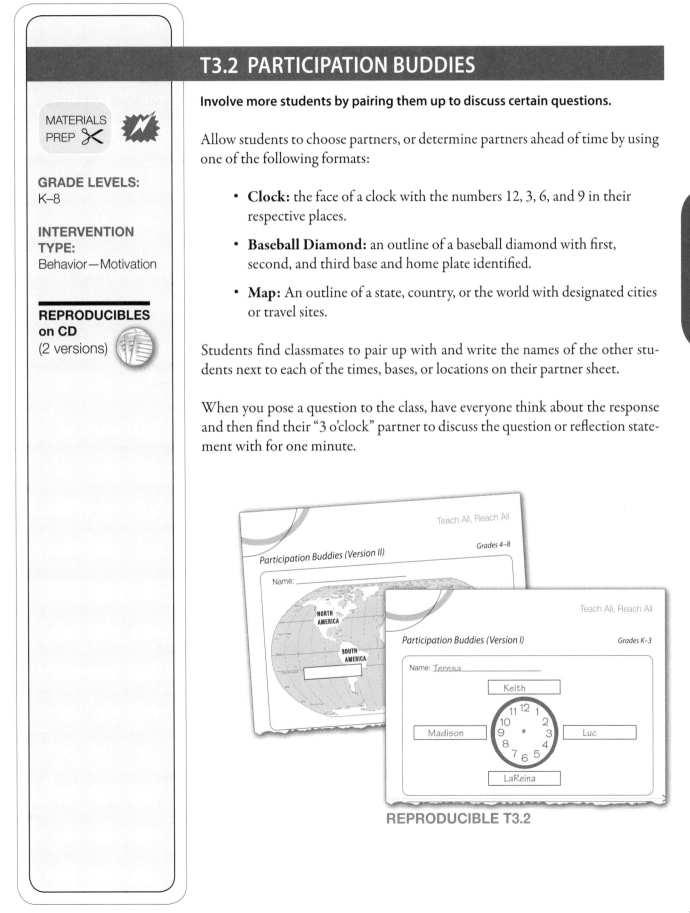

REPRODUCIBLE T3.2

T3.3 PARTICIPATION JIGSAW

GRADE LEVELS:
K–8

INTERVENTION TYPE:
Behavior—Motivation

Divide up the information and/or materials among the students so participation with others is necessary.

Break students into groups of four. Each group is responsible for completing an assignment cooperatively. Give each student a part of the assignment to complete individually, then require each individual to share their information with the rest of the group. Make it clear to the students that every group member is accountable for all the information shared in the group. Group and/or individual tests can be administered after completion of the assignment.

Source: *Johnson, Johnson, & Holubec, 1987.*

T3.4 WILD CARD SPINNER

MATERIALS PREP

GRADE LEVELS:
K–8

INTERVENTION TYPE:
Behavior—Motivation

You and your students agree on a predetermined number of participation marks the students will try to earn during the class period.

If the student earns the required number of marks, they are allowed a chance to spin. The rewards are listed on the Menu of Options, along with the unknown Wild Card. After using this procedure successfully, you can vary the number of participation marks the students must earn or write down a mystery number that is unknown to them. Students earn a chance to spin if they demonstrate the behavior at least the number of times written on the paper.

Step 1. The Spinner is divided into sections of various sizes and is numbered to correspond to the items on the Menu of Options. The number on each section represents a different positive reinforcer.

Step 2. The reinforcers are selected so that those of "higher" value (time, effort, money) correspond to the numbers in the smaller sections of the spinner. Those of "lesser" value correspond to the numbers in the larger sections of the spinner (see illustration). The section with the exclamation mark is the unknown Wild Card. The fact that this reinforcer is unknown adds an element of mystery and surprise to this technique. The Menu of Options is laminated so that the positive reinforcements can be changed periodically to maintain student interest and the effectiveness of the technique.

Step 3. The Wild Card reinforcer should be unique and of value to students. The unknown reinforcer is placed inside a large envelope or box, or the item name can be written on a slip of paper and placed inside an

T3: What can I do about the students who do not participate during my instruction?

envelope. The envelope or box is then displayed in a prominent position in the classroom.

Step 4. When the student earns a reward, he or she receives a chance to spin the Wild Card Spinner. The student then locates the corresponding number on the Menu of Options and determines the reinforcement to be received.

Menu of Options
1 half homework
2 Floating "A"
3 Pencil
4 Spin tomorrow
5 One bonus point
! Wild card

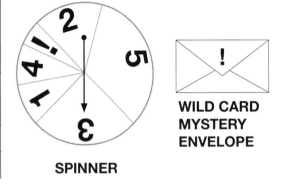

SPINNER

**WILD CARD
MYSTERY
ENVELOPE**

**T
G
I
F**

Source: Adapted from Rhode, Jenson, & Reavis, 1993.

T3.5 PARTICIPATION DOTS

**MATERIALS
PREP** ✂

GRADE LEVELS:
K–6

**INTERVENTION
TYPE:**
Behavior—Motivation

**REPRODUCIBLE
on CD**

Students track their participation by connecting the dots on a picture each time they participate in class. Obtain a dot-to-dot picture from a coloring book or create a picture with dots arranged along the outside. With each positive participation, the student is allowed to draw a line to the next dot on the picture. The student can earn rewards based on the number of dots connected during a specified period of time. The first or last dot of the day can be marked in order to visualize daily progress on the chart.

Source: Adapted from Rhode, Jenson, & Reavis, 1993.

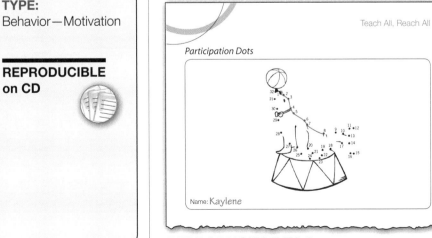

Teach All, Reach All

Participation Dots

Name: Kaylene

REPRODUCIBLE T3.5

MATERIALS
PREP

GRADE LEVELS:
K–8

INTERVENTION
TYPE:
Behavior—Motivation

NOTE:
Invisible ink pens
or Secret Agent
markers can be pur-
chased from Alex
Toys (www.alextoys.
com) or Crayola
(www.crayola.com).

T3.6 MYSTERY MOTIVATORS

Students earn mystery reinforcers by participating.

The first component of Mystery Motivators is the reinforcer itself. The name of a reinforcer is written on a slip of paper and sealed inside an envelope. The second component is the chart on which you have randomly marked reinforcement days with an X. Each day on the chart has a self-sticking dot on it. For each day or period in which the students have earned a reinforcement for positive participation, a dot is peeled off. If there is an X under the dot, the student is given the Mystery Motivator envelope to open. If there is no X, the student waits until the next day to earn a reinforcement and peel off another dot. Invisible ink pens can be used instead of self-sticking dots to mark the X's on the chart.

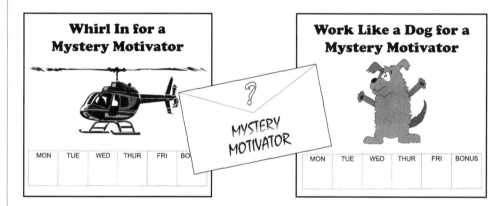

Source: Rhode, Jenson, & Reavis, 1993.

T3.7 PARTICIPATION POINTS

Provide students with a grading sheet that outlines the point system you have developed to reflect participation and effort during class.

Establish the criteria for earning participation points by identifying the particular class behaviors that demonstrate excellence in participation.

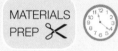

Criteria for participation and effort (up to ten points can be earned per day/class):

• Bring pencil, paper, book, and other related materials (four points).

• Answer teacher-directed questions (one point each).

MATERIALS
PREP

GRADE LEVELS:
3–8

INTERVENTION
TYPE:
Behavior—Motivation

REPRODUCIBLE
on CD

T3: What can I do about the students who do not participate during my instruction?

- Interact appropriately with other students during discussions (two points).

- Use target social behaviors such as sitting up, eyes tracking teacher, getting teacher's attention with signal, accepting feedback, and completing in-class assignments (two points).

Keep track of participation points using a recording sheet (see illustration). Record the number of points earned during the corresponding day of the week. Incorporate points earned into the quarterly academic grade. Students can also monitor each other's participation using a similar recording sheet.

Teach All, Reach All

Participation Points

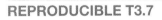

Name	WEEK 1						WEEK 2						WEEK 3						WEEK 4					
	M	T	W	Th	F	Total	M	T	W	Th	F	Total	M	T	W	Th	F	Total	M	T	W	Th	F	Total
Tasha	7	7	9	5																				

Reproducible Form T3.7
See p. 50

COPYRIGHT © 2009 · SUSAN L. MULKEY & KAREN A. KEMP

REPRODUCIBLE T3.7

T G I F

51

T4

TEACHER-DIRECTED INSTRUCTION

What can I do about the students who disrupt during my instruction?

T4.1 EVERYBODY SAY

Whenever you give information to the students, ask them to repeat it back to you or supply certain key words. When you maintain high rates of responses, students will be less likely to disrupt.

GRADE LEVELS:
K–8

INTERVENTION TYPE:
Academic—All

EXAMPLES

- Sturdy means strong. Everybody, what does sturdy mean? Class, what is another word for strong?

- Here is a rule for regrouping. Whenever you take away more than you start with, you must regroup. Everybody, get ready to say the rule with me.
  Or, Whenever you take away more then you start with, you must . . . (students supply the missing word).

- Everybody, what sound? What word?

- Class, spell the word aloud with me.

- **Au** represents what element, everybody?

- Get ready to say the name of the main character. What is the name?

- Which family did Romeo belong to?

T4.2 FREQUENT QUESTIONS

Ask the disruptive students four times as many questions as you are currently asking during the problematic time period. These should be questions that you know the students can answer correctly.

Remember to first ask the question as if it were directed to the entire group ("Everybody, get ready to give me a definition for matter.") Pause for three to five seconds and then call on the target student. Call on the student when he or she is not disrupting and remember to follow the student's answer with an acknowledgement comment.

GRADE LEVELS:
K–8

INTERVENTION TYPE:
Academic—All

T4.3 ON-TASK CHART

A laminated chart or sheet of paper can serve as a visual display to post both the number of class disruptions and tasks completed during a specified time period.

Students can be assigned to count the number in both categories. (The disruptive student can be given this responsibility!) Daily totals are charted on the bottom portion of the chart and a brief discussion with the students can follow to evaluate class performance. Reinforcement can be provided for achieving daily goals. You can also set goals for the next recording period.

MATERIALS PREP ✂

GRADE LEVELS:
3–8

INTERVENTION TYPE:
Behavior—Motivation

REPRODUCIBLE on CD

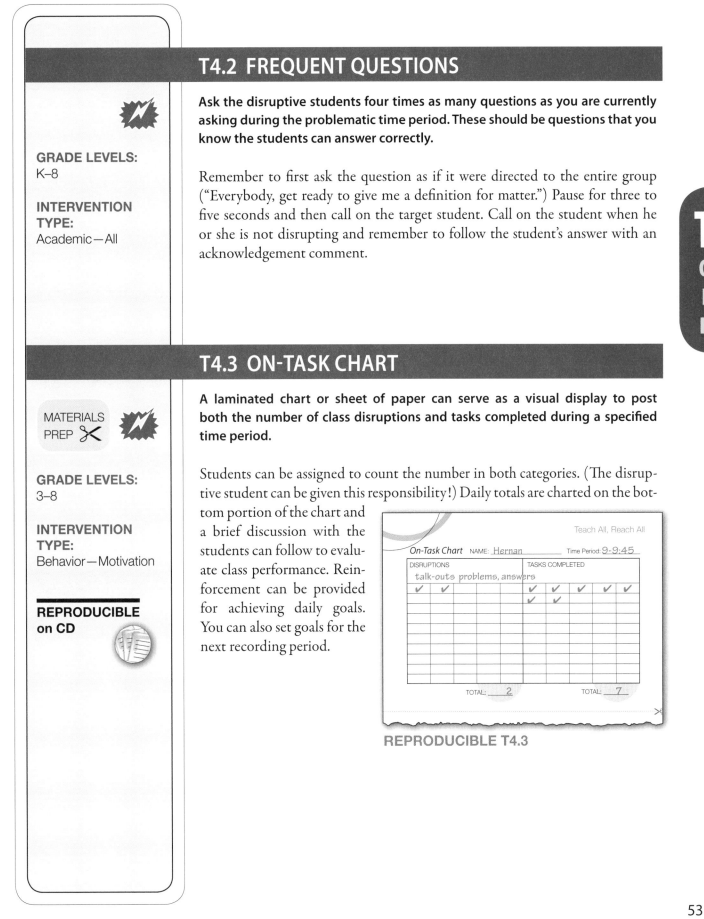

REPRODUCIBLE T4.3

T4.4 NAME'S UP LISTENING BOARD

GRADE LEVELS:
K–6

INTERVENTION TYPE:
Behavior—Motivation

A Name's Up Listening Board is a place where you can quickly write or post students' names when they demonstrate good listening or attentive behavior.

The board can be a portion of the chalk board, a flip chart, a white board, etc. (see illustration below). When you notice listening behaviors (e.g., looking at the teacher, attentive silence, quiet hand raises, relevant contributions, correct responses, etc.), write the student's name on the Listening Board and verbally recognize the behavior with an enthusiastic description of the behavior (e.g., "Wow, look at Susie. She is listening and giving quick answers!"). When students demonstrate continuing listening behaviors, simply put asterisks (*) or checkmarks (✓) next to their names as the praise is delivered. At the end of the instructional period, the names can be erased and the activity repeated.

Listening Board	
James	✔ ✔ ✔
Shawnice	✔ ✔ ✔ ✔ ✔
Ramon	✔
C.J.	✔ ✔

T4.5 FOLLOWING INSTRUCTIONS

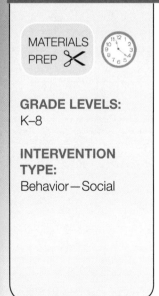

MATERIALS PREP

GRADE LEVELS:
K–8

INTERVENTION TYPE:
Behavior—Social

Teach students the steps you expect when you give instructions. See T2.5 (p. 42) for information on applying the Following Instructions technique when dealing with disruptive students.

T4: What can I do about the students who disrupt during my instruction?

T4.6 KEEPING THE NUMBERS LOW

MATERIALS PREP ✂

GRADE LEVELS:
K–8

INTERVENTION TYPE:
Behavior—Motivation

This is a classwide management system in which a limit for disruptions is pre-determined for the entire class.

Start with three cards of different colors or with the numbers 1, 2, and 3 written on them. The numbered cards indicate for the students the limits for disruptions. When a disruption occurs, turn over a card. If all cards are used, the class loses the reinforcer (which might be free time or some other privilege). When the number of disruptions decreases, the number of cards used can also decrease.

This method can also be used with small groups of students or with an individual student where the cards are placed on the student's desk.

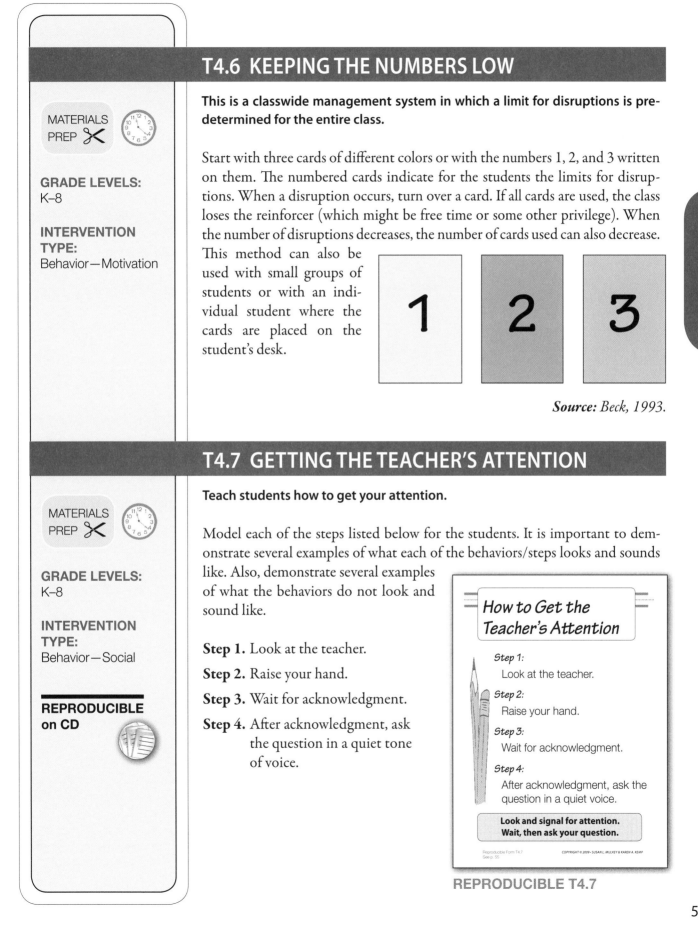

Source: Beck, 1993.

T4.7 GETTING THE TEACHER'S ATTENTION

MATERIALS PREP ✂

GRADE LEVELS:
K–8

INTERVENTION TYPE:
Behavior—Social

REPRODUCIBLE on CD

Teach students how to get your attention.

Model each of the steps listed below for the students. It is important to demonstrate several examples of what each of the behaviors/steps looks and sounds like. Also, demonstrate several examples of what the behaviors do not look and sound like.

Step 1. Look at the teacher.

Step 2. Raise your hand.

Step 3. Wait for acknowledgment.

Step 4. After acknowledgment, ask the question in a quiet tone of voice.

How to Get the Teacher's Attention

Step 1:
Look at the teacher.

Step 2:
Raise your hand.

Step 3:
Wait for acknowledgment.

Step 4:
After acknowledgment, ask the question in a quiet voice.

**Look and signal for attention.
Wait, then ask your question.**

REPRODUCIBLE T4.7

Each of the steps can be modified to fewer words, or pictures can be used to represent the steps. You may also use rhymes or short phrases such as:

- Look and signal for attention.
- Wait, then ask your question.

A T-chart such as the one in the illustration below can clarify for students what the appropriate behaviors look and sound like.

Looks Like	Sounds Like
In seat or assigned area	No noises while waiting
Signal/Hand up	Use pleasant tone of voice
Pleasant face	
Eyes on teacher	

Source: *Fister & Kemp, 1994.*

T4.8 RESPONSIBILITY ROLES

Providing a student with a specific and meaningful job may decrease disruptive behavior.

MATERIALS
PREP ✂

GRADE LEVELS:
K–8

INTERVENTION TYPE:
Behavior—Social

REPRODUCIBLE on CD

Have the target student be a timekeeper during a presentation, a note-taker during a lesson, a recorder of points earned, a facilitator during a cooperative learning group activity, a manager of materials distribution, or a counter of teacher praise statements. If appropriate, the student can mark on the role card each time the role is performed. The role needs to be clearly defined for the student, with ample practice opportunities provided. Give the student plenty of positive, specific, and descriptive feedback regarding his or her performance.

REPRODUCIBLE T4.8

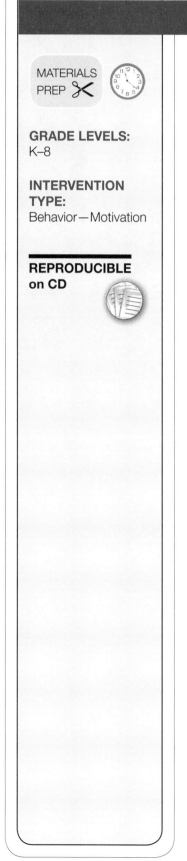

MATERIALS
PREP ✂

GRADE LEVELS:
K–8

INTERVENTION TYPE:
Behavior—Motivation

REPRODUCIBLE on CD

T4.9 COUNTOON

Students track disruptions and replacement behavior.

Target students are given a tracker card like the one in the illustration below. Teach them how to identify a disruption and mark it on the card when it occurs. Also teach students a replacement behavior to count and record, such as problems completed, hand raising, or a social skill. The replacement behavior should be an acceptable alternative to the disruptive behavior. Cartoons, hand-drawn pictures, or actual photographs representing each behavior are included on each side of the card. Reinforcement for acceptable behavior and daily improvement can be added to this strategy if necessary. (See Mystery Motivators [T3.6, p. 50] and Wild Card Spinner [T3.4, p. 48].)

Source: Fister & Kemp, 1994.

T G I F

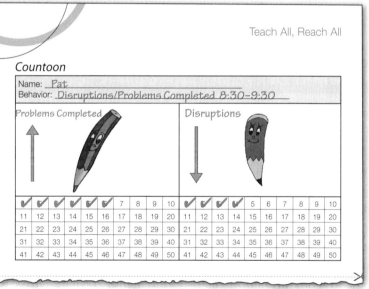

REPRODUCIBLE T4.9

T5

TEACHER-DIRECTED INSTRUCTION

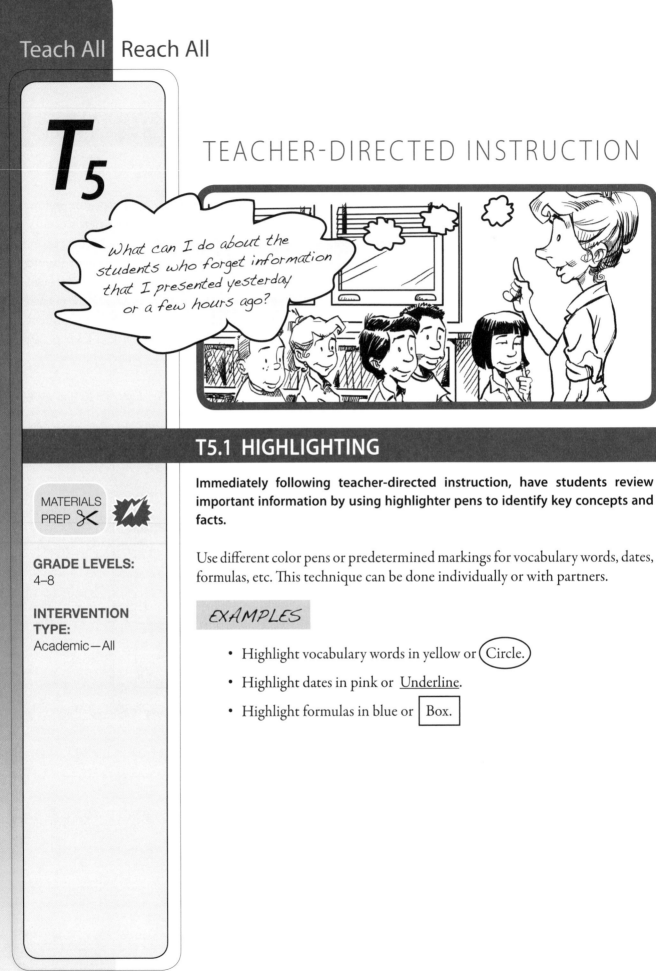

What can I do about the students who forget information that I presented yesterday or a few hours ago?

MATERIALS PREP ✂ ⚡

GRADE LEVELS:
4–8

INTERVENTION TYPE:
Academic—All

T5.1 HIGHLIGHTING

Immediately following teacher-directed instruction, have students review important information by using highlighter pens to identify key concepts and facts.

Use different color pens or predetermined markings for vocabulary words, dates, formulas, etc. This technique can be done individually or with partners.

EXAMPLES

- Highlight vocabulary words in yellow or Ⓒircle.
- Highlight dates in pink or <u>Underline</u>.
- Highlight formulas in blue or Box.

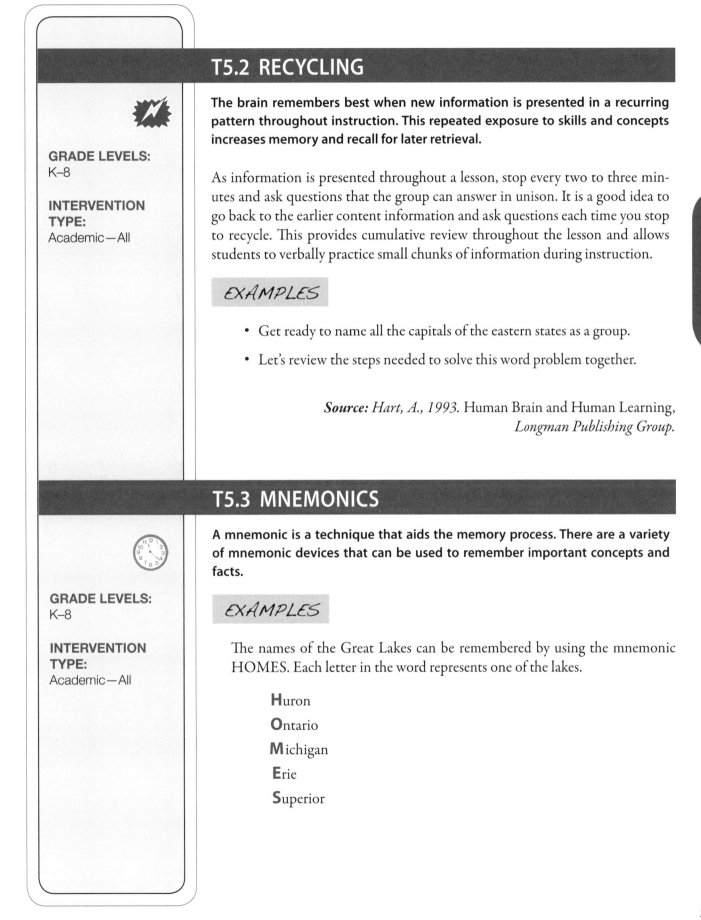

T5.2 RECYCLING

GRADE LEVELS:
K–8

INTERVENTION TYPE:
Academic—All

The brain remembers best when new information is presented in a recurring pattern throughout instruction. This repeated exposure to skills and concepts increases memory and recall for later retrieval.

As information is presented throughout a lesson, stop every two to three minutes and ask questions that the group can answer in unison. It is a good idea to go back to the earlier content information and ask questions each time you stop to recycle. This provides cumulative review throughout the lesson and allows students to verbally practice small chunks of information during instruction.

EXAMPLES

- Get ready to name all the capitals of the eastern states as a group.

- Let's review the steps needed to solve this word problem together.

***Source:** Hart, A., 1993.* Human Brain and Human Learning, *Longman Publishing Group.*

T5.3 MNEMONICS

GRADE LEVELS:
K–8

INTERVENTION TYPE:
Academic—All

A mnemonic is a technique that aids the memory process. There are a variety of mnemonic devices that can be used to remember important concepts and facts.

EXAMPLES

The names of the Great Lakes can be remembered by using the mnemonic HOMES. Each letter in the word represents one of the lakes.

Huron

Ontario

Michigan

Erie

Superior

T
G
I
F

The steps in the division process can be taught to students by using this silly sentence: Dumb Monkeys Sneak Bananas.

Divide
Multiply
Subtract
Bring Down

Students can develop their own mnemonics by using the FIRST Letter Mnemonic strategy. Model and demonstrate the following steps to students.

Form a word by using the first letters of the fact that needs to be remembered.

Insert a small letter to make a word.

Rearrange the letters if they do not need to be in order.

Sentence is created to remember the first letters of each word.

Try a combination of all of the above.

Source: *Nagel, Shumaker, & Deshler, 1986.*

T5.4 NOTE STACKS

MATERIALS
PREP

GRADE LEVELS:
3–8

**INTERVENTION
TYPE:**
Academic—All

Have students write questions or facts on one side of an index card and the corresponding information on the other side.

This can be done prior to instruction or during the "input" section of the lesson. Keep the cards in piles that can be referenced throughout the unit of instruction.

HOMES

Huron, Ontario, Michigan, Erie, Superior
(The Great Lakes)

T5: What can I do about the students who forget information that I presented yesterday or a few hours ago?

T5.5 MEMORY LOG

MATERIALS PREP ✂

GRADE LEVELS:
3–8

INTERVENTION TYPE:
Academic—All

REPRODUCIBLE on CD

T
G
I
F

Develop a format for a memory log to use during discussion or lecture.

Create the memory log on chart paper and hang it in a noticeable place in the room. Electronic chalk boards can also be used for this purpose. As you talk, have a student, an assistant, or another teacher record the important information in the memory log. Categories to be included in the log might be:

- Topic
- Rationale
- Outcome
- Important facts and concepts
- Supporting details
- Dates to remember

Logs can be used for one lesson only or throughout a unit by adding information each day. Individual versions of memory logs can also be developed and kept in student folders for personal reference.

Teach All, Reach All

Memory Log

Name: D'Neesha Quinn

Topic: Civil War

Important Facts and Concepts:

North:
manufacturing
believed in freeing the slaves

South:
plantations
used the slaves

Dates to Remember:
Compromise of 1850

Outcome: Describe important events
that led to the Civil War.

Relevance:

Supporting Details:

Vocabulary Words:

Interesting Information:

New Insights:

Reproducible Form T5.5
See p. 61

COPYRIGHT © 2009 • SUSAN L. MULKEY & KAREN A. KEMP

REPRODUCIBLE T5.5

T5.6 STUDY GUIDES (STANDARD)

MATERIALS
PREP ✂

GRADE LEVELS:
4–8

**INTERVENTION
TYPE:**
Academic—All

Study guides can be used as advance organizers for what is going to be presented in the lesson as well as review sheets for remembering important concepts taught.

The following steps are involved in creating a study guide.

Step 1. Develop an outline of the important facts and concepts to be presented during this portion of the lesson.

Step 2. Arrange the information in statement or question format.

Step 3. Allow students to use the outline to record the important information.

Review the completed study guide with the students at the end of the lesson and prior to teaching the next concept.

Study Guide—Chapter 30 Fishes
1. List two fish that belong to the class Agnatha.
2. Are lampreys parasitic in their larval stage?____ Adult stage? ____
3. Define *spawning*.
4. List common characteristics of both lampreys and hagfish.
5. List fishes that have cartilaginous skeletons.
6. The placoderm is an evolutionary link between what two classes of fishes?
7. Which of the ray's fins resemble wings?
8. What are *placoid scales*?
9. What do sharks eat?
10. Which are the most numerous of modern fishes?
11. What is the function of the swim bladder?

Source: Lovitt, Fister, Kemp, Moore, & Schroeder, 1992.

T5: What can I do about the students who forget information that I presented yesterday or a few hours ago?

T5.7 GRAPHIC ORGANIZERS (TOP DOWN)

Graphic organizers are visual displays of information that students can complete while the lesson is being presented or following the teacher's presentation. They can be used as review or completed while the lesson is presented.

Step 1. Determine important facts and concepts.

Step 2. Arrange them in sequential and logical order.

Step 3. Create a visual display of the information using boxes and pictures.

Step 4. Label reference points.

The organizer below demonstrates how information can be visually arranged to further illustrate points made during instruction.

Source: Lovitt et al., 1992.

MATERIALS PREP ✂

GRADE LEVELS:
K–8

INTERVENTION TYPE:
Academic—All

T G I F

Objective: Define and discuss the early signs and prevention of strokes.

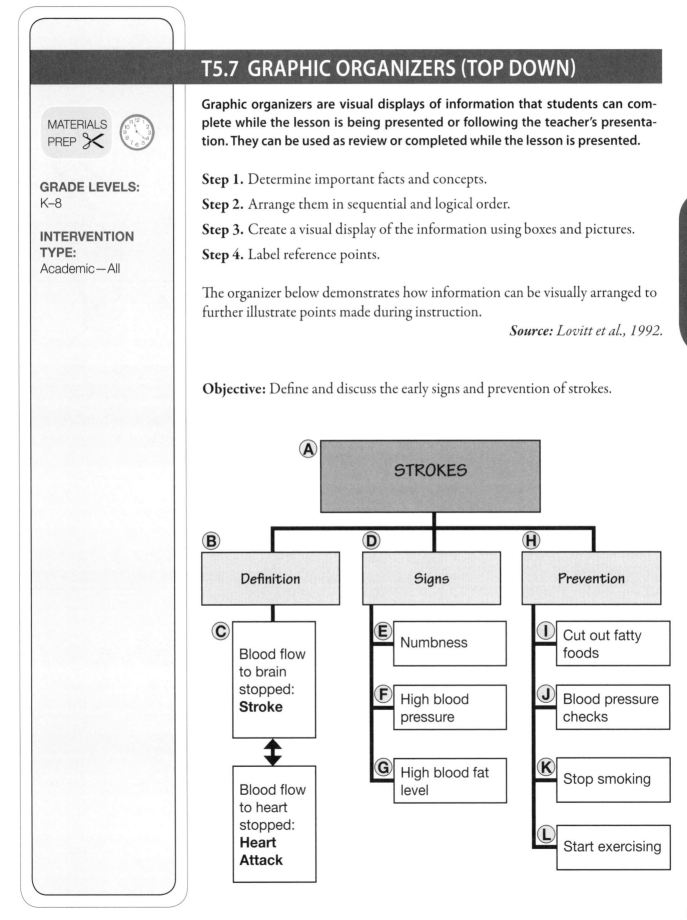

63

T_6 TEACHER-DIRECTED INSTRUCTION

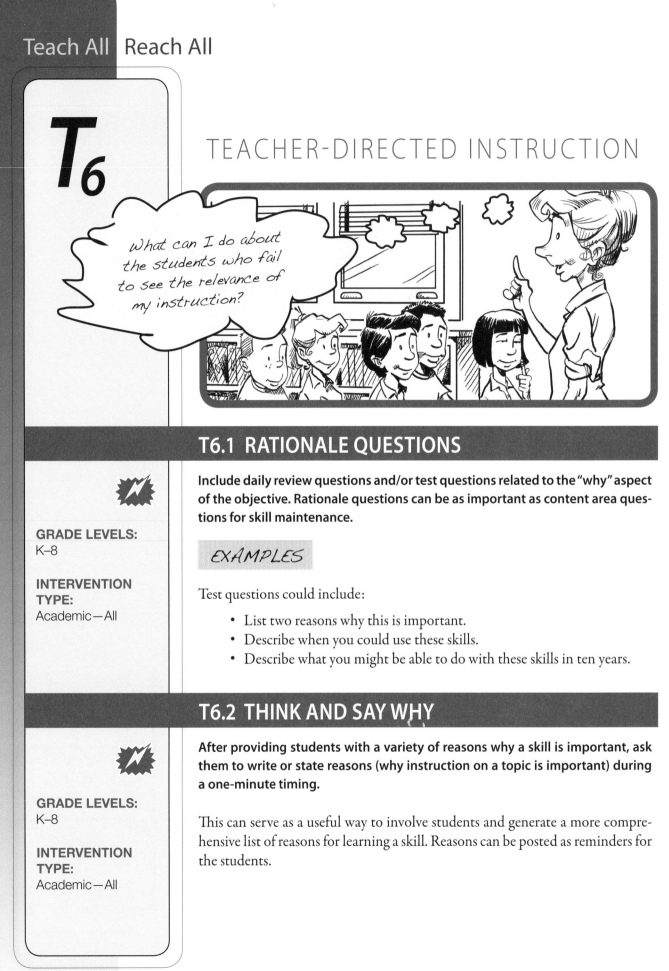

What can I do about the students who fail to see the relevance of my instruction?

T6.1 RATIONALE QUESTIONS

GRADE LEVELS:
K–8

INTERVENTION TYPE:
Academic—All

Include daily review questions and/or test questions related to the "why" aspect of the objective. Rationale questions can be as important as content area questions for skill maintenance.

EXAMPLES

Test questions could include:

- List two reasons why this is important.
- Describe when you could use these skills.
- Describe what you might be able to do with these skills in ten years.

T6.2 THINK AND SAY WHY

GRADE LEVELS:
K–8

INTERVENTION TYPE:
Academic—All

After providing students with a variety of reasons why a skill is important, ask them to write or state reasons (why instruction on a topic is important) during a one-minute timing.

This can serve as a useful way to involve students and generate a more comprehensive list of reasons for learning a skill. Reasons can be posted as reminders for the students.

T6.3 SHARE YOUR REASONS

GRADE LEVELS:
K–8

INTERVENTION TYPE:
Academic—All

Ask students to **think** of reasons why the lesson objective is important. This should first be done on their own for 10 to 30 seconds. Then, students pair up to share their reasons with a partner. Finally, they share reasons aloud with a group of four or the entire class. One student is assigned to be the reporter when sharing aloud their reasons.

Source: Kagan, 1990.

T6.4 WHAT, WHERE/WHEN, AND WHY STRATEGY

MATERIALS PREP ✂

GRADE LEVELS:
4–8

INTERVENTION TYPE:
Academic—All

REPRODUCIBLE on CD

To help students understand how they can apply new knowledge, provide students with a What, Where/When, and Why Strategy card such as the one in the illustration on the next page.

The students will fill in the card with What and Why statements or key words. At the beginning of the lesson, tell students what they will be able to do with their new knowledge that they cannot do presently.

- You will be able to use the steps for getting the teacher's attention.
- You will be able to say four new words and definitions.
- You will be able to solve a new variety of word problem.
- You will be able to identify both similarities and differences in the two characters from our story.

Then, have students fill in the **What** box with what they will be able to do. They might write:

- Use steps
- Say words and definitions
- Solve problems
- Write about same-different qualities

Likewise, tell students at the beginning of the lesson **Where** and/or **When** they can use the **What**. Provide students with situations where they can use the skill.

- You can use this strategy in this classroom and other classrooms, in the cafeteria, and at home.
- You can use these words when you read the story.

T
G
I
F

Then, instruct students to fill in the **Where/When** box with information on where and when they will be able to use the skill. They might write:

- In the classroom
- At home
- On the playground

Next, tell students at the beginning of the lesson **Why** the **What** is important. Provide students with a personal benefit (PB) rationale statement, an avoiding a negative consequence (ANC) benefit, or an effect on others (EOO) benefit.

EXAMPLES

PB: When you use the steps for getting the teacher's attention, you will get the help you need from me and get your work done on time.

ANC: When you use the steps for getting the teacher's attention, you will not lose points or your free time privileges.

EOO: When you use the steps for getting the teacher's attention, I appreciate and respect that kind of responsible behavior. So will other teachers. That's called a teacher-pleasing behavior!

Then, instruct students to fill in one of the **Why** boxes with an appropriate rationale statement. What, Where/When, Why cards can be practiced and reviewed before instruction and stored in a folder, notebook, or ring clip.

Teach All, Reach All

Name: Kory

	What, Where/When, Why Card
What	Use steps for getting attention.
Where/When	At home, in the classroom.
Why	I will get the help I need from my parents and my teachers.

REPRODUCIBLE T6.4

T6: What can I do about the students who fail to see the relevance of my instruction?

T6.5 FUTURES MAP

**MATERIALS
PREP** ✂

GRADE LEVELS:
4–8

**INTERVENTION
TYPE:**
Academic—All

**REPRODUCIBLE
on CD**

Help students connect future goals with current objectives.

Begin by providing students with a relevant goal for the future that has a connection to the current lesson objective. Create a Futures Map (see illustration) where you and the students chart the relevance of lessons as "Life Skills." Some of the categories on the map should include: Employment, Leisure/Social Recreation, and Daily Independent Living. The map should also include the lesson objective and how it can be applied both in and out of the classroom. In charting the map, ask students:

- What do you see yourself doing in 2 years, 5 years, 10 years?

- What do you want to have accomplished?

Proceed from the future vision back to the present, asking questions like, "What will you need to get there in terms of money, job, education, etc."? This activity often helps to establish the relevancy of current lessons when students fail to see their importance.

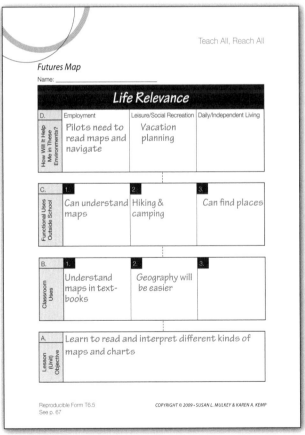

REPRODUCIBLE T6.5

**T
G
I
F**

T₇

TEACHER-DIRECTED INSTRUCTION

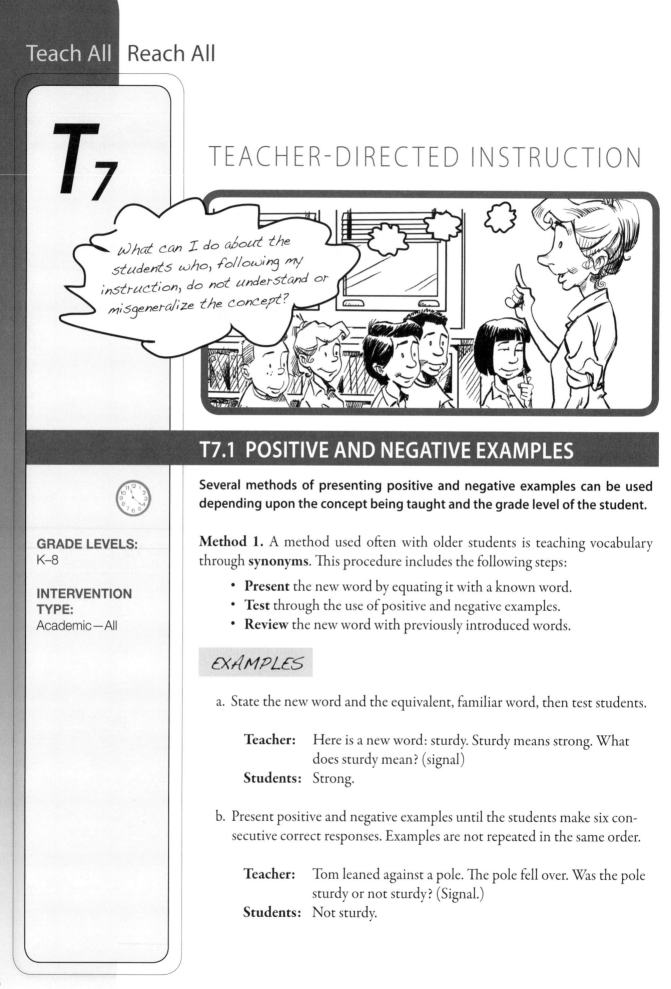

> What can I do about the students who, following my instruction, do not understand or misgeneralize the concept?

T7.1 POSITIVE AND NEGATIVE EXAMPLES

GRADE LEVELS:
K–8

INTERVENTION TYPE:
Academic—All

Several methods of presenting positive and negative examples can be used depending upon the concept being taught and the grade level of the student.

Method 1. A method used often with older students is teaching vocabulary through **synonyms**. This procedure includes the following steps:

- **Present** the new word by equating it with a known word.
- **Test** through the use of positive and negative examples.
- **Review** the new word with previously introduced words.

EXAMPLES

a. State the new word and the equivalent, familiar word, then test students.

> **Teacher:** Here is a new word: sturdy. Sturdy means strong. What does sturdy mean? (signal)
>
> **Students:** Strong.

b. Present positive and negative examples until the students make six consecutive correct responses. Examples are not repeated in the same order.

> **Teacher:** Tom leaned against a pole. The pole fell over. Was the pole sturdy or not sturdy? (Signal.)
>
> **Students:** Not sturdy.

T7: What can I do about the students who, following my instruction, do not understand or misgeneralize the concept?

Teacher: Tom leaned against another pole. The pole did not move. Was the pole sturdy or not sturdy? (Signal.)

Students: Sturdy.

Teacher: A house did not shake at all in a strong windstorm. Was the house sturdy or not sturdy? (Signal.)

Students: Sturdy.

Teacher: A different house fell down when the wind started blowing. Was the house sturdy or not sturdy? (Signal.)

Students: Not sturdy.

Note: You may also provide practice by asking the students to generate examples: "Tell me about something that is sturdy."

c. Review the new word and other previously introduced words.

- Is it mild out today? How do you know?
- Is that bench sturdy? How do you know?
- Is my desk tidy? How do you know?

In constructing definitions, you must make them understandable to students rather than make them technically correct. For example, a liquid might be defined as "something poured." Although scientists may disapprove of this definition, it is adequate to teach the meaning of liquid to young children. Definitions are kept simple and understandable by using words students already know to define words they don't.

Some sample definitions appear below. Note the effort to keep them as simple as possible.

Word	Category/Group	Differs from other things in the category/group
Container	An object	you can put things in.
Vehicle	An object	that can take you places.
Seam	A thing	where two pieces of material are sewn together.
Glare	An action	where you stare at someone as if you are angry.

Source: *Adapted from Carnine, Silbert, & Kame'enui, 1990.*

Method 2. Modeling is used when it is impossible to find the language to explain the exact meaning of a word. It is used primarily to teach concepts like color, size, and shape covered in preschool and kindergarten. The basic procedures include:

- **Provide** positive and negative examples of the new concept.
- **Test** the students on their mastery of the examples for the new word.
- **Present** different examples of the new word, along with examples of previously taught words.

	Object	Adjective (color)	Adverb	Adjective (texture)
Step 1: Teacher models positive and negative examples.	"This is a **mitten**" or "This is not a mitten." **Examples:** • brown wool mitten • brown wool glove • red nylon glove • red nylon mitten • blue sock • blue mitten	"This is **orange**" or "This is not orange." **Examples:** • a red disk • an orange disk • piece of orange construction paper • piece of brown construction paper	"This is writing **carefully**" or "This is not writing carefully." **Examples:** • Write on board, first neatly, then sloppily. • Hang up coat, first carefully, then carelessly. • Arrange books, first carelessly, then carefully.	"This is **rough**" or "This is not rough." **Examples:** • red flannel shirt • red silk shirt • piece of sandpaper • piece of paper • smooth book cover • rough book cover
Step 2: Teacher tests. Present positive and negative examples until the students make six consecutive correct responses.	"Is this a mitten or not a mitten?"	"Is this orange or not orange?"	"Is this _____ carefully or not carefully?"	"Is this rough or not rough?"
Step 3: Teacher tests by asking for names. Present examples until the students make six consecutive correct responses.	"What is this?" **Examples:** • glove • mitten • sock • mitten • mitten • glove	"What color is this?" **Examples:** • orange • brown • orange • red	"Show me how you _____ carefully" or "Tell me about how I am writing" (quickly, slowly, carefully, etc.).	"Find the _____ that is rough" or "Tell me about this shirt" (rough, red, pretty, etc.).

Source: Direct Instruction Reading *(2nd ed.)* by Douglas Carnine, Jerry Silbert, *and Edward J. Kame'enui. © 1990 by Macmillan College Publishing. Reprinted with permission.*

GRADE LEVELS:
K–8

INTERVENTION TYPE:
Academic—All

T7.2 STRATEGIES AND RULES

When introducing a new concept to students, use consistent vocabulary and provide explicit step-by-step instructions.

Students should be taught strategies they can learn relatively easily and apply to a range of related problems.

EXAMPLES

MATH STRATEGIES/RULES

- **Reading Thousand Numbers:** The number in front of the comma tells how many thousands.

- **Subtraction With Renaming:** When we take away more than we start with, we must rename.

- **Fractions:** If the top number is more than the bottom number, the fraction equals more than one whole. If the top number is less than the bottom number, the fraction equals less than one whole.

- **Metric Conversions:** When we change to a bigger unit, we divide. When we change to a smaller unit, we multiply.

Source: Silbert, Carnine, & Stein, 1990.

READING STRATEGIES/RULES

- **Identifying the Main Idea:** If it tells about the whole passage, it is the main idea.

- **Vowel Consonant Silent "e" (VCe):** When there is an "e" at the end of the word, this letter (the vowel) says its name.

- **Writing a Main Idea Sentence:** Name the person and tell the main thing the person did in all the sentences.

- **Double Consonants Following a Vowel:** If double consonants come after the vowel, pronounce the vowel's sound (hopping); if a single consonant comes after, pronounce the vowel's name (hoping).

Source: Carnine et al., 1990.

T7.3 CORRECTIVE FEEDBACK

GRADE LEVELS:
K–8

INTERVENTION TYPE:
Behavior—Social

Using a specific strategy for feedback gives you an opportunity to re-teach a concept to a student.

EXAMPLE

A student has been asked the question: "What is the capital of Utah?" and responds, "Provo." Use the following correction procedure to treat the student with dignity and respect while providing a correct answer to the question.

Step 1. Dignify the response. Do this by moving close to the student, using the student's name, and maintaining a pleasant tone of voice and facial expression. Use phrases such as:
- "You are thinking of another large city in Utah that is farther south than the capital."
- "I wonder if you are thinking of . . ."

If the answer does not make sense to you, use phrases such as:
- "Help me understand how you came up with that answer."
- "I am not sure what you are thinking—can you tell me?"

Step 2. Correct the answer. Do this by prompting the student for the answer. An example might be: "This city starts with an S and has three words." Or give the student the answer: "The capital of Utah is Salt Lake City."

Step 3. Validate the student's response. Do this by having the student give the correct answer before you move on to another question or student. Let the student know that you will be back later to see if he or she remembers the correct answer.

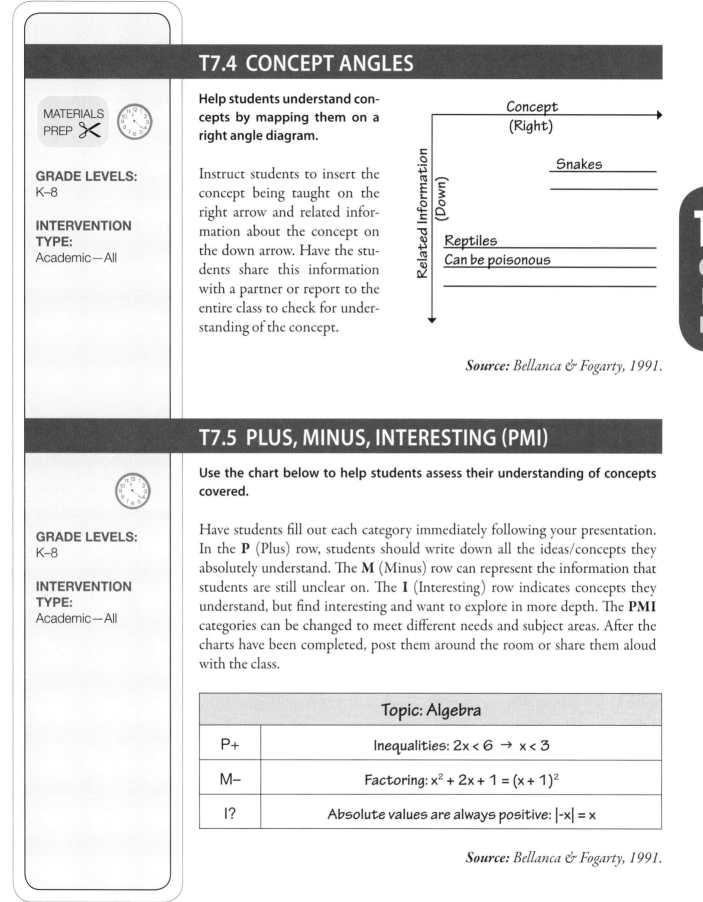

T7.4 CONCEPT ANGLES

MATERIALS PREP

GRADE LEVELS:
K–8

INTERVENTION TYPE:
Academic—All

Help students understand concepts by mapping them on a right angle diagram.

Instruct students to insert the concept being taught on the right arrow and related information about the concept on the down arrow. Have the students share this information with a partner or report to the entire class to check for understanding of the concept.

Concept
(Right)

Snakes

Reptiles
Can be poisonous

Related Information
(Down)

Source: Bellanca & Fogarty, 1991.

T7.5 PLUS, MINUS, INTERESTING (PMI)

GRADE LEVELS:
K–8

INTERVENTION TYPE:
Academic—All

Use the chart below to help students assess their understanding of concepts covered.

Have students fill out each category immediately following your presentation. In the **P** (Plus) row, students should write down all the ideas/concepts they absolutely understand. The **M** (Minus) row can represent the information that students are still unclear on. The **I** (Interesting) row indicates concepts they understand, but find interesting and want to explore in more depth. The **PMI** categories can be changed to meet different needs and subject areas. After the charts have been completed, post them around the room or share them aloud with the class.

Topic: Algebra	
P+	Inequalities: $2x < 6 \rightarrow x < 3$
M–	Factoring: $x^2 + 2x + 1 = (x + 1)^2$
I?	Absolute values are always positive: $|-x| = x$

Source: Bellanca & Fogarty, 1991.

T7.6 I QUESTION THAT!

This chart is especially useful when difficult vocabulary keeps students from understanding the concepts.

Provide students with a chart similar to the one shown to fill out as information is presented. Review what students have written down with the entire class.

MATERIALS
PREP ✂

GRADE LEVELS:
3–8

INTERVENTION TYPE:
Academic—All

Topic: Hamlet by William Shakespeare: Soliloquy "To be or not to be . . ."	
What Do I Think Is Being Said?	What Words Keep Me From Understanding?
Hamlet is debating whether or not to commit suicide.	consummation, line 63 fardels, line 76 the native hue of resolution, line 84

T7.7 KNOW/WANT TO KNOW/LEARNED (KWL)

Give students the following chart to fill out before and after information is presented. Discuss the responses with partners, cooperative groups, or the entire class.

MATERIALS
PREP ✂

GRADE LEVELS:
K–8

INTERVENTION TYPE:
Academic—All

Topic: Sewing		
What We Know	What We Want to Find Out	What We Learned
How to thread a sewing machine	How to use a serger	How to create French seams

Source: Bellanca & Fogarty, 1991.

74

T7.8 LEARNING LOGS

MATERIALS
PREP

GRADE LEVELS:
3–8

**INTERVENTION
TYPE:**
Academic—All

**REPRODUCIBLES
on CD**
(2 versions)

Have students keep a log of their lessons.

Have students write in a notebook for a specified amount of time (five minutes) during the lesson or immediately following. Use the following questions or make up your own. You can also use illustrations or icons as questions (e.g., a lightbulb, smiling face, question marks).

1. What did I learn?

2. What puzzled me?

3. What did I not enjoy?

4. How did I learn?

5. What will I remember most?

T
G
I
F

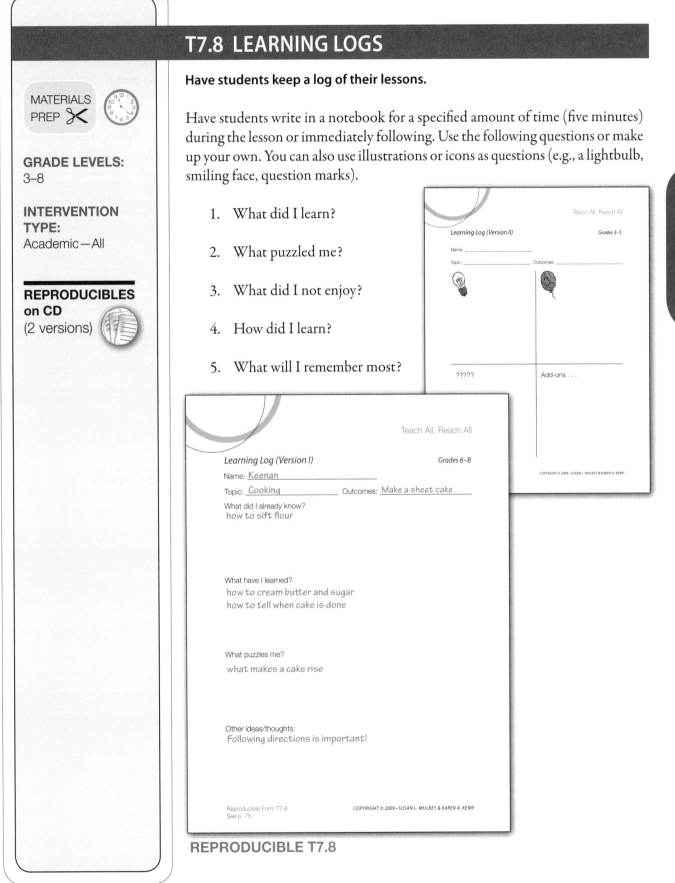

Teach All, Reach All

Learning Log (Version II)   Grades 3–5

Name: _____

Topic: _____   Outcomes: _____

?????   Add-ons . . .

COPYRIGHT © 2009 · SUSAN L. MULKEY & KAREN A. KEMP

Teach All, Reach All

Learning Log (Version I)   Grades 6–8

Name: <u>Keenan</u>

Topic: <u>Cooking</u>   Outcomes: <u>Make a sheet cake</u>

What did I already know?
how to sift flour

What have I learned?
how to cream butter and sugar
how to tell when cake is done

What puzzles me?
what makes a cake rise

Other ideas/thoughts:
Following directions is important!

Reproducible Form T7.8   COPYRIGHT © 2009 · SUSAN L. MULKEY & KAREN A. KEMP
See p. 75

REPRODUCIBLE T7.8

T7.9 STUDY GUIDES (MARGINS)

MATERIALS PREP ✂

GRADE LEVELS:
3–8

INTERVENTION TYPE:
Academic—All

Study Guides help students stay focused during a lesson and provide a logical structure to the concepts being presented.

The margins provide a space for students to write more notes. They can also indicate page numbers in a book where information can be found. The following steps can be used to develop study guides.

Step 1. Develop an outline of the important facts and concepts to be presented during this portion of the lesson.

Step 2. Arrange the information in statement or question format.

Step 3. Allow students to use the outline to record the important information.

Study Guide—Chapter 8 Sponges
1. What does the phylum name *porifera* literally mean?
2. Define *sessile*.
3. Sponge spicules may be made of what two substances?
4. Name the largest sponge. How big is it?
5. How many species of sponge exist?
6. Define *choanocytes*.
7. Name the three canal systems found in sponges.
8. What does it mean to be a filter feeder?

Source: *Lovitt et al., 1992.*

T7: What can I do about the students who, following my instruction, do not understand or misgeneralize the concept?

MATERIALS
PREP ✂

GRADE LEVELS:
3–8

**INTERVENTION
TYPE:**
Academic—All

T7.10 GRAPHIC ORGANIZERS (SEQUENCE)

Graphic organizers display information spatially and connect concepts for students in a meaningful way.

An organizer can be used to link new information to past learning and help students organize and focus on the most important concepts of the lesson. The following steps can be used to develop a graphic organizer:

Step 1. Determine important facts and concepts.

Step 2. Arrange them in sequential and logical order.

Step 3. Create a visual display of the information using boxes and pictures.

Step 4. Label reference points.

Graphic organizers can be used to present concepts in a variety of formats:

- Top Down–Bottom Up (main ideas and supporting details)
- Compare and Contrast (comparison of several critical attributes)
- Sequence (progression of events over time)
- Diagram (charts, graphs, maps, or picture representations)

Source: Lovitt et al., 1992.

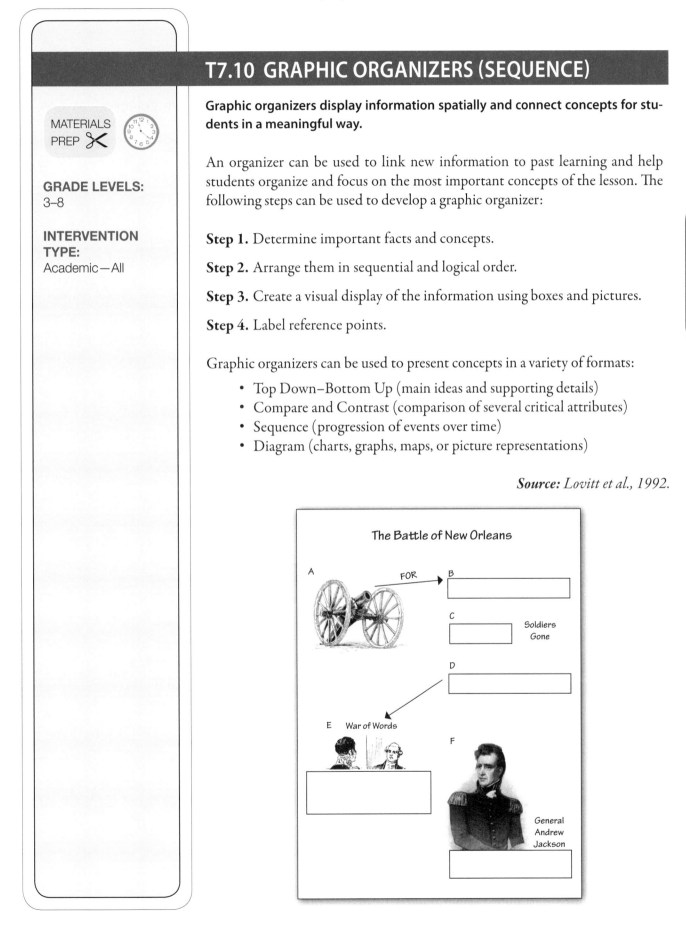

77

T7.11 ATTRIBUTE MAPS

Use an Attribute Map during instruction to provide examples and non-examples of the concept being taught.

First, supply students with a definition of the concept to be discussed. Then, describe the critical attributes or characteristics that apply to the concept.

EXAMPLE

In the illustration below, the first column is a list of attributes or characteristics that are **always** present among insects. The second column lists attributes that are **sometimes** present, and the last column lists attributes that are **never** present among insects. Give students three to six examples and non-examples of insects using information they are already familiar with or have been taught. Attribute Maps can be used as review sheets or as a measure of a student's understanding of a concept.

Insects
Definition: A group of small animals belonging to the arthropods.

ALWAYS three body parts three pairs of legs	SOMETIMES two pairs of wings	NEVER backbone
EXAMPLES flies mosquitoes grasshoppers beetles butterflies	**NON-EXAMPLES** spiders centipedes snails mites ticks	

MATERIALS PREP ✄

GRADE LEVELS:
3–8

INTERVENTION TYPE:
Academic—All

T8

TEACHER-DIRECTED INSTRUCTION

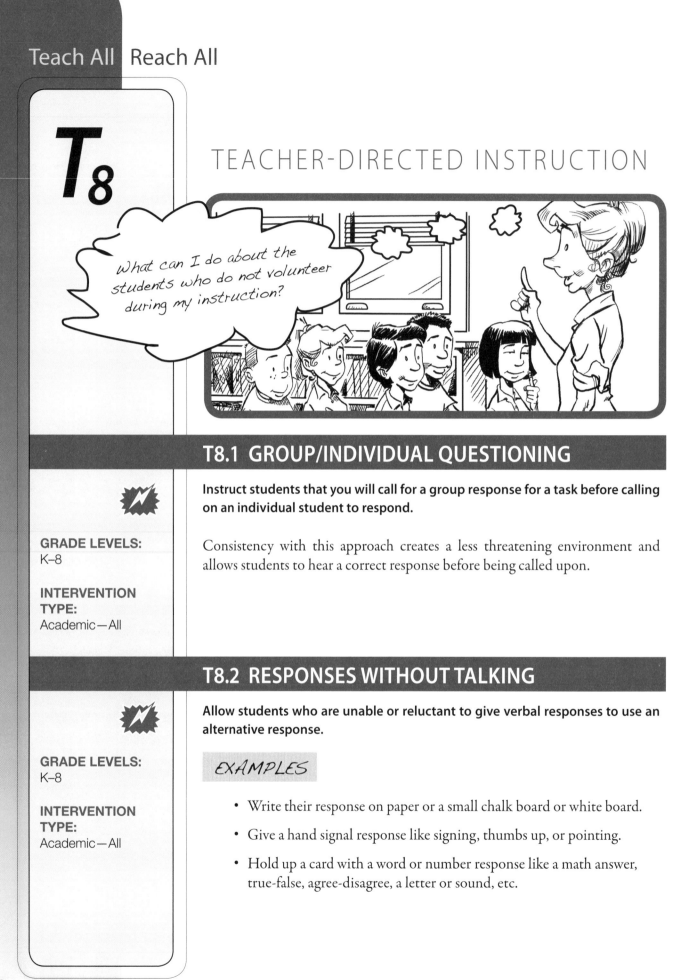

What can I do about the students who do not volunteer during my instruction?

T8.1 GROUP/INDIVIDUAL QUESTIONING

Instruct students that you will call for a group response for a task before calling on an individual student to respond.

Consistency with this approach creates a less threatening environment and allows students to hear a correct response before being called upon.

GRADE LEVELS:
K–8

INTERVENTION TYPE:
Academic—All

T8.2 RESPONSES WITHOUT TALKING

Allow students who are unable or reluctant to give verbal responses to use an alternative response.

EXAMPLES

GRADE LEVELS:
K–8

INTERVENTION TYPE:
Academic—All

- Write their response on paper or a small chalk board or white board.

- Give a hand signal response like signing, thumbs up, or pointing.

- Hold up a card with a word or number response like a math answer, true-false, agree-disagree, a letter or sound, etc.

T8.3 I AM READY

Allow students to have additional time to think of responses.

> *EXAMPLE*

Have students give you a signal like putting an index finger on their forehead or standing up a card on their desk to alert you that they are ready with answers.

GRADE LEVELS:
K–8

INTERVENTION TYPE:
Academic—All

T8.4 PLEASE COME BACK

Teach students that when they are called on to answer and they do not have a response, they say, "Please come back," or put up a sign that reads the same.

Students should understand that saying "I do not know" is not an option. "Please come back" allows a student additional time to think, research an answer, or confer with a partner or group for assistance. Additional prompts can also be provided for the student in order to guarantee a successful response. Remember to come back to the student and provide praise for a correct response.

GRADE LEVELS:
K–8

INTERVENTION TYPE:
Academic—All

Please Come Back

T8.5 NAME'S UP VOLUNTEER BOARD

A Name's Up Volunteer Board is a place where you can quickly write or post students' names when they volunteer information or responses.

The board can be a portion of the chalk board, a flip chart, or a white board (see illustration on next page). When you notice volunteering behaviors (e.g., hand raising, contributing relevant information with other students, responding in unison with the entire class or group, correct responses, etc.), write the student's name on the Volunteer Board and verbally recognize the behavior with an enthusiastic description of the behavior. ("Wow, look at Charles. He is participating and contributing answers!")

When students demonstrate subsequent volunteering information behaviors, simply put check marks ($\checkmark$) next to their names as you deliver the recognition.

MATERIALS PREP

GRADE LEVELS:
K–6

INTERVENTION TYPE:
Academic—All

T
G
I
F

At the end of the instructional period, the names can be erased and the activity repeated.

Volunteer Board	
Charles	
Susan	
Ramon	✔✔
Thuy	✔

T8.6 HEADS TOGETHER

GRADE LEVELS:
K–8

INTERVENTION TYPE:
Academic—All

Provide more opportunities to participate by arranging students in groups of four.

Each group member is assigned a number (one to four) or a color. Present a question to the entire class and tell each group of four to put their heads together and come up with an answer all members agree with. Then ask all of the ones (or twos, threes, or fours) who have an answer to raise their hands or stand up. Call on one of those students to respond. You may then ask the ones in the other groups if they agree or disagree, or ask them to expand on the answer. Repeat this process with all numbers or colors.

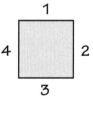 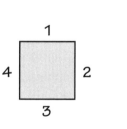 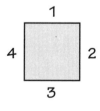

Source: Kagan, 1990.

T8: What can I do about the students who do not volunteer during my instruction?

T8.7 FOLDED CORNERS

MATERIALS
PREP ✂

GRADE LEVELS:
K–8

INTERVENTION
TYPE:
Academic—All

Students are placed in groups of four.

Each group puts its team name in the middle of one piece of paper. Each team member then writes his or her name on one corner of the paper and folds it over. Collect the papers and use them when calling on non-volunteers. Ask the entire class a question, allow the teams a few seconds to share their ideas, draw one of the papers, lift one corner, and call on that student to respond.

Source: Kagan, 1990.

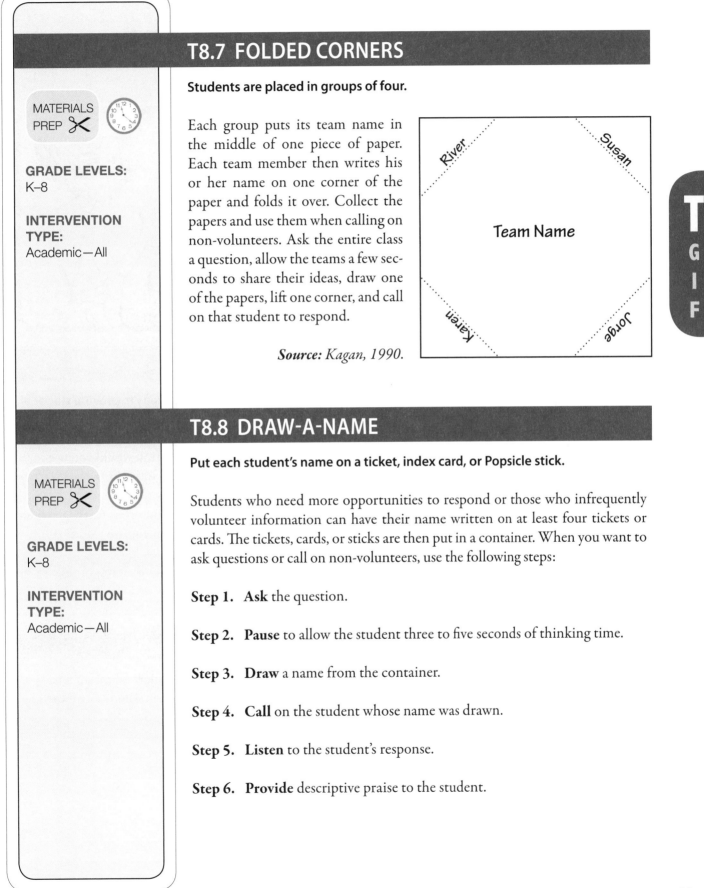

River   Susan

Team Name

Karen   Jorge

T8.8 DRAW-A-NAME

MATERIALS
PREP ✂

GRADE LEVELS:
K–8

INTERVENTION
TYPE:
Academic—All

Put each student's name on a ticket, index card, or Popsicle stick.

Students who need more opportunities to respond or those who infrequently volunteer information can have their name written on at least four tickets or cards. The tickets, cards, or sticks are then put in a container. When you want to ask questions or call on non-volunteers, use the following steps:

Step 1. **Ask** the question.

Step 2. **Pause** to allow the student three to five seconds of thinking time.

Step 3. **Draw** a name from the container.

Step 4. **Call** on the student whose name was drawn.

Step 5. **Listen** to the student's response.

Step 6. **Provide** descriptive praise to the student.

T9

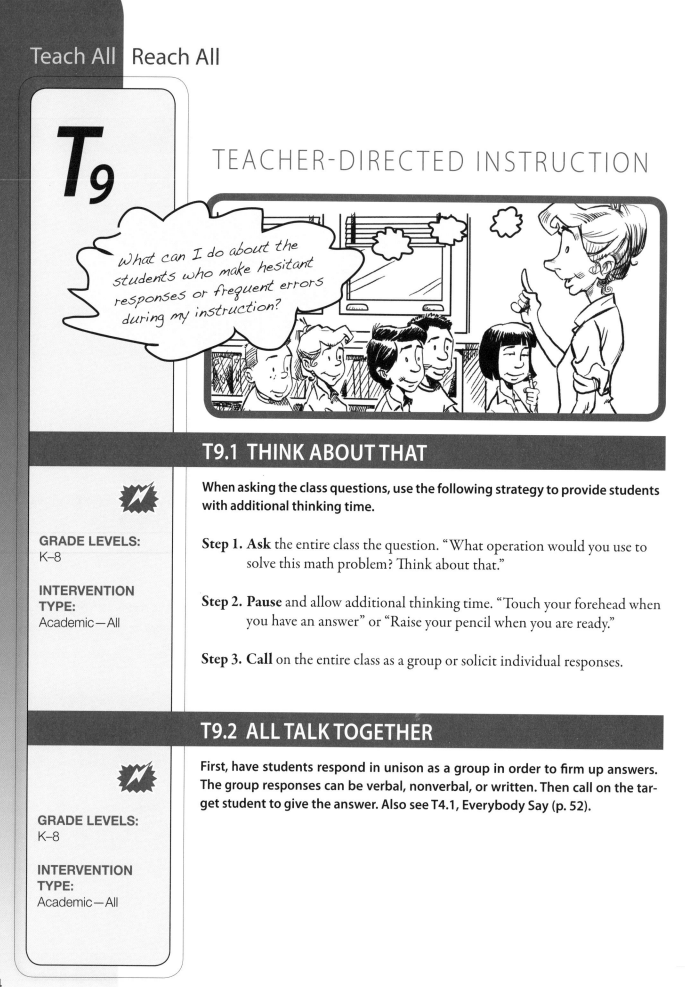

TEACHER-DIRECTED INSTRUCTION

What can I do about the students who make hesitant responses or frequent errors during my instruction?

T9.1 THINK ABOUT THAT

GRADE LEVELS:
K–8

INTERVENTION TYPE:
Academic—All

When asking the class questions, use the following strategy to provide students with additional thinking time.

Step 1. Ask the entire class the question. "What operation would you use to solve this math problem? Think about that."

Step 2. Pause and allow additional thinking time. "Touch your forehead when you have an answer" or "Raise your pencil when you are ready."

Step 3. Call on the entire class as a group or solicit individual responses.

T9.2 ALL TALK TOGETHER

GRADE LEVELS:
K–8

INTERVENTION TYPE:
Academic—All

First, have students respond in unison as a group in order to firm up answers. The group responses can be verbal, nonverbal, or written. Then call on the target student to give the answer. Also see T4.1, Everybody Say (p. 52).

T9: What can I do about the students who make hesitant responses or frequent errors during my instruction?

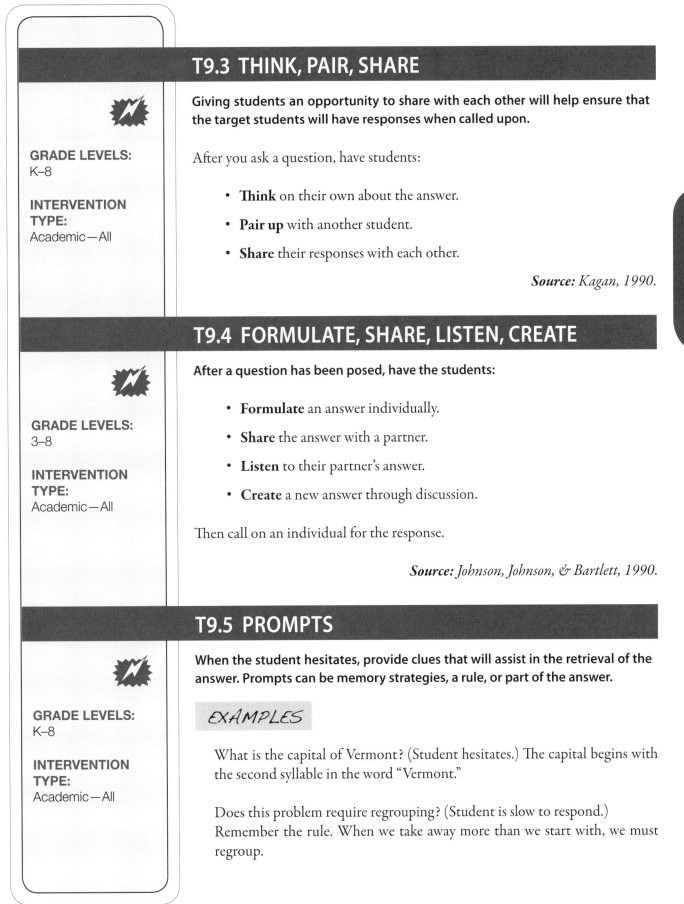

T9.3 THINK, PAIR, SHARE

GRADE LEVELS:
K–8

INTERVENTION TYPE:
Academic — All

Giving students an opportunity to share with each other will help ensure that the target students will have responses when called upon.

After you ask a question, have students:

- **Think** on their own about the answer.

- **Pair up** with another student.

- **Share** their responses with each other.

Source: Kagan, 1990.

T9.4 FORMULATE, SHARE, LISTEN, CREATE

GRADE LEVELS:
3–8

INTERVENTION TYPE:
Academic — All

After a question has been posed, have the students:

- **Formulate** an answer individually.

- **Share** the answer with a partner.

- **Listen** to their partner's answer.

- **Create** a new answer through discussion.

Then call on an individual for the response.

Source: Johnson, Johnson, & Bartlett, 1990.

T9.5 PROMPTS

GRADE LEVELS:
K–8

INTERVENTION TYPE:
Academic — All

When the student hesitates, provide clues that will assist in the retrieval of the answer. Prompts can be memory strategies, a rule, or part of the answer.

EXAMPLES

What is the capital of Vermont? (Student hesitates.) The capital begins with the second syllable in the word "Vermont."

Does this problem require regrouping? (Student is slow to respond.) Remember the rule. When we take away more than we start with, we must regroup.

T9.6 PREQUESTIONING

GRADE LEVELS:
K–8

INTERVENTION TYPE:
Academic—All

Provide students with a list of questions that will be asked during the presentation. Allow students to review them prior to the class discussion and find the answers if necessary.

T9.7 PLEASE COME BACK

GRADE LEVELS:
K–8

INTERVENTION TYPE:
Academic—All

When students do not have the answer when called on, teach them the "Please Come Back" technique (T8.4 on p. 81). This gives students time to formulate their answers or think on their options.

T9.8 RAPID-FIRE QUESTIONS

GRADE LEVELS:
K–8

INTERVENTION TYPE:
Academic—All

Have each student respond aloud to review material or previously learned information.

Move quickly around the room asking questions. If a student makes an error or hesitates, tell him or her the correct answer and move on to the next student and response/question. If all questions have been answered, start over and continue around the room until students have responded many times to the questions.

EXAMPLES

- Let us review the steps in the note-taking process. Starting with John, state the first letter, L, and the first step, Listen. Sally will say the next letter, I, and the corresponding step, Identify. We will continue until all steps have been named, and then the next person will start over again. Keep it going until I say "Stop."

- Name one thing you remember about yesterday's presentation.

The Rapid-Fire method can also be used with math facts, vocabulary, etc. This can be an effective active review technique.

T9: What can I do about the students who make hesitant responses or frequent errors during my instruction?

T9.9 THINK AND SAY IDEAS

GRADE LEVELS:
K–8

INTERVENTION TYPE:
Academic—All

Give students a specific topic or concept that has recently been presented (e.g., Natural Resources, Rhyming Words, States and Capitals).

Have them think quietly about the topic for a few minutes, then either share aloud with a partner or write down all of their ideas related to the topic during a two- to three-minute timing. Have students share the ideas generated with the class. Do this activity throughout the lesson to build the students' fluency on the topic.

T9.10 UP THE NUMBERS

GRADE LEVELS:
K–8

INTERVENTION TYPE:
Behavior—Motivation

Have students set a goal from one to ten for the number of questions they will answer during your presentation.

After the lesson, have students determine whether they met their goal or not. Encourage them to up their number by one for the next lesson. Your presentation must include an ample number of opportunities for all students to respond in order for them to achieve their goals. This can be done by having students respond as a class, by row, and by table, as well as individually.

T9.11 CORRECTIVE FEEDBACK

GRADE LEVELS:
K–8

INTERVENTION TYPE:
Behavior—Social

Using a specific strategy for feedback assists students in filing the information in their mind to reduce confusion of concepts.

EXAMPLE

The student has been asked the following question: Who is the main character in the story "The Tangled Web"? The student responds, "Josefa." (The answer is Annie.) Use the following correction procedure to treat the student with dignity and respect and provide a correct answer to the question.

Step 1. Dignify the response. Do this by moving close to the student, using the student's name, and maintaining a pleasant tone of voice and facial expression. Use phrases such as:
   • "You are thinking of another character that is in the story."
   • "I wonder if you are thinking of . . ."
If the answer does not make sense, the teacher uses phrases such as:
   • "Help me understand how you came up with that answer."
   • "I am not sure what you are thinking. Can you tell me?"

T
G
I
F

Step 2. Correct the answer. Do this by prompting the student for the answer. An example might be:

"This character is also a girl and her name starts with A."

Or you may give the student the answer:

"The main character is Annie."

Step 3. Validate the student's response. Do this by having the student give the correct answer before you move on to another question or student. Let the student know that you will be back later to see if he or she remembers the correct answer.

T9.12 QUESTION CHALLENGE

GRADE LEVELS:
K–8

INTERVENTION TYPE:
Behavior—Social

Challenge students to correctly answer fact questions during the presentation.

Tell students that you will be asking both group and individual questions and will keep score on the board. If the students answer the question correctly, they receive a point. If the group hesitates or makes an error, the response is corrected and you are awarded the point. Develop the questions beforehand and prepare the students for the type of questions that will be asked. A suggested guideline for number of questions asked is four to six per minute. Playing this game often will build fluency and reduce errors in student responses.

Approximate Number of Questions: 30	
Students	Mrs. Jones
‖‖‖‖‖ ‖‖‖‖‖ ‖	‖‖‖‖‖ ‖‖‖

T10

TEACHER-DIRECTED INSTRUCTION

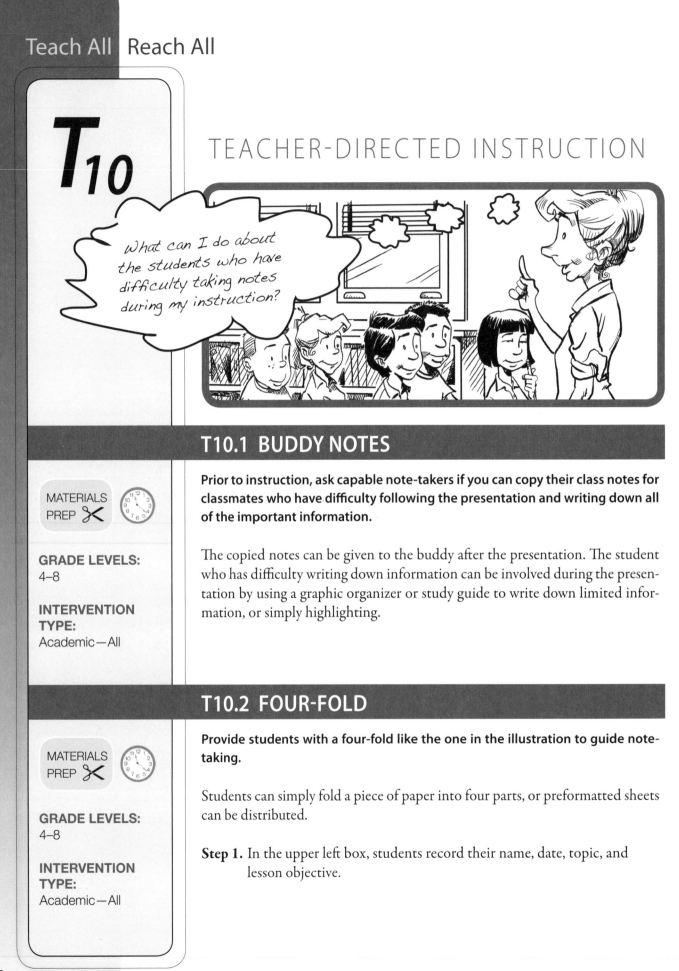

What can I do about the students who have difficulty taking notes during my instruction?

T10.1 BUDDY NOTES

MATERIALS
PREP ✂

GRADE LEVELS:
4–8

INTERVENTION TYPE:
Academic—All

Prior to instruction, ask capable note-takers if you can copy their class notes for classmates who have difficulty following the presentation and writing down all of the important information.

The copied notes can be given to the buddy after the presentation. The student who has difficulty writing down information can be involved during the presentation by using a graphic organizer or study guide to write down limited information, or simply highlighting.

T10.2 FOUR-FOLD

MATERIALS
PREP ✂

GRADE LEVELS:
4–8

INTERVENTION TYPE:
Academic—All

Provide students with a four-fold like the one in the illustration to guide note-taking.

Students can simply fold a piece of paper into four parts, or preformatted sheets can be distributed.

Step 1. In the upper left box, students record their name, date, topic, and lesson objective.

T10: What can I do about the students who have difficulty taking notes during my instruction?

REPRODUCIBLE
on CD

Step 2. In the upper right box, students record a personal relevance statement after your presentation. This is a statement that answers the question, "What personal meaning does this information have for you in your life?"

Step 3. In the lower left box, the students number and record the main ideas from the presentation.

Step 4. In the lower right box, the students number and record supporting details (e.g., definitions, examples, non-examples, clarifications) related to the main ideas.

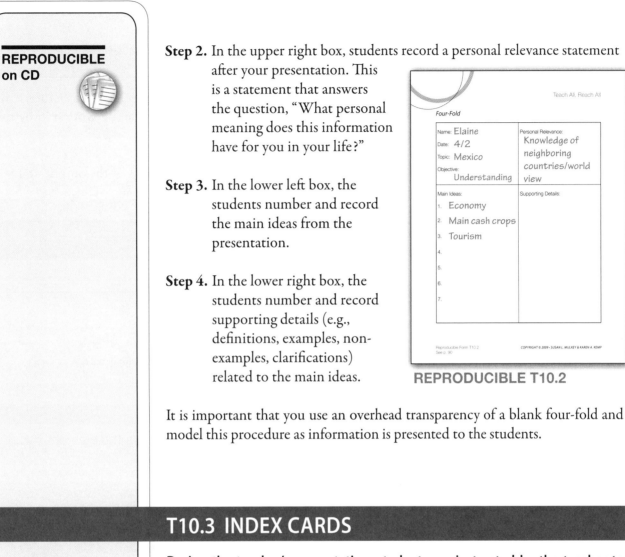

Teach All, Reach All

Four-Fold

Name: Elaine	Personal Relevance:
Date: 4/2	Knowledge of
Topic: Mexico	neighboring
Objective:	countries/world
Understanding	view

Main Ideas:	Supporting Details:
1. Economy	
2. Main cash crops	
3. Tourism	
4.	
5.	
6.	
7.	

Reproducible Form T10.2
See p. 90   *COPYRIGHT © 2009 • SUSAN L. MULKEY & KAREN A. KEMP*

REPRODUCIBLE T10.2

It is important that you use an overhead transparency of a blank four-fold and model this procedure as information is presented to the students.

T
G
I
F

T10.3 INDEX CARDS

During the teacher's presentation, students are instructed by the teacher to write down key vocabulary words or phrases on one side of an index card and the corresponding definition on the back side.

Students keep the cards in a file box or on a ring for later use during guided and independent practice activities.

MATERIALS
PREP

GRADE LEVELS:
4–8

**INTERVENTION
TYPE:**
Academic—All

Humorous

Front side

Funny

Back side

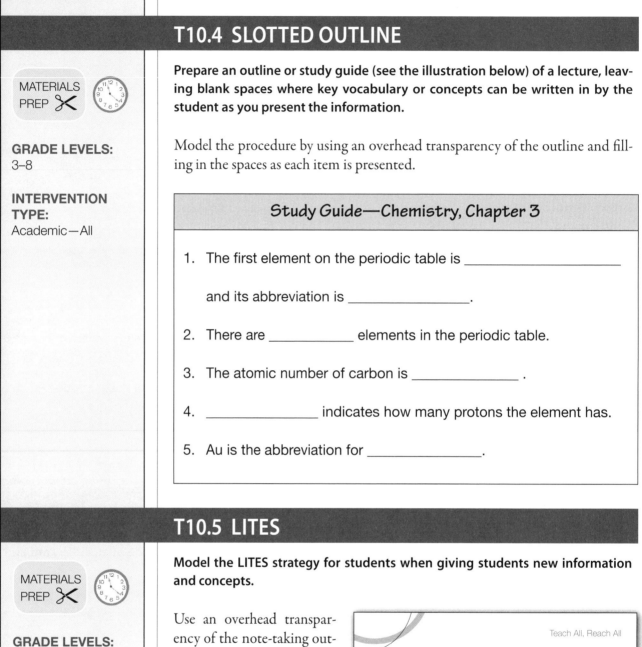

T10.4 SLOTTED OUTLINE

MATERIALS
PREP ✂

GRADE LEVELS:
3–8

INTERVENTION TYPE:
Academic—All

Prepare an outline or study guide (see the illustration below) of a lecture, leaving blank spaces where key vocabulary or concepts can be written in by the student as you present the information.

Model the procedure by using an overhead transparency of the outline and filling in the spaces as each item is presented.

Study Guide—Chemistry, Chapter 3

1. The first element on the periodic table is _____

   and its abbreviation is _____.

2. There are _____ elements in the periodic table.

3. The atomic number of carbon is _____ .

4. _____ indicates how many protons the element has.

5. Au is the abbreviation for _____.

T10.5 LITES

MATERIALS
PREP ✂

GRADE LEVELS:
4–8

INTERVENTION TYPE:
Academic—All

REPRODUCIBLES on CD
(2 versions)

Model the LITES strategy for students when giving students new information and concepts.

Use an overhead transparency of the note-taking outline similar to the one in the illustration. Students can be given a bookmark with the LITES strategy spelled out to serve as a prompt to take notes while reading.

Teach All, Reach All

Note-Taking Outline (Version I)   Name: Jayson

Topic: Bears   Date: 10/28

Objective: List and describe five important facts about bears.

Questions?	Main Ideas	Supporting Details
	1. three types of bears	grizzly, black, and polar
	2. where grizzlies live (lower 48 states)	Yellowstone, Glacier parks
	3. colors of black bears	black, brown, red, blue
	4.	

REPRODUCIBLE T10.5a

T10: What can I do about the students who have difficulty taking notes during my instruction?

Listen to the teacher and look at what he or she is saying aloud and writing.

Identify key vocabulary, important concepts, and examples/non-examples that the teacher is using or saying aloud.

Take down (write down) the key vocabulary, concepts, and examples.

Evaluate what has been taken down. Ask yourself questions like: Could I explain this to someone? Could I give more examples? If not, put a question mark in the left margin and use your strategy for asking a question or asking for clarification.

Save your notes by dating them, coding chapters or topics, and putting them in a folder or notebook.

Remember that it will be necessary to actively teach and model the LITES strategy while using the note-taking outlines. It will require several weeks of prompted practice before students will be able to use this strategy independently.

Source: Lovitt et al., 1992.

Note-Taking Strategy

LITES

Listen

Identify Main Ideas and Supporting Details

Take Down Information

Evaluate

Save and Review

Copyright © 2009

NOTE-TAKING OUTLINE (VERSION I)

Name:
Topic: _____ Date:
Objective:

Questions?	Main Ideas	Supporting Details

REPRODUCIBLE T10.5b

TGIF

T10.6 NOTE CHECKS

Develop a daily point system for taking notes or using a Note-Taking Outline (described in LITES, T10.5).

These points should be tied to students' participation grades. Points can also be awarded for dating the notes, coding the notes to chapters or topics, and maintaining them in an orderly fashion in folders or notebooks. Note checks can occur on a regular basis or as unannounced random checks.

Note Check Cards

NOTE CHECK

Name: _Julio_

Date Checked: _5/16_

• Notes Dated	yes/no	points _5_
• Notes Coded	yes/no	points _5_
• Notes Filed	yes/no	points ___
• Notes Sequenced	yes/no	points ___

REPRODUCIBLE T10.6

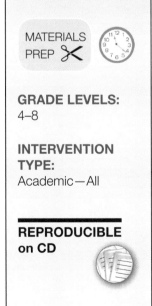

MATERIALS PREP ✂

GRADE LEVELS:
4–8

INTERVENTION TYPE:
Academic—All

REPRODUCIBLE on CD

T10.7 COOPERATIVE NOTES

MATERIALS
PREP ✂

GRADE LEVELS:
4–8

INTERVENTION TYPE:
Academic—All

REPRODUCIBLE on CD

Before your presentation, arrange students into note-taking groups of four. Each student is assigned a number (one through four), and each group is provided with one set of paper for taking notes (see illustration).

All number ones begin with the note paper, writing down their name and start time as shown in the illustration. Set a timer for five minutes. All number ones begin taking notes. At the end of five minutes, the note paper rotates to the number two person, and the procedure is repeated throughout teacher-directed instruction. At the end of each time block, you can provide feedback to the students on the notes by showing a transparency modeling an example set of notes for the previous five-minute time block. The note-taker can check his or her notes against the model and add or delete information. At the end of the note-taking session, groups can switch notes for other activities such as editing, evaluating, and rewriting.

Teach All, Reach All

Cooperative Notes

Note-Taker # __1__

Name: __Jane__   Starting Time: __10:45__

Ending Time: _____

REPRODUCIBLE T10.7

T10: What can I do about the students who have difficulty taking notes during my instruction?

T10.8 GRAPHIC ORGANIZERS (PARTIAL)

MATERIALS
PREP ✂

GRADE LEVELS:
K–8

**INTERVENTION
TYPE:**
Academic—All

Provide students with a blank, partially completed, or completely filled out graphic organizer of your presentation (see illustration below).

As you present information, students can fill in or add important information on their copy of the organizer. For example, a completely filled out version of the graphic organizer can be given to students who have limited writing skills. Give them a highlighter pen to mark the key concepts as information is presented and/or add additional words next to the boxes. Other students can use a partially completed or blank organizer to write down additional information. (See T5.7, p. 63, for a completed organizer on strokes.)

T
G
I
F

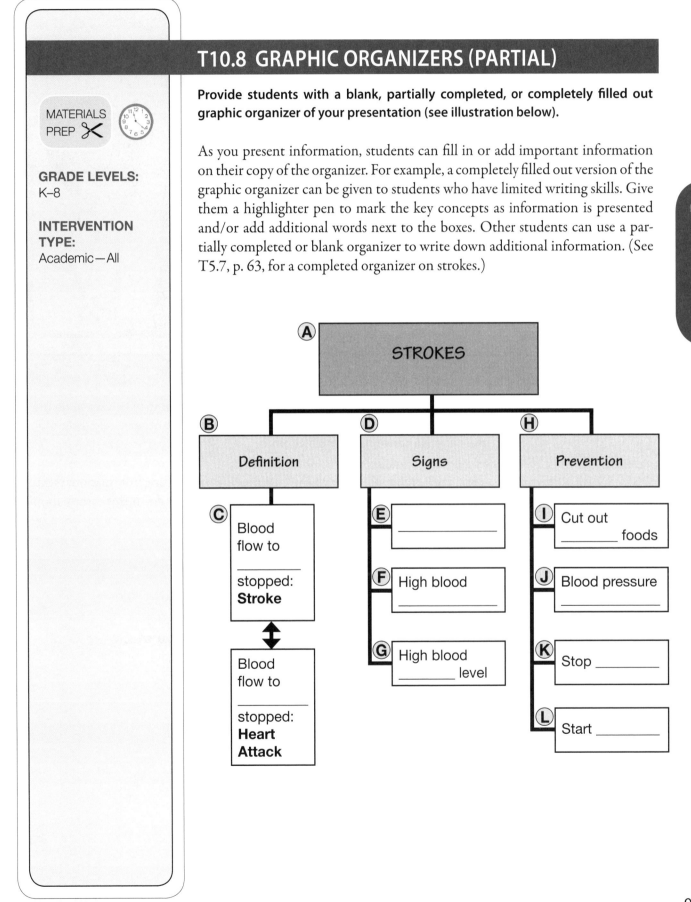

T11

TEACHER-DIRECTED INSTRUCTION

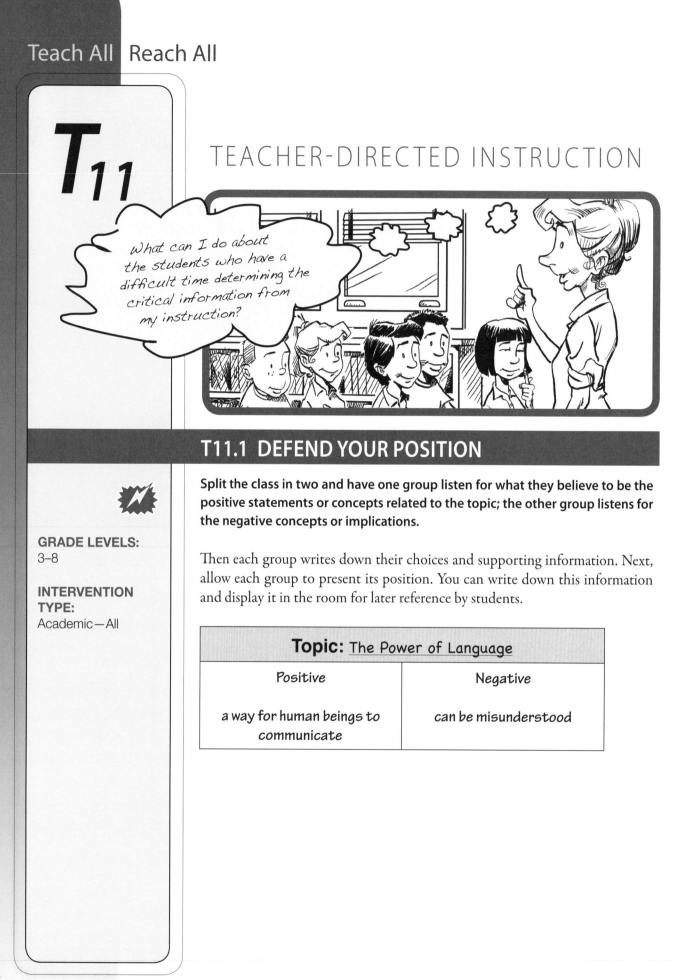

What can I do about the students who have a difficult time determining the critical information from my instruction?

T11.1 DEFEND YOUR POSITION

GRADE LEVELS:
3–8

INTERVENTION TYPE:
Academic—All

Split the class in two and have one group listen for what they believe to be the positive statements or concepts related to the topic; the other group listens for the negative concepts or implications.

Then each group writes down their choices and supporting information. Next, allow each group to present its position. You can write down this information and display it in the room for later reference by students.

Topic: The Power of Language	
Positive	Negative
a way for human beings to communicate	can be misunderstood

T11.2 FIVE-MINUTE REVIEWS

GRADE LEVELS:
3–8

INTERVENTION TYPE:
Academic — All

Check student comprehension by setting a timer to ring every five minutes.

When the timer rings, stop the presentation to review the critical information presented to that point. Have students compare what they have recorded with a partner and give them additional time to add any information that was not included in their notes. Ask questions (individual and group) related to the critical information to discover if students have interpreted it correctly, or show an overhead transparency that has been completed with the critical information.

T **G** **I** **F**

T11.3 ADVANCE ORGANIZERS

MATERIALS PREP ✂

GRADE LEVELS:
3–8

INTERVENTION TYPE:
Academic — All

Provide students with organizers that will alert them in advance to the important information that will be presented in class. Explain to the students how the completed outline will be used during instruction.

Topic: The Heart

Vocabulary Words:
    1. ventricle
    2. atrium
    3. pulmonary
 	
Key Concepts:
  • Atriums pump blood into the ventricles.
  • Right and left ventricle and right and left atrium make up four chambers of human heart.
  • Pulmonary vein carries blood from the lungs to the heart.
 	
Other Important Facts:

T11.4 THINK AND WRITE QUESTIONS

MATERIALS PREP ✂

GRADE LEVELS:
4–8

INTERVENTION TYPE:
Academic—All

REPRODUCIBLE on CD

Prior to the presentation, have students think of and write down questions related to what they want to know about this topic or what they think may be presented.

The questions should relate to the who, what, when, where, and why of the upcoming material. Add any questions that have not been suggested but are critical to students' understanding.

As a final step, assist the students in rearranging the questions or topics into the sequence in which they will be presented.

Teach All, Reach All

Think and Write Questions

Name: _Ahmed_____

Topic: _Wuthering Heights_____

Who?

Who is a key character in the novel?

What?

In what time period does this story take place?

When?

When does the main character come into the story?

Where?

Where does most of the story take place?

Why?

Why is it important to read this novel?

Reproducible Form T11.4
See p. 98

COPYRIGHT © 2009 • SUSAN L. MULKEY & KAREN A. KEMP

REPRODUCIBLE T11.4

T11: What can I do about the students who have a difficult time determining the critical information from my instruction?

T11.5 PRESENTATION CUES

MATERIALS PREP ✂

GRADE LEVELS:
4–8

INTERVENTION TYPE:
Academic—All

Teach students that teachers will use different types of cues during a presentation.

Discuss both spoken and unspoken cues. After teaching students the cues, play games with lectures to see who can identify how many cues were used and/or what the cues were. The following chart provides some presentation cues for students.

	Verbal	Nonverbal
Emphasis	This is important! You will need to remember _____. This will be on the test. Repeating information Voice inflections Volume of voice Pacing of information	Signals: • Pointing • Hand movement Facial expressions Body language Other gestures
Organization	The first step is . . . Number three . . . Next . . . In summary . . .	Writing on board Gestures Pauses Finger counting

T G I F

T12

TEACHER-DIRECTED INSTRUCTION

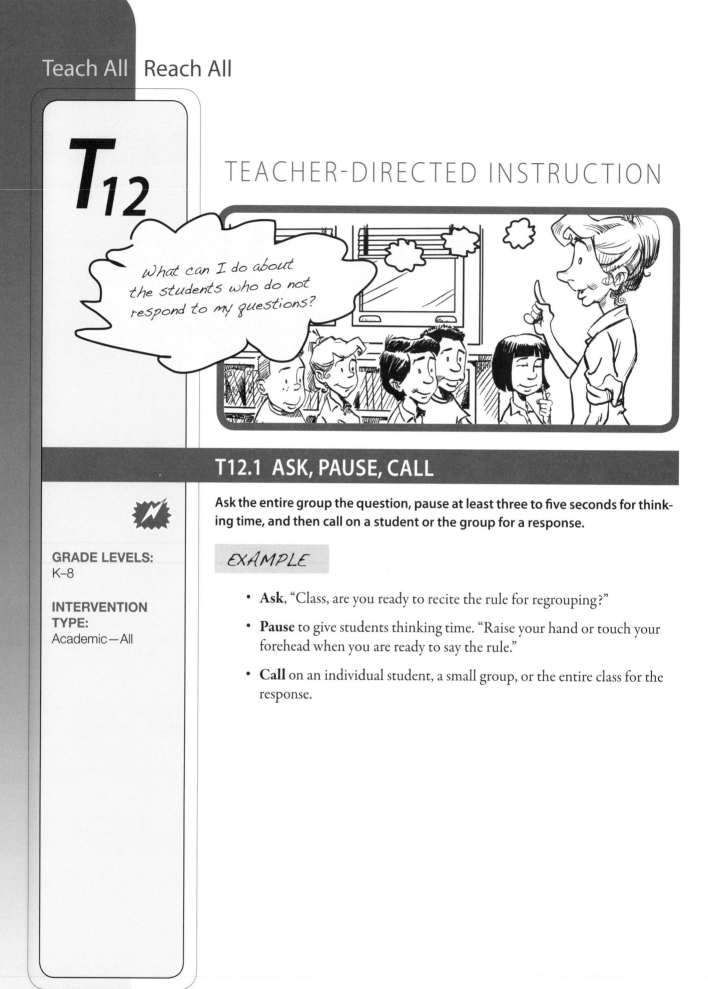

What can I do about the students who do not respond to my questions?

T12.1 ASK, PAUSE, CALL

GRADE LEVELS:
K–8

INTERVENTION TYPE:
Academic—All

Ask the entire group the question, pause at least three to five seconds for thinking time, and then call on a student or the group for a response.

EXAMPLE

- **Ask**, "Class, are you ready to recite the rule for regrouping?"

- **Pause** to give students thinking time. "Raise your hand or touch your forehead when you are ready to say the rule."

- **Call** on an individual student, a small group, or the entire class for the response.

T12.2 RESTATE

GRADE LEVELS:
K–8

INTERVENTION TYPE:
Academic — All

Ask the student or entire class to restate the question that has been presented. Or, ask the student or class to restate the answer to the question after another student has responded correctly.

EXAMPLES

- Class, get ready to repeat my question. What is another way of saying "minus"?

- Susan, repeat Mark's answer in your own words.

You can also tell students ahead of time that you are going to play Restate for points. When a student or the class can restate correctly, a class point is earned. If the student or class is incorrect, you earn a point.

T12.3 PASS FOR NOW

GRADE LEVELS:
K–8

INTERVENTION TYPE:
Academic — All

This is the same strategy as discussed in Please Come Back. See T8.4 (p. 81) for more information on how to apply its principles to unresponsive students.

T12.4 CONSULT

GRADE LEVELS:
3–8

INTERVENTION TYPE:
Academic — All

Teach students to quickly and quietly choose and consult with another person when they need assistance with an answer.

When students are called upon and they are unable to respond, they can say, "Consult," and then quickly choose a helping partner.

This technique empowers students and can be used in place of the teacher saying, "Who can help Susan?"

T G I F

T12.5 ALL TOGETHER

GRADE LEVELS:
K–8

INTERVENTION TYPE:
Academic—All

Use choral, unison, group, or entire class responses before calling on individual students.

Tell students you will be using the all-together strategy and review the procedure with them:

- Use talking voices, not shouting voices.
- Respond when the teacher gives you a signal to respond, not before or after the signal.

You can use signals such as a verbal cue and a hand drop or finger touch to keep students in unison.

EXAMPLE

Get ready to recite the words. What word? (finger touch)
Next word. (finger touch)

If students do not respond in unison, use a pleasant tone of voice, then repeat the item until the desired unison response is obtained. Add variety and fun to the verbal responses by asking students to recite (the word or task) in their softest voices, their deepest voices, or their highest voices.

T12.6 NO SURPRISES

GRADE LEVELS:
3–8

INTERVENTION TYPE:
Academic—All

Prearrange a subtle, no-surprise signal with target students that can be used to cue them in advance of being called upon.

EXAMPLE

You might arrange with a student that when you are standing next to his or her desk, you will be calling on him or her next.

T12: What can I do about the students who do not respond to my questions?

T12.7 ANSWER, PAIR, SPOTLIGHT

GRADE LEVELS:
K–8

INTERVENTION TYPE:
Academic — All

After presenting the question, instruct students to think of an answer on their own for 30 to 60 seconds, then pair with a partner and quietly share responses with each other.

Next, use a **spotlighting** technique by calling on pairs to share their responses. One partner (the reporter) can share both responses. When other pairs are spotlighted, they should report only new ideas or information.

T12.8 CLARIFICATION

MATERIALS
PREP ✂

GRADE LEVELS:
K–8

INTERVENTION TYPE:
Behavior — Social

**REPRODUCIBLE
on CD**

Teach the students a strategy to ask for a clarification when they do not understand the question or when they need to have the question restated.

EXAMPLE

Step 1. Use the strategy for getting the teacher's attention (look, signal, wait to be acknowledged).

Step 2. Use a pleasant tone of voice.

Step 3. Say, "I do not understand the question." Or say, "Could you please restate the question?"

Step 4. Say, "Thank you."

Step 5. Each of the steps can be modified to fewer words, or pictures can be used to represent the steps. Rhymes or short phrases can also be used, such as: **Listen, wait, then ask for a restate.**

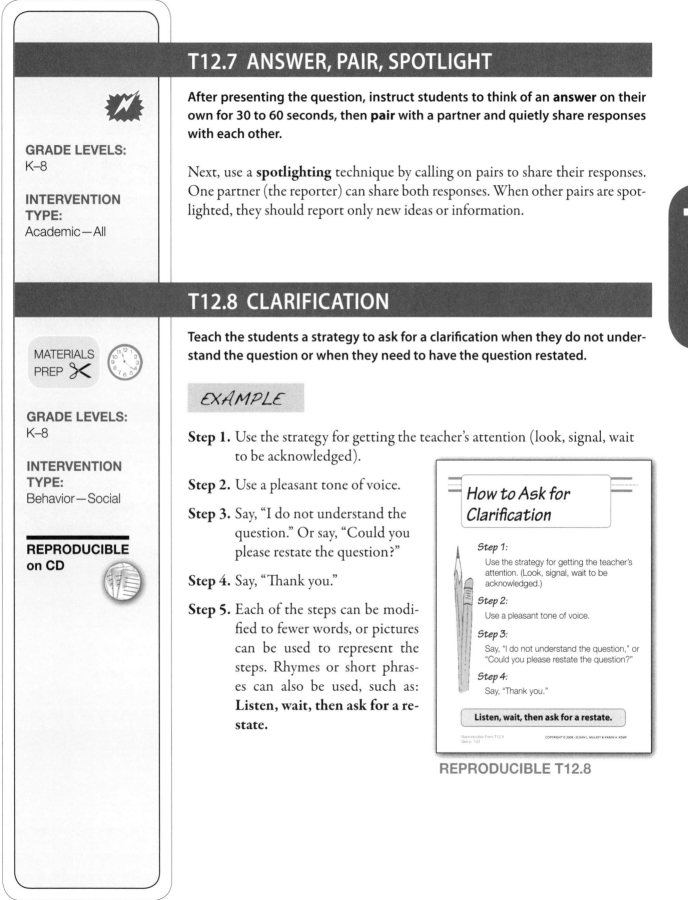

How to Ask for Clarification

Step 1:
Use the strategy for getting the teacher's attention. (Look, signal, wait to be acknowledged.)

Step 2:
Use a pleasant tone of voice.

Step 3:
Say, "I do not understand the question," or "Could you please restate the question?"

Step 4:
Say, "Thank you."

Listen, wait, then ask for a restate.

REPRODUCIBLE T12.8

A T-chart can be used to teach students what specific behaviors are necessary for each step.

Looks Like	Sounds Like
Signal for teacher Pleasant facial expression In seat	No noises while signaling Pleasant tone of voice "I do not understand." "Could you please restate?" "Thank you."

T12.9 DRAW-A-NAME

MATERIALS
PREP ✂

GRADE LEVELS:
K–8

**INTERVENTION
TYPE:**
Academic—All

This strategy is explained in full in T8.8 (p. 83). Please reference for information that can be applied to this question as well.

T12.10 COUNTING RESPONSES

MATERIALS
PREP ✂

GRADE LEVELS:
K–8

**INTERVENTION
TYPE:**
Behavior—Motivation

**REPRODUCIBLE
on CD**

Provide the student with an index card to self-monitor the number of questions answered during a portion of class time.

The student can simply mark a box each time a response is given when he or she is called upon by the teacher. The boxes can be checked whether the responses are volunteer or non-volunteer.

Teach All, Reach All

Counting Responses

Questions Answered

Name: Drew   Time Period: 10:00-10:30

X	X	?	?	?	?	?	?	?	?	?	?
?	?	?	?	?	?	?	?	?	?	?	?
?	?	?	?	?	?	?	?	?	?	?	?

REPRODUCIBLE T12.10

Throughout **G**, the teacher leads and prompts students through structured activities designed to provide frequent opportunities for students to practice new skills and eliminate errors. Practice may be individual or through peer-mediated structures.

GUIDED PRACTICE ACTIVITIES

G_1 GUIDED PRACTICE ACTIVITIES

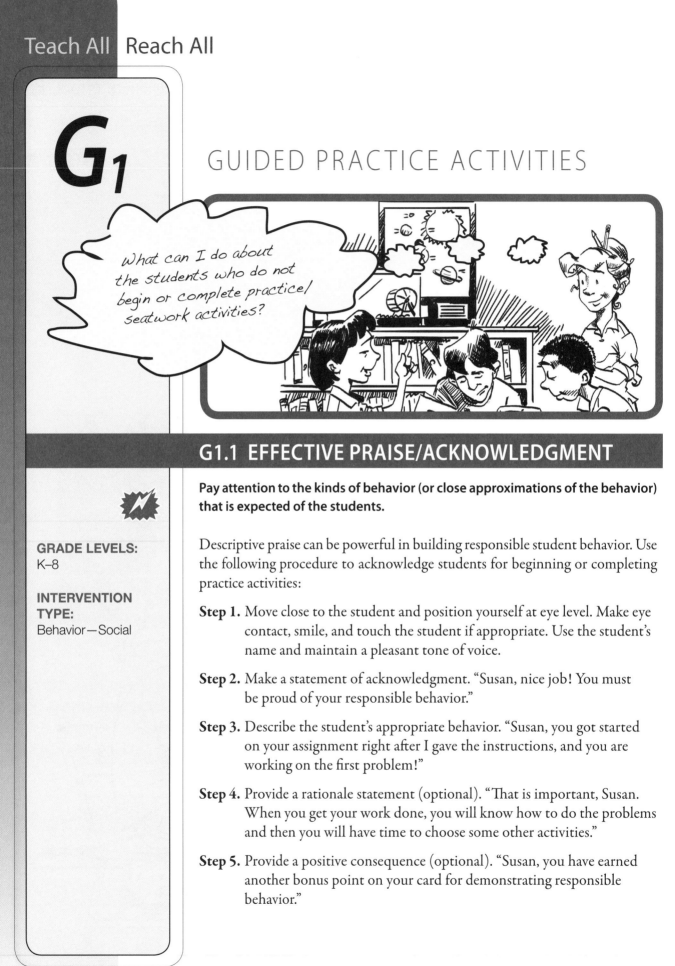

G1.1 EFFECTIVE PRAISE/ACKNOWLEDGMENT

GRADE LEVELS:
K–8

INTERVENTION TYPE:
Behavior—Social

Pay attention to the kinds of behavior (or close approximations of the behavior) that is expected of the students.

Descriptive praise can be powerful in building responsible student behavior. Use the following procedure to acknowledge students for beginning or completing practice activities:

Step 1. Move close to the student and position yourself at eye level. Make eye contact, smile, and touch the student if appropriate. Use the student's name and maintain a pleasant tone of voice.

Step 2. Make a statement of acknowledgment. "Susan, nice job! You must be proud of your responsible behavior."

Step 3. Describe the student's appropriate behavior. "Susan, you got started on your assignment right after I gave the instructions, and you are working on the first problem!"

Step 4. Provide a rationale statement (optional). "That is important, Susan. When you get your work done, you will know how to do the problems and then you will have time to choose some other activities."

Step 5. Provide a positive consequence (optional). "Susan, you have earned another bonus point on your card for demonstrating responsible behavior."

G1: What can I do about the students who do not begin or complete practice/seatwork activities?

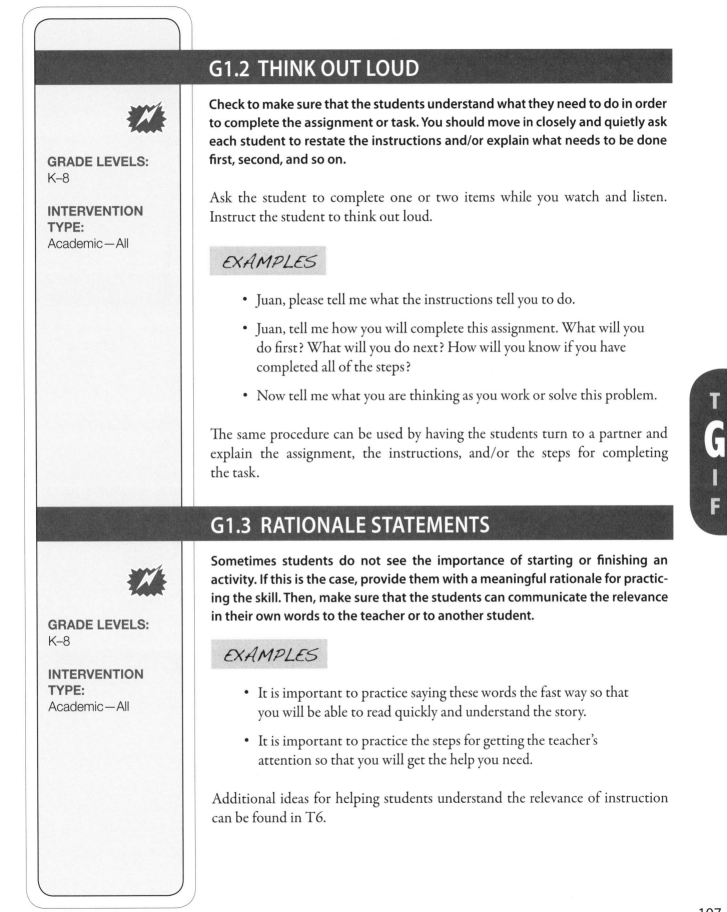

G1.2 THINK OUT LOUD

GRADE LEVELS:
K–8

INTERVENTION TYPE:
Academic—All

Check to make sure that the students understand what they need to do in order to complete the assignment or task. You should move in closely and quietly ask each student to restate the instructions and/or explain what needs to be done first, second, and so on.

Ask the student to complete one or two items while you watch and listen. Instruct the student to think out loud.

EXAMPLES

- Juan, please tell me what the instructions tell you to do.

- Juan, tell me how you will complete this assignment. What will you do first? What will you do next? How will you know if you have completed all of the steps?

- Now tell me what you are thinking as you work or solve this problem.

The same procedure can be used by having the students turn to a partner and explain the assignment, the instructions, and/or the steps for completing the task.

G1.3 RATIONALE STATEMENTS

GRADE LEVELS:
K–8

INTERVENTION TYPE:
Academic—All

Sometimes students do not see the importance of starting or finishing an activity. If this is the case, provide them with a meaningful rationale for practicing the skill. Then, make sure that the students can communicate the relevance in their own words to the teacher or to another student.

EXAMPLES

- It is important to practice saying these words the fast way so that you will be able to read quickly and understand the story.

- It is important to practice the steps for getting the teacher's attention so that you will get the help you need.

Additional ideas for helping students understand the relevance of instruction can be found in T6.

T
G
I
F

G1.4 ALTERNATING BUDDIES

Allow students to pair up to copmlete practice assignments.

Students alternate between writing the answers down and talking through the answer aloud. The partner who writes the answer for a problem should initial that item.

GRADE LEVELS:
3–8

INTERVENTION TYPE:
Academic—All

G1.5 STRATEGIC SKILLS

Rather than asking the students to complete the entire practice assignment, focus on just the strategic skills that are necessary for completing the task.

EXAMPLES

- For a math assignment, ask the students to mark the problems that require regrouping rather than solving all the problems.

- For a reading assignment, ask the students to indicate page numbers and paragraphs where certain information can be found relating to comprehension rather than answering all questions.

- For a language assignment, ask the students to list the steps for writing a good paragraph rather than creating an entire paragraph.

- For a punctuation activity, ask the students to mark the sentences that require capital letters.

GRADE LEVELS:
3–8

INTERVENTION TYPE:
Academic—All

G1.6 BEAT THE CLOCK

Establish reasonable time limits for beginning and/or completing a small number of items on the practice assignment.

EXAMPLES

- Place a timer on the target student's desk. Have the student set the timer for the amount of time estimated to complete the tasks.

- Using a timer, challenge the student. For instance, "Finish these problems in five minutes to beat the clock!"

GRADE LEVELS:
K–8

INTERVENTION TYPE:
Behavior—Motivation

G1: What can I do about the students who do not begin or complete practice/seatwork activities?

G1.7 ASSIGNMENT QUESTIONS

GRADE LEVELS:
4–8

INTERVENTION TYPE:
Academic—All

After distributing practice assignments and explaining the steps for completion, instruct students to think of questions about the assignment and write them down during a two-minute timing.

Then, students pair up and share their questions and answers. The teacher then calls for questions that dyads cannot answer on their own. Questions can be answered by the teacher or other dyads.

G1.8 STAR STICKERS

GRADE LEVELS:
K–6

INTERVENTION TYPE:
Academic—All
Behavior—Motivation

Reinforce on-task behavior.

Continually move around the classroom as students are completing a practice activity. As a student starts or completes an item, acknowledge the student by describing the appropriate behavior and then drawing a star or placing a star sticker on the practice sheet.

EXAMPLES

- As a student completes a math problem, say something like, "Nice work, you just finished a problem!" Then put a star on that problem.

- As a student writes one sentence during a writing activity, say something like, "Wow, you wrote one sentence and remembered to include the period!" Then place a star at the end of the sentence. (Colored marking pens or a pre-made ink stamp can also be used to make the stars.)

T
G
I
F

G1.9 CUT-UP

MATERIALS PREP ✂

GRADE LEVELS:
K–6

INTERVENTION TYPE:
Academic—All
Behavior—Motivation

Divide assignments into sections so students don't feel overwhelmed.

Cut the practice assignment into small strips or pieces. After one piece has been completed, acknowledge the students and then give them the next piece of the assignment.

EXAMPLES

- A page of math problems can be cut up into strips or rows.

- A reading assignment can be cut up into paragraphs.

- A list of comprehension questions can be cut up into individual questions.

- A study guide can be cut up into groups of two or three questions.

$$8 \quad\quad 5 \quad\quad 6$$
$$-3 \quad -1 \quad -5$$

$$7 \quad\quad 2 \quad\quad 3$$
$$+1 \quad +5 \quad +1$$

$$4 \quad\quad 3 \quad\quad 5$$
$$+3 \quad +2 \quad +3$$

G1.10 COLORED PENCILS

MATERIALS PREP ✂

GRADE LEVELS:
3–8

INTERVENTION TYPE:
Academic—All
Behavior—Motivation

Give the target student five different colored pencils. Have the student complete each practice item or row of items with a different colored pencil.

After a predetermined number of items have been completed, provide the student with a tangible reinforcer or positive comment. The different colors may make it clearer for the student to see what has been accomplished and provide a goal for reinforcement.

G1.11 SPLIT THE ASSIGNMENT

GRADE LEVELS:
3–8

INTERVENTION TYPE:
Behavior—Motivation

Put students into groups of four or five when working on practice assignments.

Each group is given one practice assignment. Each student in the group is responsible for completing a small portion of the task (e.g., questions one to three). The completed tasks are then combined onto one sheet.

Students who are responsible for the same numbered item(s) across all the classroom groups can meet in "expert" groups to complete the task. After they have finished, they return to their "home" group and share the information and record it on the practice assignment.

G1.12 CHANGE THE CHANNEL

MATERIALS PREP ✂

GRADE LEVELS:
K–8

INTERVENTION TYPE:
Academic—All

Change the Channel involves changing the input and/or the output channel that is required in the practice assignment.

EXAMPLES

A math assignment that requires the student to **look** at math facts on a page and then **write** answers could be changed to:

1. **Look** at facts and **say** answers aloud.
2. **Look** at facts and **calculate** answers with a calculator.
3. **Hear** the facts dictated and **write** answers.
4. **Hear** the facts dictated and **circle** answers on a piece of paper.

A reading assignment that requires the student to look at words on a page and then write definitions for them could be changed to:

1. **Hear** the words and **say** the definitions aloud.
2. **Hear** the words and **mark** the definitions on a sheet of paper.
3. **See** the words and **say** the definitions aloud.

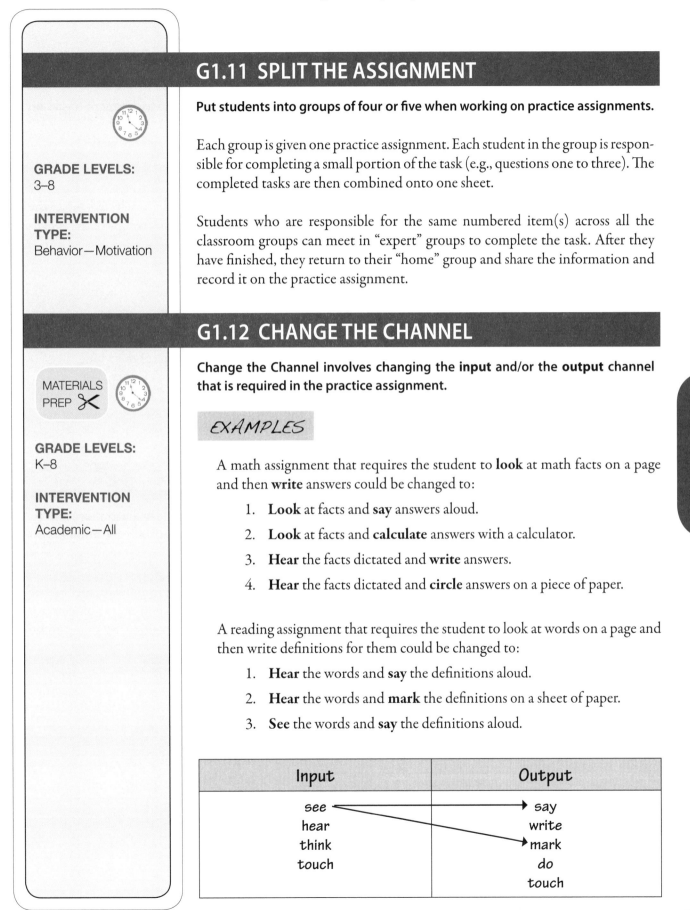

Input	Output
see	say
hear	write
think	mark
touch	do
	touch

G1.13 SLICE BACK

MATERIALS PREP ✂

GRADE LEVELS:
K–8

INTERVENTION TYPE:
Academic—All

With some students it may be necessary to scaffold the assignment based on the level of difficulty.

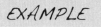

EXAMPLE

If the outcome requires students to write paragraphs on a selected topic, the assignment may be broken into smaller pieces so students complete the assignment a step at a time to achieve the outcome. For instance:

- Mark the words that describe a certain character.
- Mark the words that tell about the setting.
- Circle the different names of characters.
- Highlight the sentence that describes the content of the whole paragraph.
- Draw a graphic representation of the story.
- Write a sentence about the story on an index card.

G1.14 BEHAVIOR BINGO

MATERIALS PREP ✂

GRADE LEVELS:
K–8

INTERVENTION TYPE:
Behavior—Motivation

Provide the target students with Behavior Bingo Cards (see illustration) and an envelope containing numbered squares that correspond with the numbers on the students' cards.

Each time a student completes one item on the practice assignment, the teacher draws a number from the envelope and the student places it on the bingo card. When a bingo is achieved, the student earns a reinforcement, such as one minute of free time or a special privilege.

Source: Jenson et al., 1992.

B	I	N	G	O
2	9	12	16	25
4	8	15	19	24
1	6	14	17	21
5	7	11	20	22
3	10	13	18	23

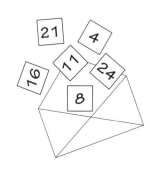

G1: What can I do about the students who do not begin or complete practice/seatwork activities?

MATERIALS PREP ✂

GRADE LEVELS:
4–8

INTERVENTION TYPE:
Academic—All

REPRODUCIBLE
on CD

G1.15 DESIGN YOUR OWN ASSIGNMENT

Allow students the option of designing their own practice assignment.

Students can complete the Design Your Own Assignment form on an individual basis, with a partner, or within the context of a small group. Students are required to provide answers for questions such as: what skills will they be practicing, what materials will they need, how will they determine if the goal has been met, where and how long will they practice, what student/students are accountable for completing the assignment, and what are their start and finish estimates. Teacher approval must be obtained after students have designed their own assignment.

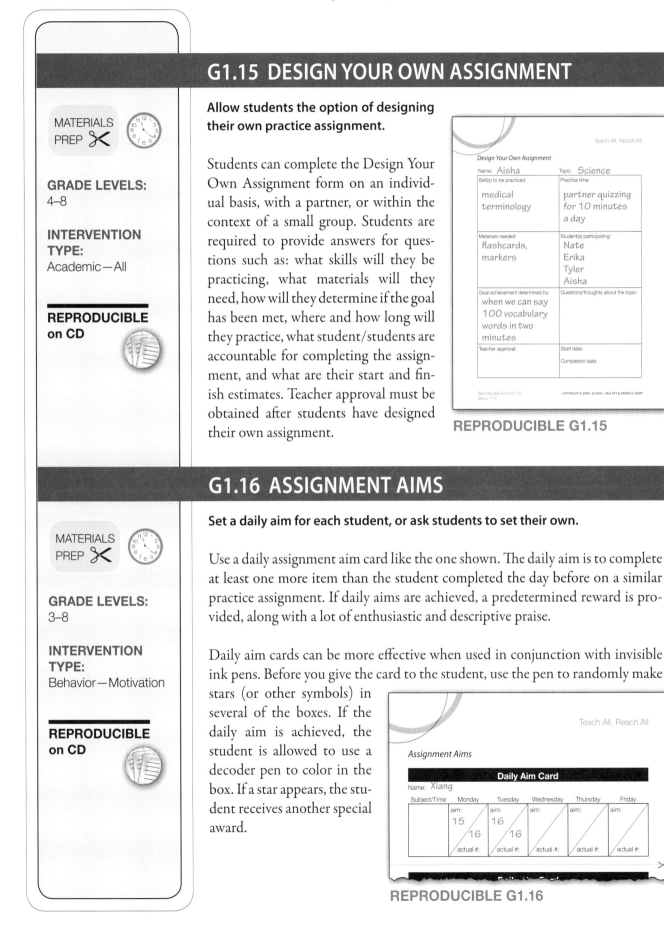

REPRODUCIBLE G1.15

MATERIALS PREP ✂

GRADE LEVELS:
3–8

INTERVENTION TYPE:
Behavior—Motivation

REPRODUCIBLE
on CD

G1.16 ASSIGNMENT AIMS

Set a daily aim for each student, or ask students to set their own.

Use a daily assignment aim card like the one shown. The daily aim is to complete at least one more item than the student completed the day before on a similar practice assignment. If daily aims are achieved, a predetermined reward is provided, along with a lot of enthusiastic and descriptive praise.

Daily aim cards can be more effective when used in conjunction with invisible ink pens. Before you give the card to the student, use the pen to randomly make stars (or other symbols) in several of the boxes. If the daily aim is achieved, the student is allowed to use a decoder pen to color in the box. If a star appears, the student receives another special award.

REPRODUCIBLE G1.16

G1.17 COMPLETION DOTS

MATERIALS PREP ✂

GRADE LEVELS:
K–8

INTERVENTION TYPE:
Behavior—Motivation

NOTE:
For Completion Dots, use the T3.5 (p. 49) Participation Dots reproducible found on the CD.

Provide the student with a dot-to-dot illustration.

Each time the student completes a task on a practice activity, he or she draws a line between two dots, beginning with number one. This procedure can be combined with the use of invisible ink pens as described in G1.16. Invisible ink stars can be pre-marked under random dots. The student can use a decoder pen to color over dots that have been joined by a connecting line. If a star appears, the student can be given an award.

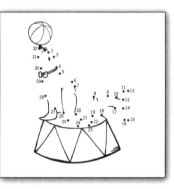

Source: *Rhode et al., 1993.*

G1.18 ASK FOR HELP

MATERIALS PREP ✂

GRADE LEVELS:
K–8

INTERVENTION TYPE:
Behavior—Social

REPRODUCIBLE on CD

Teach students a strategy for how to ask for help when it is apparent that they are unclear on the assignment.

Model examples and non-examples of each of the steps in the strategy. Provide a lot of opportunities for the students to practice the strategy in controlled settings.

Step 1. Use the steps for getting the teacher's attention (look, signal, wait to be acknowledged).

Step 2. Use a pleasant tone of voice.

Step 3. Use the "please" word when requesting help. ("Could you please help me?")

Step 4. Make a specific statement or question about the kind of help

REPRODUCIBLE G1.18

you need, where you need help, or what you do not understand ("I need help with this problem.")

Step 5. Smile and say "thank you" after help has been given.

Step 6. Ask another specific question if you need more help.

A pleasant request is best, then a thank you does the rest.

G1.19 START/STOP TIME

MATERIALS
PREP ✂

GRADE LEVELS:
K–8

**INTERVENTION
TYPE:**
Behavior—Motivation

Have the target students use a Start/Stop Time card to record when the first assignment or task begins.

The ending time is recorded when the assignment or task is finished. The elapsed time is then figured and recorded in the third column. The procedure can be repeated for all items within an assignment. When the assignment is completed, each student indicates a plus for improvement in time, a minus if the time spent was longer, or a circle if the time was the same. Points can be awarded for improved times or the number of pluses on the card.

Item #	Start Time	Stop Time	Elapsed Time	+	–	◯
1. Sentences	9:00	9:10	10 min.		x	
2. Paragraphs	9:10	9:15	5 min.	x		
3.						
4.						
5.						
6.						
7.						
8.						
9.						
10.						

T
G
I
F

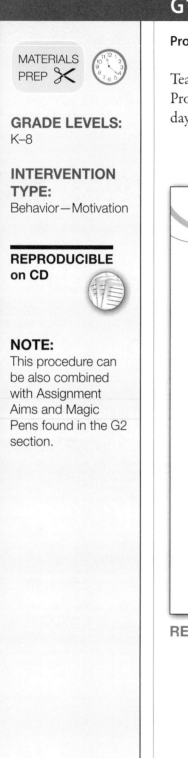

MATERIALS
PREP ✂

GRADE LEVELS:
K–8

INTERVENTION TYPE:
Behavior—Motivation

REPRODUCIBLE on CD

NOTE:
This procedure can be also combined with Assignment Aims and Magic Pens found in the G2 section.

G1.20 MONITORING SEATWORK

Provide the student with a self-monitoring chart like the one in the illustration.

Teach students to slash a number after each problem, item, or task is completed. Provide many opportunities for success by numbering the chart 1–40 for each day. See Counting Responses (T12.10, p. 104) for additional ideas.

Source: *Fister & Kemp, 1994.*

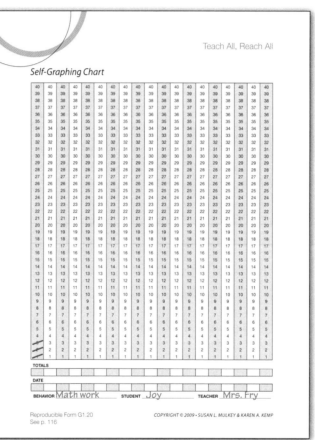

REPRODUCIBLE G1.20

G₂ GUIDED PRACTICE ACTIVITIES

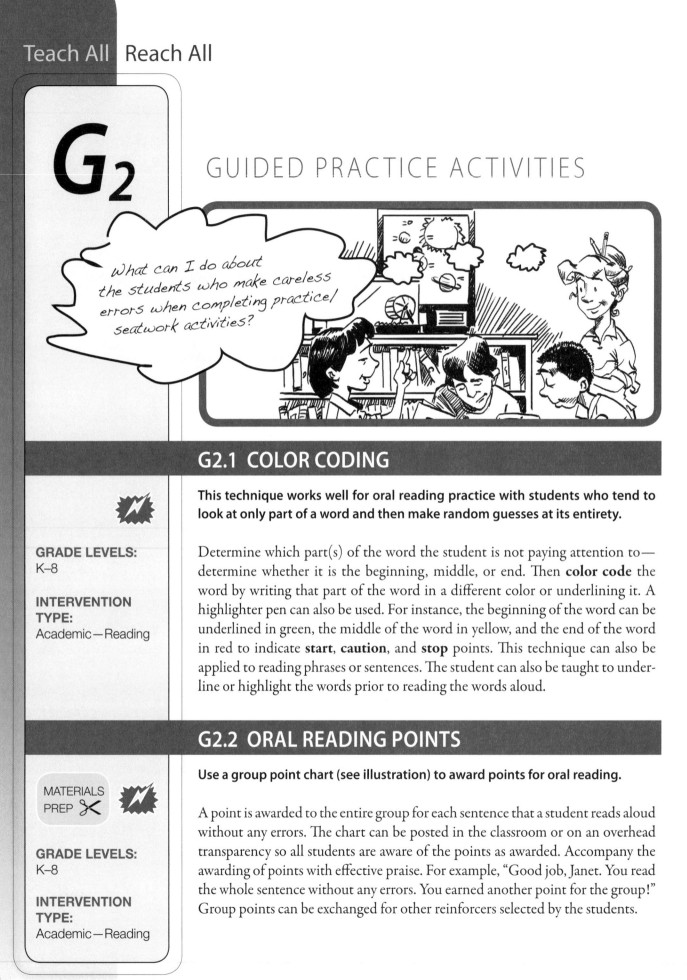

What can I do about the students who make careless errors when completing practice/ seatwork activities?

G2.1 COLOR CODING

This technique works well for oral reading practice with students who tend to look at only part of a word and then make random guesses at its entirety.

GRADE LEVELS:
K–8

INTERVENTION TYPE:
Academic—Reading

Determine which part(s) of the word the student is not paying attention to—determine whether it is the beginning, middle, or end. Then **color code** the word by writing that part of the word in a different color or underlining it. A highlighter pen can also be used. For instance, the beginning of the word can be underlined in green, the middle of the word in yellow, and the end of the word in red to indicate **start**, **caution**, and **stop** points. This technique can also be applied to reading phrases or sentences. The student can also be taught to underline or highlight the words prior to reading the words aloud.

G2.2 ORAL READING POINTS

Use a group point chart (see illustration) to award points for oral reading.

MATERIALS PREP ✂

GRADE LEVELS:
K–8

INTERVENTION TYPE:
Academic—Reading

A point is awarded to the entire group for each sentence that a student reads aloud without any errors. The chart can be posted in the classroom or on an overhead transparency so all students are aware of the points as awarded. Accompany the awarding of points with effective praise. For example, "Good job, Janet. You read the whole sentence without any errors. You earned another point for the group!" Group points can be exchanged for other reinforcers selected by the students.

REPRODUCIBLE on CD

Note: Points can be awarded for other behaviors like students knowing their place when it is their turn to read, reading with expression, following along, not blurting out, etc.

Oral Reading Points

Group Point Chart

Group Name: *Centipedes*

DATE	POINTS	DAILY TOTAL
4/20	𝍷𝍷𝍷 𝍷𝍷𝍷 𝍷𝍷𝍷𝍷	14
4/21	𝍷𝍷𝍷 𝍷𝍷𝍷 𝍷𝍷𝍷 𝍷𝍷	17
4/22	𝍷𝍷𝍷 𝍷𝍷𝍷 𝍷𝍷𝍷 𝍷𝍷𝍷𝍷𝍷 𝍷𝍷	27
	WEEKLY TOTAL	58

REPRODUCIBLE G2.2

G2.3 STOP AND SWITCH

MATERIALS PREP ✂

GRADE LEVELS:
3–8

INTERVENTION TYPE:
Academic—Reading, Math

Divide the class into two or more teams. (Rows or tables can also constitute teams.)

Students are assigned a partner at the beginning of a practice activity. The pairs, or dyads, also participate on one of the teams. At any time while students are working on the practice assignment, you can call out, "Stop and switch!" Students immediately trade papers with their partner for checking. You may randomly select specific problems for students to check, or have them check all of the items from the point where the last switch occurred. Accuracy points can be written in the margin of the assignment. Partners can add their accuracy points together for a combined total. The total number of points for the partners are then reported and recorded toward their team score. Each member of the winning team of the day can receive a special reward such as a reduced homework certificate, free time activity, etc.

Team 1	M	T	W	Th	F	Total
Guillermo & Janet	4	9				
Ling & Tyler	6	8				
Mykael & Madison	8	2				
Team Total:						

Team 2	M	T	W	Th	F	Total
...ex & ...ome	3	7				
... Luis	10	6				
...&	10	4				

G2.4 SELF-CHECK AND COUNT

Provide students with an answer key upon completion of the practice assignment.

Teach the students how to check and count their own work by circling or marking every component of their answer that matches the answer key, rather than looking at only the final answer. By counting each component of the answer, students are reinforced for partially correct answers and are provided with corrective feedback.

EXAMPLES

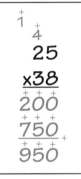

- In counting math answers, every correct digit written should be given a count, along with counts for correct alignment, drawing lines, and other critical elements necessary for solving the problem. In the example above, there could be a possible correct count of 12 (8 digits, 2 numbers carried, 1 alignment, and 1 line above the answer) when counting digits, alignment, carried numbers, and the line.

- In counting spelling, the student can be taught to count every correct letter written in sequence. The following demonstrates how students could self-check their spelling of "black." If the student wrote blak for black: count of three correct letters in sequence (b-l-a), count of one error (left the "c" out altogether). If the student wrote blakc for black: count of three correct letters in sequence (b-l-a), count of two errors ("k" and "c" are out of sequence).

- In checking handwriting, counts could be given for correct formation of each letter, correct size on line for each letter, and correct ending stroke.

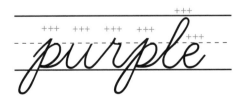

- In checking writing, counts could be given for each word written, punctuation mark, capital letter, complete sentence, etc.

G2: What can I do about the students who make careless errors when completing practice/seatwork activities?

A recording sheet can be used for corrects and errors. Points can then be awarded for correct answers and subtracted for incorrect responses.

Teach All, Reach All

Self-Check and Count

Name: *Zoe*   Subject:

DATE	CORRECTS	—	ERRORS	= TOTAL POINTS
5/1	63	–	4	= 59

REPRODUCIBLE G2.4

G2.5 MAGIC PENS

MATERIALS PREP

GRADE LEVELS:
K–8

INTERVENTION TYPE:
Academic
Behavior—Motivation

NOTE:
Invisible ink pens or Secret Agent markers can be purchased from Alex Toys (www.alextoys.com) or Crayola (www.crayola.com).

Before practice assignments are handed out, use an invisible ink pen and randomly draw stars close to where the answers will be written.

Start by marking one or two stars for every five problems. Tell the students that several items are marked with the invisible ink pen. If they have written a correct answer on one of those items, they will earn special rewards.

After the students have completed the entire assignment, a designated portion of the assignment, or have been working for a specified time period, have them use one of the decoder pens and mark over their answers. If a star shows through **and** the answer is correct, an additional reward is provided (points, free time minutes, lottery tickets, etc.).

Be sure to select items that are reinforcing to the student. Since the student does not know ahead of time where the stars have been placed on the practice assignment, there is added incentive to complete all of the problems carefully and accurately. This technique can be combined with the Mystery Motivator (T3.6, p. 50) and Wild Card Spinner (T3.4, p. 48) techniques.

4 x 5 ☆20	3 x 6 18	8 x 4 32
6 x 7 42	9 x 3 ☆27	7 x 2 14

T
G
I
F

G₃

GUIDED PRACTICE ACTIVITIES

What can I do about the students who do not comprehend and/or respond to written material during practice/seatwork activities?

G3.1 CHANGE THE CHANNEL

GRADE LEVELS:
K–8

INTERVENTION TYPE:
Academic—All

NOTE:
This is an accelerated version of the Change the Channel technique discussed in G1.12, p. 111. Refer to this earlier version for more in-depth ideas.

Use different input or output channels for completing assignments as an alternative to writing answers to questions after reading the material.

EXAMPLES

- Have the students **read** the material and **say** the answers aloud.
- Have the students **listen** to the material and **say** the answers aloud.
- Have the students **read** the material and **mark** the answers.
- Have the students **listen** to the material and **mark** the answers.
- Have the students **listen** to the material and **write** the questions.
- Have the students **listen** to the material and **say** the questions aloud.

G3: What can I do about the students who do not comprehend and/or respond to written material during practice/seatwork activities?

G3.2 PAGE NUMBERS

GRADE LEVELS:
3–8

INTERVENTION TYPE:
Academic—All

After reading or listening to the questions, ask the students to locate and write down page and paragraph numbers where the information related to the question can be found.

Students would not be required to write answers to the questions, but rather **locate information**.

G3.3 QUESTIONS FIRST

GRADE LEVELS:
3–8

INTERVENTION TYPE:
Academic—All

Provide the students with the questions related to the reading selection prior to the actual reading.

The questions can also reference page numbers where the information that includes the answer can be found. Read the questions to the students or have them read to themselves. Ask each student to restate the question. Next, have the students read the first section of material, stopping at the end of the pages indicated for question one. After the students answer question one, have them go on to repeat the procedure for the remaining questions.

G3.4 QUESTION/INSTRUCTION REPEAT

GRADE LEVELS:
K–8

INTERVENTION TYPE:
Academic—All

Students who have difficulty answering questions may not understand the question or the instructions.

Check for understanding by having each student read the question/instruction aloud. Then, ask students to repeat or restate the information in their **own words**. Or, the students could be asked to rewrite the question or the instructions in their own words.

T
G
I
F

G3.5 LISTEN, WRITE, LISTEN, SAY

GRADE LEVELS:
3–8

INTERVENTION TYPE:
Academic—All

The following procedure is a series of steps to enhance comprehension. It is important to be consistent in using this format so that students learn a pattern for responding.

Step 1. Begin by **reading a question** related to the information contained in a short paragraph.

Step 2. Then, **read the paragraph** to the students.

Step 3. Next, **read the question** again to the students and wait for a few seconds. Do not allow answers to be blurted out. This is a silent time for the students to think of the answer.

Step 4. Then, **give the answer** to the question. Demonstrate this procedure several times with a variety of different paragraphs.

Step 5. Next, **read the same question** as used in the above activity for one of the paragraphs.

Step 6. Instruct the students to **write their answer**. Wait until students have made a response.

Step 7. Then, **give the correct answer**.

Repeat this procedure with the remaining questions. You may also repeat the procedure as often as needed for each paragraph or ask for a verbal group response.

Source: Adapted from Buchanan, 1994.

G3.6 KEY WORDS

MATERIALS PREP ✂

GRADE LEVELS:
3–8

INTERVENTION TYPE:
Academic—All

Identifying and defining key words from students' practice assignments is a useful strategy for helping students to understand the importance of vocabulary/definitions.

Step 1. Write the definitions for the vocabulary words on index cards. Count up the number of words in the definition and write it on the card. (If the word is "igloo" and the definition is "a house made of ice blocks," the definition has a total of six possible points.

G3: What can I do about the students who do not comprehend and/or respond to written material during practice/seatwork activities?

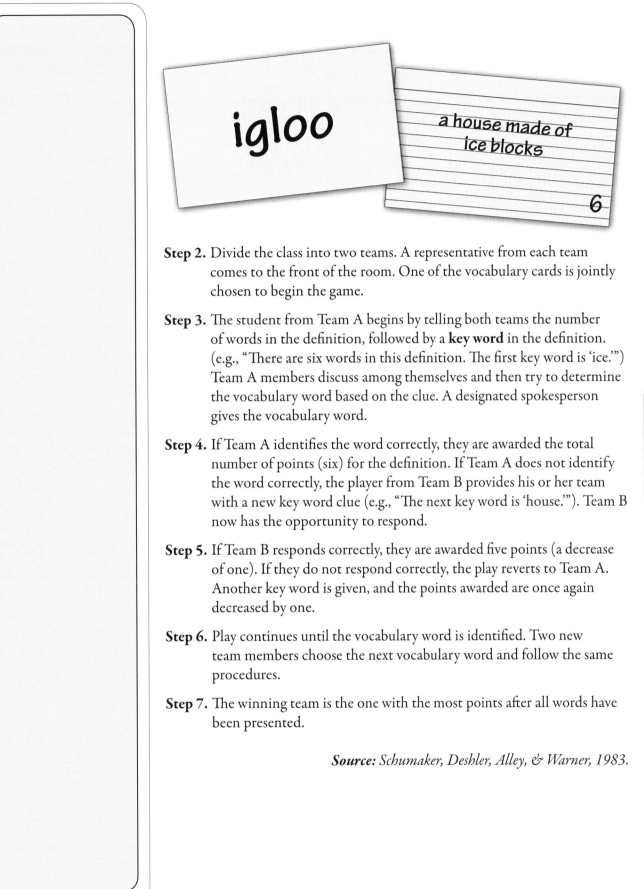

Step 2. Divide the class into two teams. A representative from each team comes to the front of the room. One of the vocabulary cards is jointly chosen to begin the game.

Step 3. The student from Team A begins by telling both teams the number of words in the definition, followed by a **key word** in the definition. (e.g., "There are six words in this definition. The first key word is 'ice.'") Team A members discuss among themselves and then try to determine the vocabulary word based on the clue. A designated spokesperson gives the vocabulary word.

Step 4. If Team A identifies the word correctly, they are awarded the total number of points (six) for the definition. If Team A does not identify the word correctly, the player from Team B provides his or her team with a new key word clue (e.g., "The next key word is 'house.'"). Team B now has the opportunity to respond.

Step 5. If Team B responds correctly, they are awarded five points (a decrease of one). If they do not respond correctly, the play reverts to Team A. Another key word is given, and the points awarded are once again decreased by one.

Step 6. Play continues until the vocabulary word is identified. Two new team members choose the next vocabulary word and follow the same procedures.

Step 7. The winning team is the one with the most points after all words have been presented.

Source: Schumaker, Deshler, Alley, & Warner, 1983.

G3.7 I AM READY TO FIND OUT

MATERIALS
PREP ✂

GRADE LEVELS:
4–8

INTERVENTION TYPE:
Academic—All

REPRODUCIBLE on CD

To guide students in identifying key points, provide them with the I Am Ready to Find Out index card prior to reading the selection.

Instruct students to complete who/what/where/when questions they want answered.

EXAMPLES

- Who is the story about?

- What happened to the main character?

- What is the sequence of events?

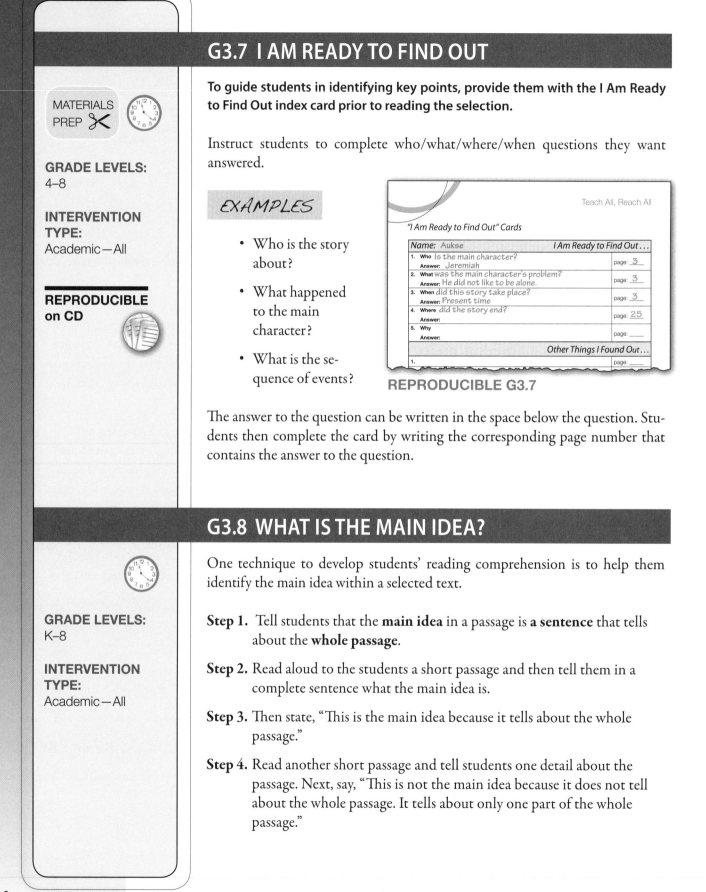

"I Am Ready to Find Out" Cards

Name: Aukse	I Am Ready to Find Out...
1. **Who** Is the main character? **Answer:** Jeremiah	page: 3
2. **What** was the main character's problem? **Answer:** He did not like to be alone.	page: 3
3. **When** did this story take place? **Answer:** Present time	page: 3
4. **Where** did the story end? **Answer:**	page: 25
5. **Why** **Answer:**	page:
	Other Things I Found Out...
1.	page: ____

Teach All, Reach All

REPRODUCIBLE G3.7

The answer to the question can be written in the space below the question. Students then complete the card by writing the corresponding page number that contains the answer to the question.

G3.8 WHAT IS THE MAIN IDEA?

GRADE LEVELS:
K–8

INTERVENTION TYPE:
Academic—All

One technique to develop students' reading comprehension is to help them identify the main idea within a selected text.

Step 1. Tell students that the **main idea** in a passage is **a sentence** that tells about the **whole passage**.

Step 2. Read aloud to the students a short passage and then tell them in a complete sentence what the main idea is.

Step 3. Then state, "This is the main idea because it tells about the whole passage."

Step 4. Read another short passage and tell students one detail about the passage. Next, say, "This is not the main idea because it does not tell about the whole passage. It tells about only one part of the whole passage."

G3: What can I do about the students who do not comprehend and/or respond to written material during practice/seatwork activities?

NOTE:
The sentence that tells about the whole passage does not necessarily appear verbatim in the passage.

Step 5. Repeat this modeling procedure with at least three to six other short passages using examples and non-examples.

Step 6. Then read a short passage and tell students a detail **or** the main idea. Ask, "Is this the main idea?" Wait for a group response of yes or no. Then ask, "Why?" Call on individual students or the entire group to respond with statements such as:

- Because it tells about the whole passage.

- Because it tells about only one part of the whole passage.

G3.9 MARK AND SAY MAIN IDEA

MATERIALS
PREP

GRADE LEVELS:
4–8

INTERVENTION TYPE:
Academic—All

This technique will work best in conjunction with What Is the Main Idea? as described in G3.8 above.

Give students a card or piece of paper and read a paragraph to them. Tell students to put a mark on an index card when they think they can identify the main idea. After students have made a mark, such as an "M," state the main idea. Then ask the students to repeat the main idea in unison or call on individual students to repeat the main idea. Repeat this procedure with several other short paragraphs. Later, you can drop the modeling step and ask students to give the main idea after reading short passages.

G3.10 ANSWER EXPERTS

MATERIALS
PREP

GRADE LEVELS:
4–8

INTERVENTION TYPE:
Academic—All

REPRODUCIBLE on CD

Assign students to "home" groups of four or five.

The number of students in a group should be the same as the number of questions to be answered. Each student in the group is assigned one question related to the reading selection to answer. After reading or listening to the selection, students move to "expert" groups, joining students from the other groups who have been assigned the same question. The expert groups answer their question and write notes on an index card (see illustration). Students then return to their home group and share the answer to their question with the entire group. All students in the home group are then responsible for answering all the questions.

Teach All, Reach All

Answer Expert Cards

What was significant about the way the students
Name: *Quintell*   Question #: __3__   Question: *solved the problem?*
Main ideas related to the question: Other details to remember:
1. _____
2. _____
3. *They did not panic. They brainstormed ideas. They picked the solution that everyone liked.*
4. _____

REPRODUCIBLE G3.10

T
G
I
F

G3.11 ADD IT UP

MATERIALS PREP ✂

GRADE LEVELS:
3–8

INTERVENTION TYPE:
Academic—ELA

REPRODUCIBLE on CD

Students are taught to fill out the Add It Up organizer to arrive at the main idea.

This organizer can be completed while reading aloud, reading silently, or just listening to a passage. Details can also be written in the boxes after the reading of the passage.

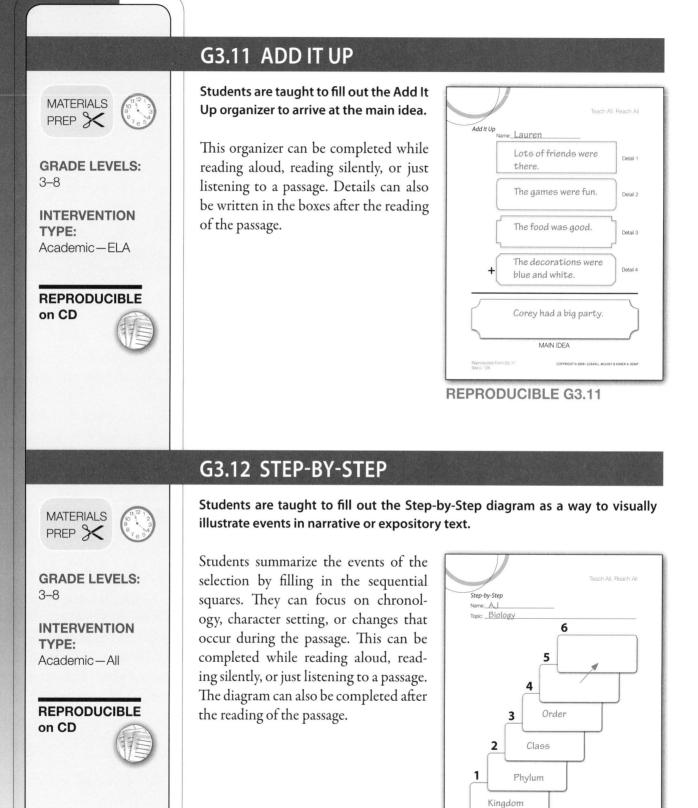

REPRODUCIBLE G3.11

G3.12 STEP-BY-STEP

MATERIALS PREP ✂

GRADE LEVELS:
3–8

INTERVENTION TYPE:
Academic—All

REPRODUCIBLE on CD

Students are taught to fill out the Step-by-Step diagram as a way to visually illustrate events in narrative or expository text.

Students summarize the events of the selection by filling in the sequential squares. They can focus on chronology, character setting, or changes that occur during the passage. This can be completed while reading aloud, reading silently, or just listening to a passage. The diagram can also be completed after the reading of the passage.

REPRODUCIBLE G3.12

G3: What can I do about the students who do not comprehend and/or respond to written material during practice/ seatwork activities?

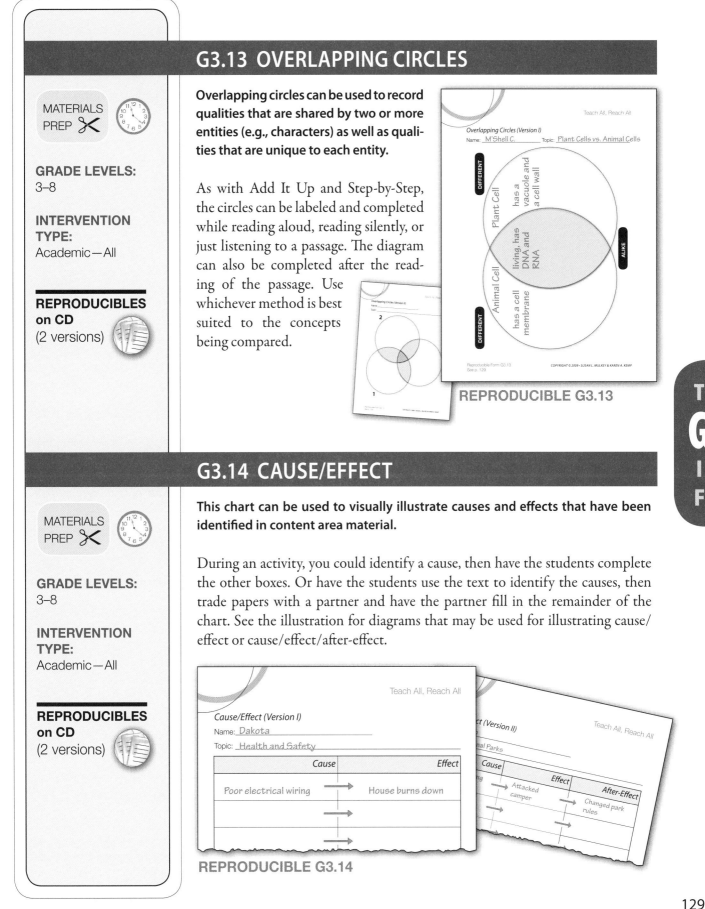

G3.13 OVERLAPPING CIRCLES

MATERIALS PREP ✂

GRADE LEVELS:
3–8

INTERVENTION TYPE:
Academic—All

REPRODUCIBLES on CD
(2 versions)

Overlapping circles can be used to record qualities that are shared by two or more entities (e.g., characters) as well as qualities that are unique to each entity.

As with Add It Up and Step-by-Step, the circles can be labeled and completed while reading aloud, reading silently, or just listening to a passage. The diagram can also be completed after the reading of the passage. Use whichever method is best suited to the concepts being compared.

Teach All, Reach All

Overlapping Circles (Version I)
Name: M'Shell C.   Topic: Plant Cells vs. Animal Cells

DIFFERENT — Plant Cell: has a vacuole and a cell wall

ALIKE — living, has DNA and RNA

DIFFERENT — Animal Cell: has a cell membrane

Reproducible Form G3.13
See p. 129   COPYRIGHT © 2009 • SUSAN L. MULKEY & KAREN A. KEMP

REPRODUCIBLE G3.13

G3.14 CAUSE/EFFECT

MATERIALS PREP ✂

GRADE LEVELS:
3–8

INTERVENTION TYPE:
Academic—All

REPRODUCIBLES on CD
(2 versions)

This chart can be used to visually illustrate causes and effects that have been identified in content area material.

During an activity, you could identify a cause, then have the students complete the other boxes. Or have the students use the text to identify the causes, then trade papers with a partner and have the partner fill in the remainder of the chart. See the illustration for diagrams that may be used for illustrating cause/ effect or cause/effect/after-effect.

Teach All, Reach All

Cause/Effect (Version I)
Name: Dakota
Topic: Health and Safety

Cause	Effect
Poor electrical wiring	House burns down

...ct (Version II)   Teach All, Reach All
...nal Parks

Cause	Effect	After-Effect
...ng	Attacked camper	Changed park rules

REPRODUCIBLE G3.14

T
G
I
F

G3.15 STAR BOOK REPORT

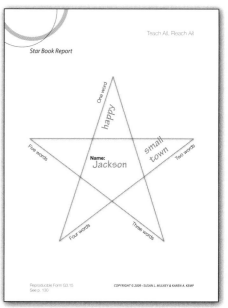

MATERIALS PREP ✂

GRADE LEVELS:
3–8

INTERVENTION TYPE:
Academic—All

REPRODUCIBLE on CD

Star book reports can be used as a way to simplify the task of writing a book report.

The students answer the five questions using only the number of words indicated next to each star point.

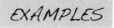
EXAMPLES

- Describe how the book made you feel in one word.

- Describe in four words where most of the story took place.

Different questions may be used depending on the objectives and reading level of the student. Stars can be posted and shared as an oral book report or as a way to advertise the book.

REPRODUCIBLE G3.15

Source: *Livingston, 1991.*

G3.16 HERRINGBONE

MATERIALS PREP ✂

GRADE LEVELS:
3–8

INTERVENTION TYPE:
Academic—All

REPRODUCIBLE on CD

Herringbone is a way to visually display literal information along with the main idea of a story.

Answers to who, what, where, why, and how questions are written on the herringbones. Questions that appear along the Herringbone are:

- Who was involved?

- What did they do?

- When did it happen?

- Where was it done?

- How did they do it?

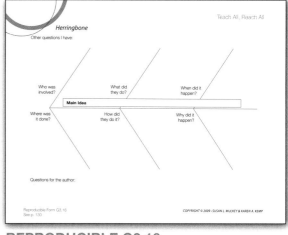

REPRODUCIBLE G3.16

G3: What can I do about the students who do not comprehend and/or respond to written material during practice/ seatwork activities?

The Herringbone diagram can also be expanded to include inferential information by adding a Question the Author component and changing the questions. As before, the responses can be written while reading aloud or reading silently, or while listening to the passage. It can also be completed following the reading of the passage.

EXAMPLES

What does this remind you of?

What is the author saying about . . . ?

What is the effect of . . . ?

G3.17 COMPREHENSION WHEELS

Comprehension wheels are used before reading a story or passage and are completed during or after the reading of the story.

The story or passage topic is written in the center circle (e.g., whales). Students are then asked to generate questions they would like answered about the topic. These are then written separately on the outer rim of the Comprehension Wheel. Prompts can be provided to help students generate questions, such as "Think of a 'what' or 'who' question." The story or passage is read, and the students record the answers in the spaces between spokes. (Some questions may not be answered through reading the story and can be researched using other materials.)

Students may write paragraphs using the information on the wheel. Questions can be numbered to assist students in sequencing the information on the wheel. Topic and main idea sentences can also be inserted. Paragraphs that result from the Comprehension Wheels can be traded and edited among students.

MATERIALS PREP

GRADE LEVELS:
3–8

INTERVENTION TYPE:
Academic—All

REPRODUCIBLE on CD

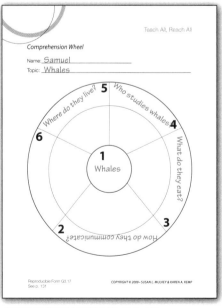

Teach All, Reach All

Comprehension Wheel

Name: Samuel
Topic: Whales

5 Who studies whales
Where do they live?
6
4 What do they eat?
1 Whales
2 How do they communicate?
3

Reproducible Form G3.17
See p. 131

COPYRIGHT © 2009 • SUSAN L. MULKEY & KAREN A. KEMP

REPRODUCIBLE G3.17

TGIF

G3.18 STORY CHARTS

MATERIALS
PREP

GRADE LEVELS:
3–8

INTERVENTION
TYPE:
Academic—All

REPRODUCIBLE
on CD

Story Charts are a way to visually record the information in a story, chapter, or passage.

The responses can be written while reading aloud, silently, or just listening to a passage. Primary information in each column can be expanded to include other descriptive information.

In the Who? column, primary information might include the characters and their names. Expanded information can include words that describe the characters. In the Did What? column, primary information might include actions and events from the passage. Expanded information can include words describing the actions and events from the passage. In the Said/ Thought column, primary information might include words spoken or thought by a character. Expanded information can include words that describe how the information was spoken.

Who?	Did What?	Said/ Thought?	Where?	When?	Why?
child/ Erica	went to far-away university to learn Spanish	I'm excited and afraid.	Madrid, Spain	summer of '93	applied and got scholarship
only child, 16		anxious, scared			

Name: Chaz Topic: trip

REPRODUCIBLE G3.18

G3.19 KNOW/DO NOT KNOW

MATERIALS
PREP

GRADE LEVELS:
3–8

INTERVENTION
TYPE:
Academic—All

REPRODUCIBLE
on CD

Students can be taught to use the Know/Do Not Know format while they are reading narrative or expository text.

They record what they think is being said in the Know column and vocabulary words that are unknown or prevent their understanding of the material in the Do Not Know column. A variation of this technique uses three columns: Know/ Acquainted/Use. Students can identify their level of knowledge by recording the concept or vocabulary words accordingly. Other activities for teaching vocabulary can be used with the unknown words, such as Practice Sheets/Cards (G3.21, p. 133) and ideas found in T5 and T7.

Teach All, Reach All

Know/Do Not Know

Name: Trina
Topic: Spiders

Know	Do Not Know
Spin webs	Cephalothorax?
Predators	Are all arachnids spiders?

REPRODUCIBLE G3.19

G3: What can I do about the students who do not comprehend and/or respond to written material during practice/ seatwork activities?

G3.20 COMPREHENSION OUTLINES

MATERIALS PREP ✂

GRADE LEVELS:
K–8

INTERVENTION TYPE:
Academic — All

REPRODUCIBLES on CD
(2 versions)

A generic outline can be used as an alternative for acquiring information about a passage.

Additional prompts (as shown below in the version at left) can be added to assist students who need more clues to complete the outline.

The version on the right requires students to write more in-depth information.

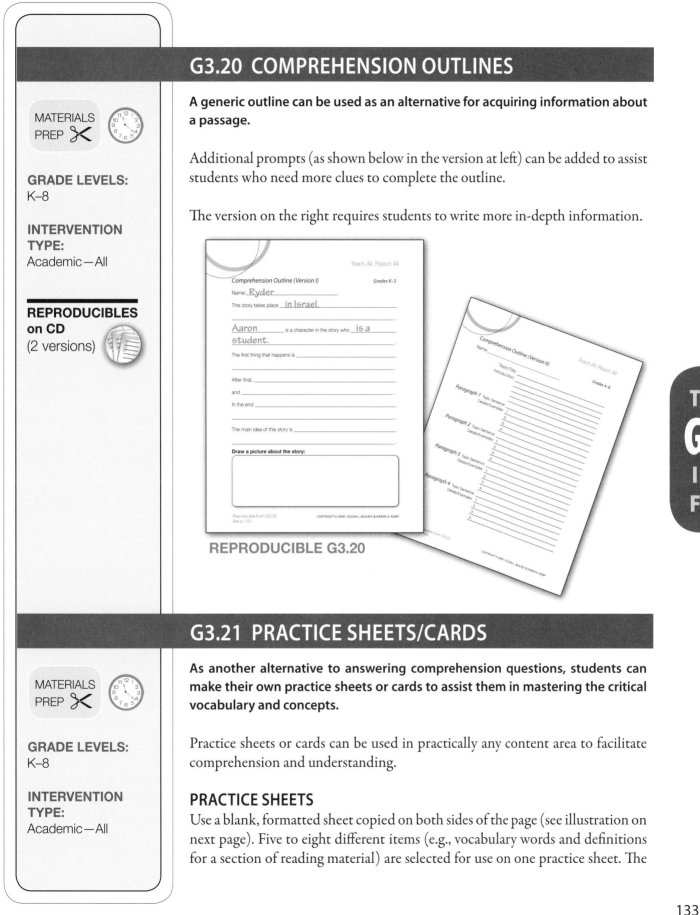

REPRODUCIBLE G3.20

G3.21 PRACTICE SHEETS/CARDS

MATERIALS PREP ✂

GRADE LEVELS:
K–8

INTERVENTION TYPE:
Academic — All

As another alternative to answering comprehension questions, students can make their own practice sheets or cards to assist them in mastering the critical vocabulary and concepts.

Practice sheets or cards can be used in practically any content area to facilitate comprehension and understanding.

PRACTICE SHEETS
Use a blank, formatted sheet copied on both sides of the page (see illustration on next page). Five to eight different items (e.g., vocabulary words and definitions for a section of reading material) are selected for use on one practice sheet. The

**REPRODUCIBLES
on CD
(3 versions)**

items are written, one per box, and repeated randomly at least two to three times on the page. The corresponding answers/definitions are written on the back side of the practice sheet in matching positions. With a partner, students practice the information during two-minute timed drills. Student A shows the vocabulary side of the page to Student B. Student B pronounces the word and then states the definition. Student A (who is looking at the answer side of the sheet) checks and gives feedback to Student B. After two minutes, partners switch roles. Student B shows the vocabulary side of the page to Student A and the process is repeated.

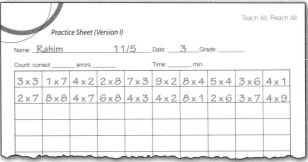

Practice Sheet (Version I)

Name: Rahim   11/5   Date: 3   Grade:

Count: correct _____ errors _____   Time: _____ min.

3 x 3	1 x 7	4 x 2	2 x 8	7 x 3	9 x 2	8 x 4	5 x 4	3 x 6	4 x 1
2 x 7	8 x 8	4 x 7	6 x 8	4 x 3	4 x 2	8 x 1	2 x 6	3 x 7	4 x 9

REPRODUCIBLE G3.21

PRACTICE CARDS

Students make their own index cards for critical vocabulary and concepts. On one side of the card the student writes the key concept or vocabulary word. On the back side of the card, the student writes the key points associated with the concept or the definition. Students then practice by looking at the information on one side of the card and stating what is on the reverse side of the card. They then look at the reverse side of the card to check their answer. Students use only five to eight different cards at a time during a two-minute timed drill. This allows students to go through the stack of cards at least two to three times during the practice session. This activity can also be conducted with partners. One partner shows one side of the card to the partner and is able to check the answer with the information that appears on the back side of the card.

***Source:** Lovitt et al., 1992.*

G3: What can I do about the students who do not comprehend and/or respond to written material during practice/seatwork activities?

G3.22 STOP AND THINK

MATERIALS
PREP ✂

GRADE LEVELS:
4–8

INTERVENTION TYPE:
Academic—All

REPRODUCIBLE on CD

Stop and Think is a strategy that allows students to think about what they are reading while they are reading or while they are listening to information.

Students are taught to stop at designated points (such as after each paragraph) and ask questions or make notations about the material. Notations and marks can be made on the actual material, or students can use a format with prompts to record information (see illustration). The Stop and Think format should include prompts that promote a broad-based understanding of the written materials. Students should be able to record impressions, disagreements, challenges, affirmations, and expansions in their own terms.

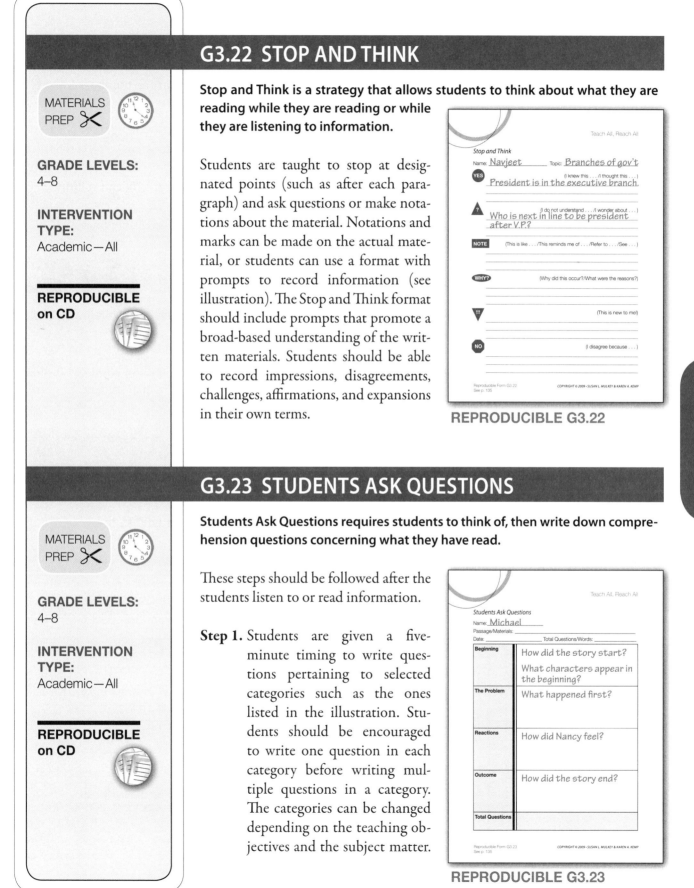

Teach All, Reach All

Stop and Think
Name: Navjeet Topic: Branches of gov't

YES (I knew this . . . /I thought this . . .)
President is in the executive branch.

? (I do not understand . . . /I wonder about . . .)
Who is next in line to be president after V.P.?

NOTE (This is like . . . /This reminds me of . . . /Refer to . . . /See . . .)

WHY? (Why did this occur?/What were the reasons?)

!!! (This is new to me!)

NO (I disagree because . . .)

Reproducible Form G3.22
See p. 135   COPYRIGHT © 2009 • SUSAN L. MULKEY & KAREN A. KEMP

REPRODUCIBLE G3.22

G3.23 STUDENTS ASK QUESTIONS

MATERIALS
PREP ✂

GRADE LEVELS:
4–8

INTERVENTION TYPE:
Academic—All

REPRODUCIBLE on CD

Students Ask Questions requires students to think of, then write down comprehension questions concerning what they have read.

These steps should be followed after the students listen to or read information.

Step 1. Students are given a five-minute timing to write questions pertaining to selected categories such as the ones listed in the illustration. Students should be encouraged to write one question in each category before writing multiple questions in a category. The categories can be changed depending on the teaching objectives and the subject matter.

Teach All, Reach All

Students Ask Questions
Name: Michael
Passage/Materials:
Date: _____ Total Questions/Words: _____

Beginning	How did the story start? What characters appear in the beginning?
The Problem	What happened first?
Reactions	How did Nancy feel?
Outcome	How did the story end?
Total Questions	

Reproducible Form G3.23
See p. 135   COPYRIGHT © 2009 • SUSAN L. MULKEY & KAREN A. KEMP

REPRODUCIBLE G3.23

Step 2. Students then count the number of questions written or the total number of words written in the questions.

Step 3. Students then record the number of questions or the number of words on a chart or graph.

Step 4. Students try to improve their question and word-writing score the next time a Students Ask Questions timing is administered.

Alternate categories could include characters, setting, problem, and solution.

Source: *Lovitt et al., 1992.*

G3.24 STUDY GUIDES (PROMPTS)

A study guide with page numbers can be used to assist students in locating answers to questions in textbooks.

Other prompts can be incorporated into the study depending upon the needs of the student. Study guides can be completed by an individual student, by partners, or in cooperative learning groups.

MATERIALS PREP

GRADE LEVELS:
4–8

INTERVENTION TYPE:
Academic — All

Study Guide—Chapter 11, Worms

1. How many roundworm species have been identified? _____

2. In roundworms, hydrostatic pressure is antagonistic to the
   _____

3. Most roundworms are monoecious. T or F

4. Name two body systems that are missing in roundworms.
   _____

5. Roundworms are in what phylum? _____

6. Name the roundworm parasite that:
   a. burrows through the bottoms of the feet _____
   b. causes itching _____
   c. is obtained by ingesting undercooked pork _____
   d. is often found in all members of a family _____
   e. has eggs that are killed by sunlight and high temperatures
      _____
   f. causes elephantiasis _____

G3: What can I do about the students who do not comprehend and/or respond to written material during practice/ seatwork activities?

G3.25 GRAPHIC ORGANIZERS

MATERIALS PREP ✂

GRADE LEVELS:
3–8

INTERVENTION TYPE:
Academic—All

NOTE:
See T5.7, p. 63, and T10.8, p. 95, for examples of completed and partial graphic organizers.

Visual-spatial maps or graphic organizers may be appropriate aids, depending on the comprehension task that is required of the students.

The use of graphic organizers should be introduced, modeled, and demonstrated for the students before use as a comprehension activity or for answering questions. After instruction, the organizers can be completed by an individual student, by partners, or in a cooperative group setting. Determine whether to use a **blank copy** of the organizer (see illustration), a partially completed version that includes some of the information, or a complete copy that contains all of the information. Additionally, an appropriate format should be selected based on the practice activity and the objective.

Source: Lovitt et al., 1992.

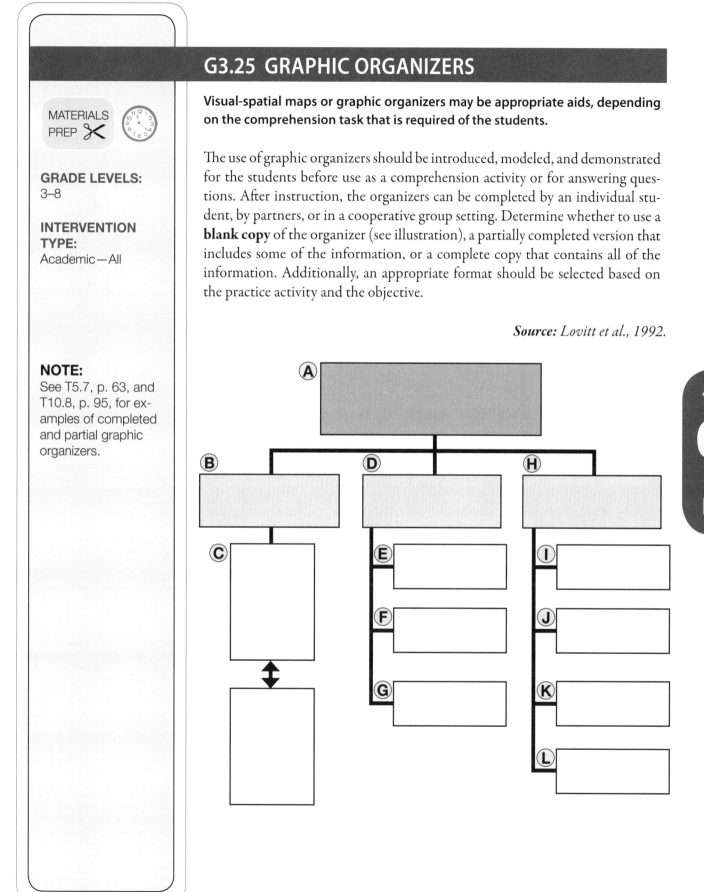

T
G
I
F

G3.26 SR.I.SRV (SCANNING)

SR.I.SRV is a six-step scanning-for-information strategy.

SR.I.SRV is ideal for answering questions at the end of a chapter or other questions related to printed material. Scanning does not require the student to read all of the information.

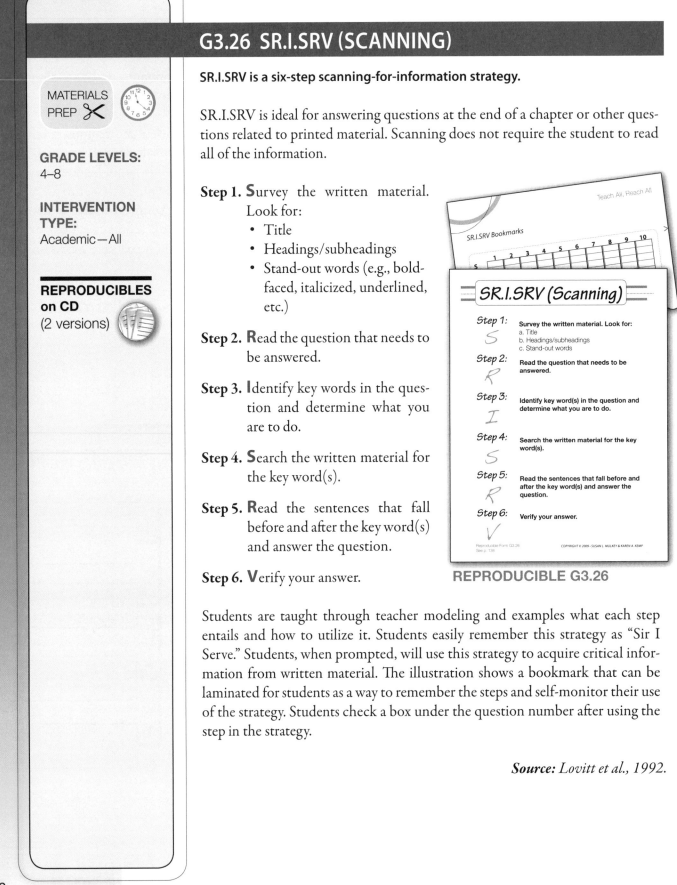

MATERIALS PREP ✂ 🕐

GRADE LEVELS:
4–8

INTERVENTION TYPE:
Academic—All

REPRODUCIBLES on CD
(2 versions)

Step 1. Survey the written material. Look for:
- Title
- Headings/subheadings
- Stand-out words (e.g., bold-faced, italicized, underlined, etc.)

Step 2. Read the question that needs to be answered.

Step 3. Identify key words in the question and determine what you are to do.

Step 4. Search the written material for the key word(s).

Step 5. Read the sentences that fall before and after the key word(s) and answer the question.

Step 6. Verify your answer.

REPRODUCIBLE G3.26

Students are taught through teacher modeling and examples what each step entails and how to utilize it. Students easily remember this strategy as "Sir I Serve." Students, when prompted, will use this strategy to acquire critical information from written material. The illustration shows a bookmark that can be laminated for students as a way to remember the steps and self-monitor their use of the strategy. Students check a box under the question number after using the step in the strategy.

Source: *Lovitt et al., 1992.*

G3: What can I do about the students who do not comprehend and/or respond to written material during practice/
seatwork activities?

G3.27 SQ3R WORKSHEETS

MATERIALS
PREP ✂

GRADE LEVELS:
4–8

**INTERVENTION
TYPE:**
Academic—All

**REPRODUCIBLE
on CD**
(2 pages)

**SQ3R Worksheets is a five-step study skill designed to improve reading compre-
hension.**

Students are first taught each of the steps in the strategy through teacher modeling and examples. During structured practice activities, the worksheet shown
below can be used to assist students in more purposeful reading.

Step 1. Survey: The students look over the entire written selection before
reading it. Items that should be surveyed include the title, subheadings,
pictures, charts, graphs, stand-out words (bold, italic, etc.), bullets,
summary section, and any questions at the end of the selection.

Step 2. Question: The students formulate questions that the selection is
likely to answer. For example, if the title of the selection is *Events That
Shaped the Revolution*, students might ask, "What happened to help
start the American Revolution?" All questions should be written down
on the worksheet.

Step 3. Read: The students read (or listen to) the selection while looking for
the answers to the formulated questions. Key words or notes could be
written next to each question to assist in recall.

Step 4. Recite: After the selection has been read, the students should recite or
write the answers to the questions. If the questions cannot be answered,
the selection can be read again or another resource may be used to
locate the answer.

Step 5. Review: Some-
time later, and al-
ways before a test
on the material,
the reader should
go back over the
worksheet ques-
tions and check
for retention.

Source: *Lovitt et al., 1992.*

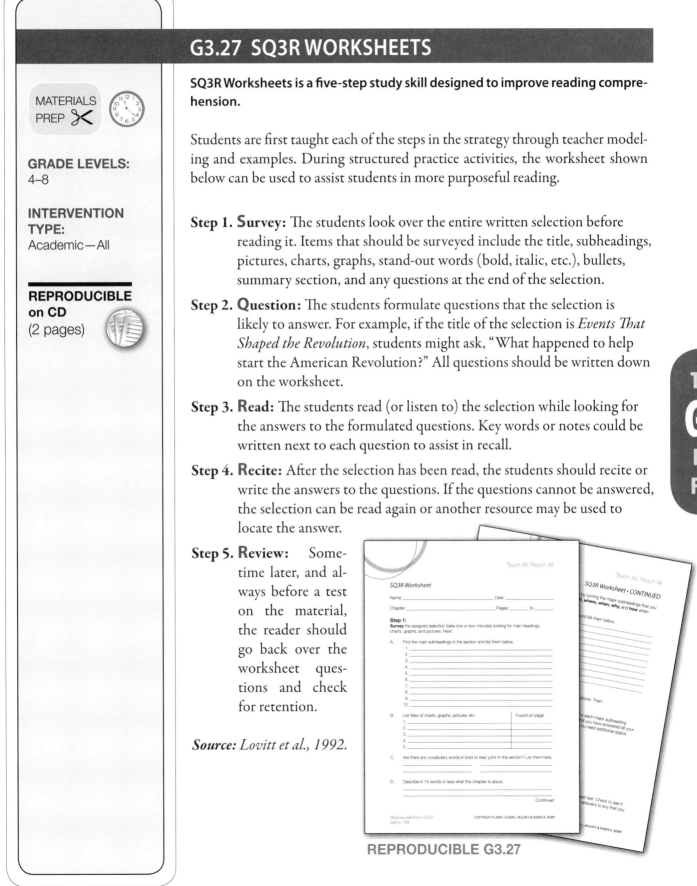

REPRODUCIBLE G3.27

G4

GUIDED PRACTICE ACTIVITIES

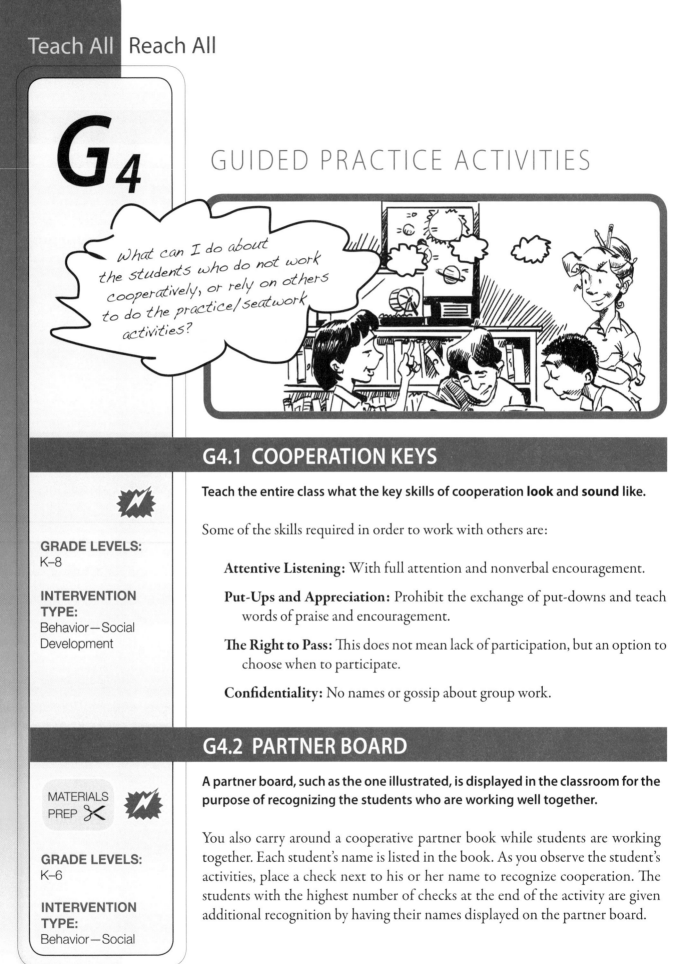

What can I do about the students who do not work cooperatively, or rely on others to do the practice/seatwork activities?

G4.1 COOPERATION KEYS

GRADE LEVELS:
K–8

INTERVENTION TYPE:
Behavior—Social Development

Teach the entire class what the key skills of cooperation look and sound like.

Some of the skills required in order to work with others are:

Attentive Listening: With full attention and nonverbal encouragement.

Put-Ups and Appreciation: Prohibit the exchange of put-downs and teach words of praise and encouragement.

The Right to Pass: This does not mean lack of participation, but an option to choose when to participate.

Confidentiality: No names or gossip about group work.

G4.2 PARTNER BOARD

MATERIALS PREP

GRADE LEVELS:
K–6

INTERVENTION TYPE:
Behavior—Social

A partner board, such as the one illustrated, is displayed in the classroom for the purpose of recognizing the students who are working well together.

You also carry around a cooperative partner book while students are working together. Each student's name is listed in the book. As you observe the student's activities, place a check next to his or her name to recognize cooperation. The students with the highest number of checks at the end of the activity are given additional recognition by having their names displayed on the partner board.

G4: What can I do about the students who do not work cooperatively or rely on others to do the practice/
seatwork activities?

PARTNER BOARD		
<u>SHARING</u>	<u>COOPERATION</u>	<u>EFFORT</u>
Shelley	Franco	Vivian
Campbell	Mary	
Ahmed		

G4.3 STEP OUT

Designate a place in the classroom where students go to step out of the group if they are not using the appropriate cooperative skills for working in a group.

GRADE LEVELS:
K–8

INTERVENTION TYPE:
Behavior—Social, Motivation

Determine and announce ahead of time the criteria for being moved to the step-out area, such as the length of stay, expected behavior during the step-out time period, and the reentry procedures. You signal students when it is necessary for them to step out. If a student steps out more than once during an activity, additional consequences can be given.

G4.4 TEAM SKILLS

Assign students specific team skills to practice while working on a group project.

GRADE LEVELS:
3–8

INTERVENTION TYPE:
Behavior—Social Development

Step 1. Students are first assigned an individual task to accomplish. This could be a specific portion of a state report, a set of math problems, or individual thoughts and important learnings from a text.

Step 2. The students are assigned a group product that incorporates the individual task. The product might be an entire state report, an entire math assignment, or a compilation of individual learnings in order of importance.

Step 3. Explain to the students that they are expected to work in groups to produce the final product while practicing specific teamwork skills. Some examples of team skills include:

- Taking turns
- Listening to others
- Disagreeing appropriately
- Keeping everyone involved
- Contributing to group work

T
G
I
F

Step 4. Choose one or two specific team skills for the groups to work on and carefully define what each looks and sounds like. In addition, students are given a specific timeline for completing the group project.

Step 5. After the final product is completed, you debrief with the groups to discuss and evaluate their use of the team skills. (See G4.6, p. 144, and G4.8, p. 145, for additional ideas.) Some questions to use might include:

- How did you use the skills in your group?
- How often did the group members use the skill?
- How did you feel using the skill?
- What might you change for the next time?
- How would you rate your own use of the skill?

Step 6. Questionnaires or surveys can be used as well as group discussion. Feedback should be given to the groups by the teacher as well as by the team members.

Step 7. You may also have students write down the skills they used and their goal for improvement in a teamwork skills notebook. These goals can be referred to from time to time, and you or the group can note progress.

Step 8. Time should also be spent reviewing the academic task in order to further the group's understanding of the subject matter.

G4.5 ROLE CARDS

MATERIALS PREP ✂

GRADE LEVELS:
K–8

INTERVENTION TYPE:
Academic — All
Behavior — Social

Prior to having students work with others, assign specific roles for each student to perform in the group.

Provide students with specific behavioral descriptions for each role. Some roles that can be assigned are:

Summarizer/Checker: Ensures that everyone in the group understands the information.

Research/Runner: Retrieves the necessary materials for the group and is the communication link with other groups and the teacher.

Recorder/Writer: Writes down the group's conclusions and edits the final copy.

Encourager: Reinforces group members' contributions.

Observer: Keeps track of the group's performance and how well everyone is collaborating.

G4: What can I do about the students who do not work cooperatively or rely on others to do the practice/
seatwork activities?

Quiet Captain: Makes sure the group does not disturb others.

The Gatekeeper: Keeps everyone participating and makes sure that no one person is dominating the group.

Other names can be assigned to these roles to fit the age level of the students and content being taught. For instance:

MATH GROUP ROLES

Calculator: Verifies work on a calculator.

Analyst: Determines which strategies the group should use.

Bookkeeper: Verifies final work and records time spent.

Inventory Controller: Keeps track of materials and supplies.

NOVEL DISCUSSION GROUP ROLES

Discussion Leader: Prepares and leads questions with the group.

Vocabulary Enricher: Selects enrichment questions for review.

Literary Illuminary: Reads critical passages and information.

Agent: Retrieves materials and supplies and is the communication link with the teacher.

SCIENCE GROUP ROLES

Scientist: Observes group progress and keeps track of time.

Researcher: Provides guidelines for the group to follow.

Observer: Records information about the lesson and/or the group.

Lab Technician: Sets up materials and equipment the group is to use.

SOCIAL STUDIES GROUP ROLES

Presiding Officer: Facilitates what goes on in the group.

Secretary: Records information that is processed by the group.

Parliamentarian: Observes group progress with the topic.

Sergeant at Arms: Keeps time, retrieves supplies, and serves as communication link with the teacher.

PRIMARY GROUP ROLES

Happy Talker: Makes positive comments about student contributions.

Turn Taker: Makes sure everyone is involved and has a turn participating.

Helper: Retrieves materials and serves as communication link with the teacher.

Source: Johnson et al., 1987.

T
G
I
F

GRADE LEVELS:
3–8

INTERVENTION TYPE:
Behavior—Social

REPRODUCIBLE on CD

G4.6 REFLECTION CARDS

After group work, have students complete individual and/or group assessments related to the social/responsibility skill(s) used while working with one another.

This type of assessment requires a high level of trust among students and some training in feedback procedures. Reflections to include are:

1. Name one thing you learned about working with others.

2. Name something another team member may have learned.

3. Name one skill you could improve upon.

If a particular student is having a difficult time, have the individual student fill out the form and process the information with you privately.

REPRODUCIBLE G4.6

G4.7 ASSIGNMENT CO-OP

GRADE LEVELS:
3–8

INTERVENTION TYPE:
Academic—All
Behavior—Social

Assign students to groups of three or four. Divide up the assignment so each group member is responsible for completing only a portion of the assignment.

Establish time frames for completing the assignment and allow students to work within the group while completing their individual portions. When all portions of the assignment are completed, each student in the group must share the information he or she was responsible for with the entire group. A group product can be compiled using each member's information. Tests should be administered individually, and bonus points should be awarded to teams whose members all score above a specified grade. The purpose of the bonus point is to encourage group work, sharing of information, and cooperation.

G4.8 PROCESSING

GRADE LEVELS:
K–8

INTERVENTION TYPE:
Behavior—Social

Processing is discussing, reflecting, and evaluating with students how partners or groups functioned during an activity.

Classwide processing can include feedback from observations you make and some observations from members of the class. Names should not be used when processing with the whole group, but the feedback should be as specific as possible. Groups that are new to processing often need an agenda, including specific questions each group must address. A simple agenda might include: Name two things the group/dyad did well and one thing they need to do even better. Group processing should focus on member's contributions to the learning along with questions regarding the maintenance of effective working relationships among partners/groups. Some possible questions for group processing follow.

EXAMPLES

- What did you do that helped your team work together?
- What could you change in order to improve next time?
- How is your team working as a group?
- What would you do differently next time?
- How did you feel about your group?
- What did you notice that might help the team?
- What was the best thing that happened to your group?
- What changes would make your group even more successful?

Processing can be done on an individual basis by having students fill out a simple rating scale regarding their own performance. Students can then share their self-rating with their partners by explaining why they rated themselves as they did and what they could do next time to improve.

EXAMPLES

- How well did you check to make sure your partners understood the material you presented?

1	2	3	4	5	6	⑦	8	9	10
no checking									checked thoroughly

- How well did you share supplies with your group?

1	2	3	4	5	6	7	8	⑨	10
not at all									all the time

T G I F

G4.9 CLASSWIDE PEER TUTORING

MATERIALS PREP ✂

GRADE LEVELS:
K–8

INTERVENTION TYPE:
Academic—All
Behavior—Social

Classwide peer tutoring is a structured tutoring situation where students practice material but also earn rewards and bonus points for working cooperatively with others. The following steps will help you set up classwide peer tutoring in the classroom.

Step 1. Divide the classroom into two teams. Students can be randomly assigned to teams, or you can make team assignments. Teams should choose a team name, color, or logo.

Step 2. Assign students to dyads (tutoring pairs). Students can be randomly assigned, or you may want to make assignments based on individual needs.

Step 3. Train the dyads to conduct tutoring sessions. Carefully demonstrate and model the tutoring procedure described in this section. Students also need to be taught to use an individual scorecard (see illustration) to keep track of correct and error responses. Students should practice the procedure prior to implementation.

Step 4. Total the points from the tutoring session. The students in each dyad add the points earned from the questions and the bonus points together for a daily total.

Step 5. Record the dyad point totals on a game chart. Collect the total scores for each dyad, either by having students call out their total or through an individual student recorder. Because these scores are combined for each dyad, the chance of embarrassment is greatly reduced and students work cooperatively to raise their combined scores. Dyads with the highest daily score can be recognized.

Step 6. Recognize the winning team of the week. After all dyad scores are totaled by team, the team with the highest total score is the winning team for the week. Some form of recognition should be given to this team. Ideas for reinforcement could be:
- Posting results on a class or school bulletin board
- Printing results in a weekly newsletter
- Providing all team members with achievement certificates
- Notes home to parents
- Rewards tied into the classroom management system

Step 7. Assess student performance on material practiced by tutors. Quizzes or some other type of evaluation should be administered individually on a regular basis to determine student growth on the practiced material.

G4: What can I do about the students who do not work cooperatively or rely on others to do the practice/seatwork activities?

SCORECARD

Step 1. A scorecard can have any number of items. This example is based on 15 items.

Step 2. A plus (+) or minus (-) is recorded for each item.

Step 3. If no errors occur during round one, 25 points are awarded.

SCORING ERRORS

Step 1. If one or more errors occur during the first round, the student goes to the second round.

Step 2. In the second round, only the missed items from round one are presented and responded to.

Step 3. If the student responds correctly to the items in round two, 20 points are awarded.

Step 4. If an error occurs in round two, the student goes to round three (15 points) or round four (15 points), if necessary.

Student Scorecard				
Tutoring Items	Round 1 (25)	Round 2 (20)	Round 3 (15)	Round 4 (15)
1.				15
2.		20		
3.			15	
4.	25			
5.	25			
6.				
7.				
8.				
9.				
10.				
11.				
12.				
13.				
14.				
15.				
Round				
Bonus				
Total				

T
G
I
F

CLASSWIDE SCORE SHEET

Step 1. Total the points from tutoring sessions.

Step 2. Dyads total their daily round points and bonus points from their individual scorecards.

Step 3. Dyads record their total daily points on a classwide score sheet posted in the classroom.

Classwide Score Sheet		M	T	W	Th	F
Dyad Points						
1.	Tutoring	48				
	Quiz					
2.	Tutoring	39				
	Quiz					
3.	Tutoring	54				
	Quiz					
4.	Tutoring	35				
	Quiz					
5.	Tutoring					
	Quiz					
6.	Tutoring					
	Quiz					
7.	Tutoring					
	Quiz					
8.	Tutoring					
	Quiz					
9.	Tutoring					
	Quiz					
10.	Tutoring					
	Quiz					
Total						
Weekly Total						

Source: *Lovitt et al., 1992.*

G4.10 TEAM-BUILDING EXERCISES

Prior to placing students with partners or in groups, have the entire class participate in activities that promote belonging and trust.

If students do not feel included in a classroom, they will create their own inclusion by grabbing influence (attracting attention, creating controversy, demanding power, or taking control).

GRADE LEVELS:
K–8

G4: What can I do about the students who do not work cooperatively or rely on others to do the practice/seatwork activities?

INTERVENTION TYPE:
Behavior—Social Development

EXAMPLES

WISHFUL THINKING

Students sit in a circle. Each person makes a brief statement beginning with "I wish…" There is no discussion during the activity, and statements can be related to personal life, feelings about school, the group, friends, etc. After everyone has had a chance to make a statement, debrief with questions such as:

- Do we share common wishes?
- How did you feel?
- Did others listen to you?
- How did you know they listened to you?

SOMETHING GOOD

Students sit in a circle. Each person shares one positive experience that happened during the past week, with no discussion occurring until all have shared. Ask follow-up questions such as:

- Were there any similarities about the good things shared?
- When was the last time you told someone about a positive experience?
- Was it hard to think of something good to share?

BUILD A BETTER BATHTUB

Break students into small groups of three or five. Have each group appoint a recorder. (Younger groups can use an aide or older student as recorder.) Provide groups with the rules for brainstorming:

D (defer judgment)

O (off-beat, original)

V (vast number of ideas)

E (expand, elaborate on other's ideas)

Tell groups they have five minutes to call out and write down as many ideas as possible on the subject: How could we design a better bathtub—one that provides more enjoyment, efficiency, and comfort than ordinary tubs? The recorder jots down all ideas. Stop the brainstorming after five minutes and ask each recorder to read the list. Lead the applause after each group's presentation.

Afterward, the teacher asks questions such as:
- Are many heads better than one in producing a wide range of ideas?
- What would have happened if we had judged, commented, or discussed ideas as they were being offered?
- Did each group have fun?

Source: *Gibbs, 1987.*

T G I F

G5 GUIDED PRACTICE ACTIVITIES

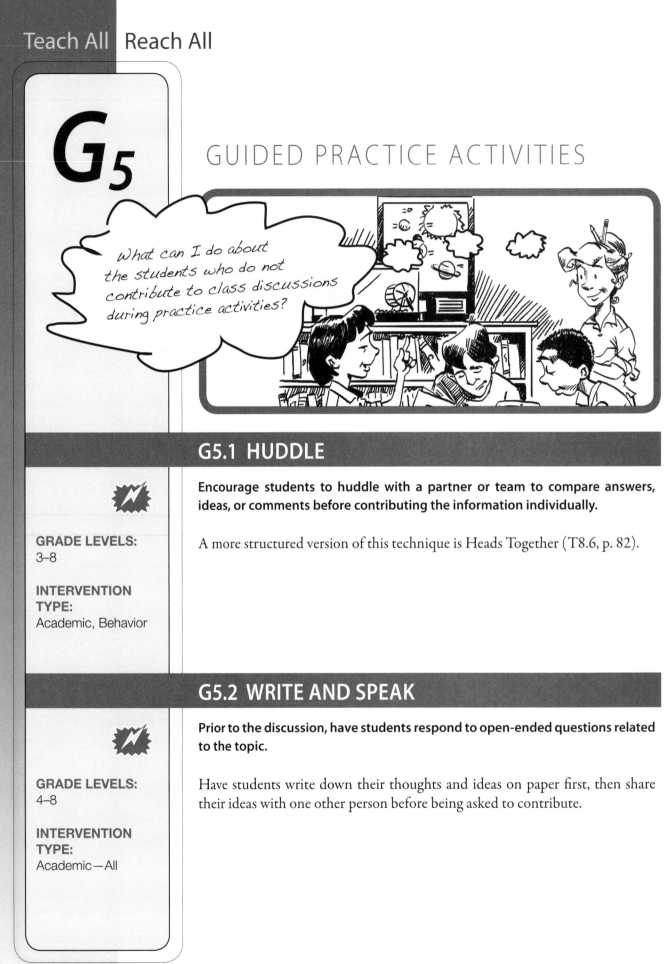

What can I do about the students who do not contribute to class discussions during practice activities?

G5.1 HUDDLE

GRADE LEVELS:
3–8

INTERVENTION TYPE:
Academic, Behavior

Encourage students to huddle with a partner or team to compare answers, ideas, or comments before contributing the information individually.

A more structured version of this technique is Heads Together (T8.6, p. 82).

G5.2 WRITE AND SPEAK

GRADE LEVELS:
4–8

INTERVENTION TYPE:
Academic—All

Prior to the discussion, have students respond to open-ended questions related to the topic.

Have students write down their thoughts and ideas on paper first, then share their ideas with one other person before being asked to contribute.

G5: What can I do about the students who do not contribute to class discussions during practice activities?

G5.3 SIGNALS

GRADE LEVELS:
K–8

INTERVENTION TYPE:
Academic—All

Set up a signal or cue ahead of time to let students know when they will be expected to contribute.

A brief consultation about what will take place during the discussion and examples of ideas or comments for contribution will give the student additional preparation time.

G5.4 CONTRIBUTION POINTS

GRADE LEVELS:
K–8

INTERVENTION TYPE:
Academic
Behavior—Motivation

Keep track of student contributions with the use of a contribution checklist or board.

Award points for number or type of contributions made (facts, opinions, additional ideas, or insights). Points can be tallied for individual rewards, or they can be added into each student's participation grade.

T
G
I
F

G5.5 CONTRIBUTION CHIPS

MATERIALS
PREP ✂

GRADE LEVELS:
K–8

INTERVENTION TYPE:
Academic
Behavior—Motivation

Break students into smaller groups to encourage participation.

Put four or five students in a small discussion group. Each group member is allotted an equal number of chips he or she must use throughout the discussion. When members contribute information, they place a chip in the middle of the table. When a student's chips run out, he cannot talk again until everyone in the group has contributed. Chips cannot be taken or given away by any member of the group.

Source: Kagan, 1990.

G5.6 PENS IN THE JAR

MATERIALS
PREP ✂

GRADE LEVELS:
K–8

**INTERVENTION
TYPE:**
Academic
Behavior—Motivation

Put four or five students in a small discussion group.

Place a jar in the middle of the table with different colored pens, sticks, or markers representing each student. When a student makes a contribution, she pulls out her pen or marker and places it in front of her. Before that student can speak again, the other group members must make a contribution. After all members of the group have contributed, the pens are placed back in the jar and the discussion continues following the same procedure.

Source: Kagan, 1990.

G5.7 CORNERS

GRADE LEVELS:
K–8

**INTERVENTION
TYPE:**
Academic—All

Write different ideas or questions related to a specific topic on chart paper and post them in the four corners of the classroom.

When you give the signal, each student moves to one of the corners. Once in their selected corner, students pair up and discuss the reasons for their choice. After a specified time of discussion, randomly select pairs to report their thinking to the class.

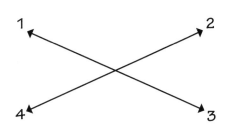

EXAMPLES

- **Volleyball skills:** Serve, bump, set, spike. (What skill would you like most to develop?)

- **Current issues:** Poverty, drug abuse, gang violence, pollution. (If you were governor of this state, which issue would be top priority? Why?)

- **Novels/Storybooks:** Characters and events from the story. (Who was your favorite character? Which character do you think was most responsible for the dilemma? Why?)

- **Controversial issues:** Strongly agree, disagree, agree, strongly disagree. (All students are treated fairly at our school. Why do you believe this? Defend your position.)

Source: Kagan, 1990.

G5.8 GRAFFITI PAPERS

MATERIALS
PREP ✂

GRADE LEVELS:
3–8

**INTERVENTION
TYPE:**
Academic—All

Students are placed in groups of three or four. Each group is given a sheet of butcher paper with a different topic/question printed on the top and different colored marking pens.

For a specified period of time (three to five minutes), every group writes "graffiti" (words, phrases, pictures) on their particular topic. Graffiti could be the students' reactions, impressions, interpretations, or creative response to the topic or question. When the specified time is up, stop the groups and have each group pass its graffiti sheet to the next group. Then repeat the process. After each group has had an opportunity to respond to every question, the papers are given to the original group, and the members of that group present a brief summary of what was written by all groups.

Source: Gibbs, 1987.

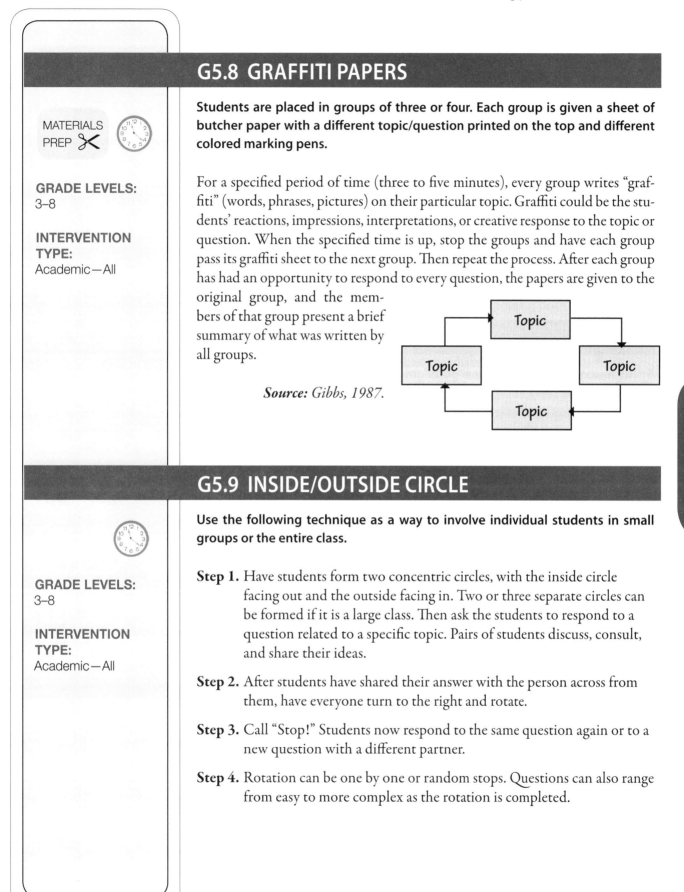

G5.9 INSIDE/OUTSIDE CIRCLE

GRADE LEVELS:
3–8

**INTERVENTION
TYPE:**
Academic—All

Use the following technique as a way to involve individual students in small groups or the entire class.

Step 1. Have students form two concentric circles, with the inside circle facing out and the outside facing in. Two or three separate circles can be formed if it is a large class. Then ask the students to respond to a question related to a specific topic. Pairs of students discuss, consult, and share their ideas.

Step 2. After students have shared their answer with the person across from them, have everyone turn to the right and rotate.

Step 3. Call "Stop!" Students now respond to the same question again or to a new question with a different partner.

Step 4. Rotation can be one by one or random stops. Questions can also range from easy to more complex as the rotation is completed.

**T
G
I
F**

G5.10 MAKING A CONTRIBUTION

MATERIALS PREP ✂

GRADE LEVELS:
3–8

INTERVENTION TYPE:
Academic
Behavior

REPRODUCIBLE on CD

Describe and model the following steps for contributing to a discussion in class.

Be sure students have ample opportunity for structured practice of the skill before expecting them to use it on their own. This strategy can be used along with contribution points or a contribution scoreboard.

Step 1. For one minute, think about the topic being discussed.

Step 2. Signal your desire to talk by using a hand raise or another appropriate signal.

Step 3. Look at the person or group.

Step 4. Make a comment related to the topic.

Step 5. Listen for a response and follow up with another comment if appropriate.

Think, **then say a comment related in some way.**

Making a Contribution

Step 1:
Think about the topic being discussed for one minute.

Step 2:
Signal your desire to talk by raising your hand or using another appropriate signal.

Step 3:
Look at the person or group.

Step 4:
Make a comment related to the topic.

Step 5:
Listen for a response and follow up with another comment if appropriate.

Think, then say a comment related in some way.

Reproducible Form G5.10
See p. 154   COPYRIGHT © 2009 • SUSAN L. MULKEY & KAREN A. KEMP

REPRODUCIBLE G5.10

G5.11 PAIR INTERVIEWS

MATERIALS PREP ✂

GRADE LEVELS:
3–8

INTERVENTION TYPE:
Academic

Use pair interviews at the beginning or end of a lesson to engage all students in discussion.

Students are placed in groups of four and then paired off. The partners interview each other first and then reconvene with their group for a round robin. A round robin consists of all students on the team sharing in turn what they learned from the person they interviewed. The content of the interview questions can include anything. Questions that are related to the subject but do not have one right answer are best.

G5: What can I do about the students who do not contribute to class discussions during practice activities?

EXAMPLES

ANTICIPATORY OR CLOSURE QUESTIONS

- What do you want to learn about this topic?

- What experiences have you had with the information we are going to talk about?

- What was the most important thing you learned about this topic?

- When would you use this information?

- What would you like to know more about?

CONTENT-SPECIFIC QUESTIONS

- How would you feel if you were Huck Finn?

- What math problem did you find the most difficult?

- If you were a scientist, how would you solve this?

- What would you bring if you were a pioneer traveling west?

Source: Kagan, 1990.

T G I F

G5.12 CONTRIBUTION AIMS

After teaching students the strategy for making a contribution (see G5.10, p. 154), have the students self-monitor their performance.

MATERIALS
PREP

GRADE LEVELS:
K–8

INTERVENTION TYPE:
Behavior—Motivation

REPRODUCIBLE on CD

Set aims for the number of contributions expected during the class period and have the student record the number of contributions made. Give the students tracker cards (see illustration) or have them make their own.

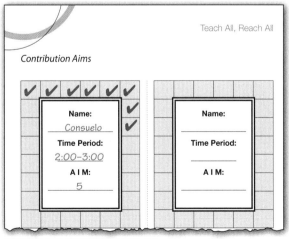

Teach All, Reach All

Contribution Aims

Name:
Consuelo

Time Period:
2:00–3:00

A I M:
5

Name:

Time Period:

A I M:

REPRODUCIBLE G5.12

G5.13 S.M.A.R.T.S. REVIEW

MATERIALS PREP ✂

GRADE LEVELS:
4–8

INTERVENTION TYPE:
Academic

REPRODUCIBLE on CD
(2 pages)

S.M.A.R.T.S. stands for Self-Motivational and Recreational Teaching Strategies. Students are assigned to heterogeneous teams of five in order to answer the questions related to the topic of study.

The student who does not often contribute to discussions could be appointed as a team captain. Select a performing team (PT) to start. All other teams become opposing teams (OT). A S.M.A.R.T.S. class score sheet is used to identify questions and point values that will be used during the game. The performing team begins by playing a complete round (parts one and two) of the game.

PART ONE
The team captain confers with the team and selects a question from the chart. Students can choose from who/what, when/where, or how/why questions. The team must answer the question after only one minute of conferencing. Only the team captain can answer aloud. All other teams are conferencing at the same time in case the PT answers incorrectly.

If the PT answers correctly, it is awarded the predetermined point value, which is recorded on the team's score sheet by the recorder. If the team is incorrect, an opposing team chosen by the teacher can give the answer and be awarded the points.

PART TWO
The PT must now answer an extended question related to the original question (e.g., spell or define a word or term). If the answer is correct, points are awarded to the team. If the team's answer is incorrect, then an opposing team may answer and receive the points. After the round of play is completed, a new team becomes the performing team and play continues.

This game can be played in one class period or over a number of days. Teams keep track of their points and are recognized for their performance.

REPRODUCIBLE G5.13

Source: Buchanan, 1989.

Throughout **I**, the teacher facilitates activities that provide continued or extended practice opportunities. These activities involve fewer prompts and less guidance from the teacher as students are building fluency and generalizing the information.

INDEPENDENT PRACTICE ACTIVITIES

I1 INDEPENDENT PRACTICE ACTIVITIES

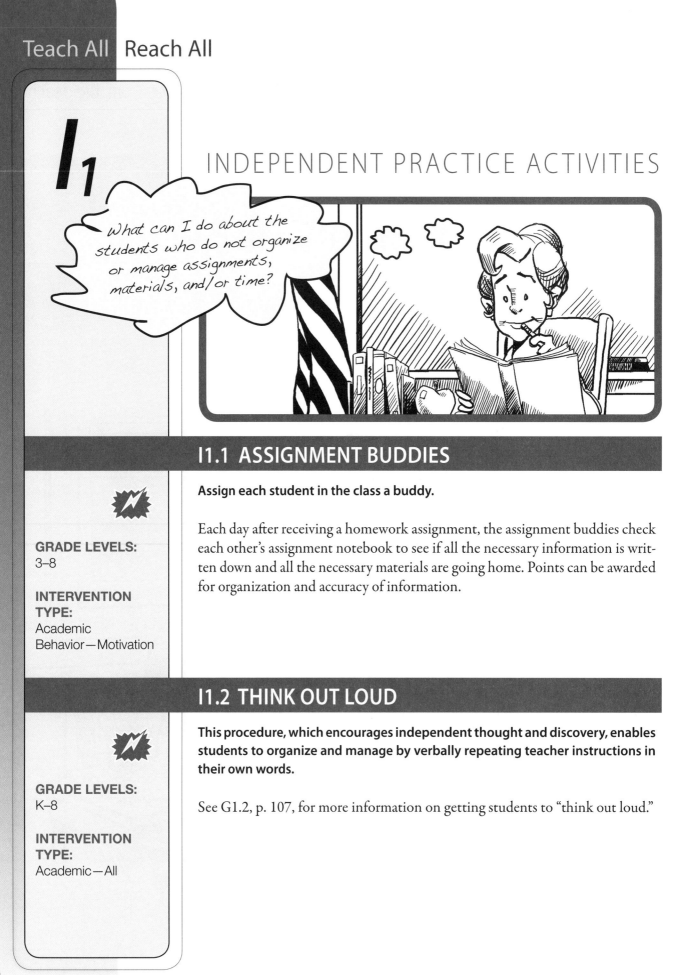

What can I do about the students who do not organize or manage assignments, materials, and/or time?

I1.1 ASSIGNMENT BUDDIES

GRADE LEVELS:
3–8

INTERVENTION TYPE:
Academic
Behavior—Motivation

Assign each student in the class a buddy.

Each day after receiving a homework assignment, the assignment buddies check each other's assignment notebook to see if all the necessary information is written down and all the necessary materials are going home. Points can be awarded for organization and accuracy of information.

I1.2 THINK OUT LOUD

GRADE LEVELS:
K–8

INTERVENTION TYPE:
Academic—All

This procedure, which encourages independent thought and discovery, enables students to organize and manage by verbally repeating teacher instructions in their own words.

See G1.2, p. 107, for more information on getting students to "think out loud."

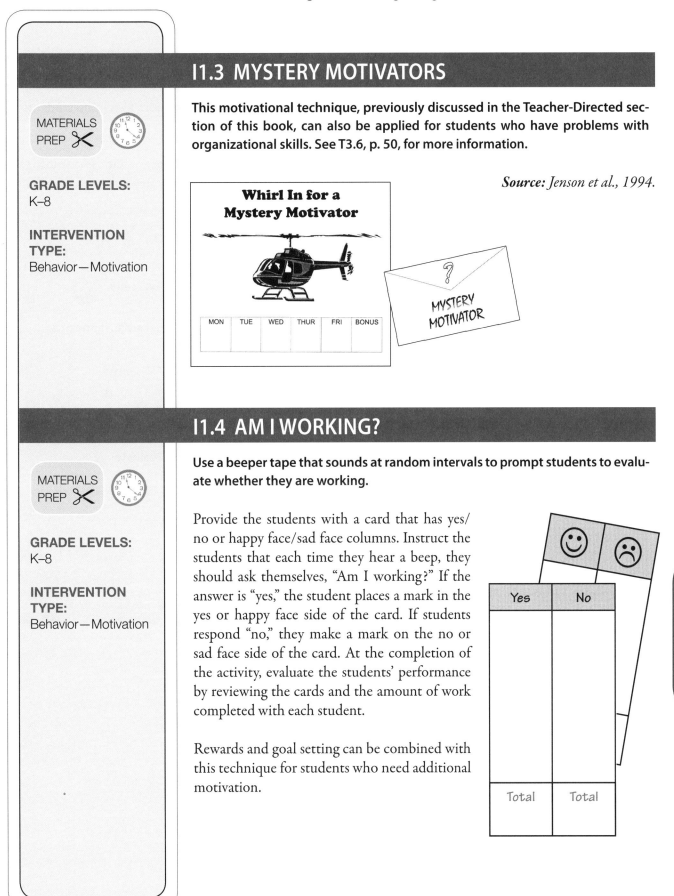

I1.3 MYSTERY MOTIVATORS

MATERIALS PREP ✂

GRADE LEVELS:
K–8

INTERVENTION TYPE:
Behavior—Motivation

This motivational technique, previously discussed in the Teacher-Directed section of this book, can also be applied for students who have problems with organizational skills. See T3.6, p. 50, for more information.

Source: Jenson et al., 1994.

Whirl In for a Mystery Motivator

MON	TUE	WED	THUR	FRI	BONUS

MYSTERY MOTIVATOR

I1.4 AM I WORKING?

MATERIALS PREP ✂

GRADE LEVELS:
K–8

INTERVENTION TYPE:
Behavior—Motivation

Use a beeper tape that sounds at random intervals to prompt students to evaluate whether they are working.

Provide the students with a card that has yes/no or happy face/sad face columns. Instruct the students that each time they hear a beep, they should ask themselves, "Am I working?" If the answer is "yes," the student places a mark in the yes or happy face side of the card. If students respond "no," they make a mark on the no or sad face side of the card. At the completion of the activity, evaluate the students' performance by reviewing the cards and the amount of work completed with each student.

Rewards and goal setting can be combined with this technique for students who need additional motivation.

Yes	No
Total	Total

T G I F

I1.5 MAKE THE GRADE

MATERIALS PREP ✂

GRADE LEVELS:
3–8

INTERVENTION TYPE:
Academic — All
Behavior — Motivation

REPRODUCIBLE on CD

Design a Make the GRADE poster to hang in the classroom to remind students of good work habits.

Model examples of what each step in the mnemonic means and how students can be successful in the classroom if they use each of the steps.

Step 1. Get ready. Arrive on time for class and be prepared with the necessary materials.

Step 2. Record assignments. Use an assignment notebook to keep track of required work.

Step 3. Ask questions. Get clarification if you are not sure about an assignment or activity.

Step 4. Design a plan. Come up with a plan of action for completing assignments.

Step 5. Evaluate. How did you do? What worked or did not work in the plan you designed?

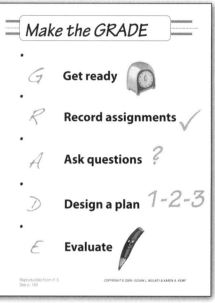

REPRODUCIBLE I1.5

Source: Pidek, 1993.

I1.6 ASSIGNMENT INITIALS

MATERIALS PREP ✂

GRADE LEVELS:
3–8

INTERVENTION TYPE:
Behavior — Motivation

Choose a behavior that needs to be reinforced, such as recording assignments or managing materials.

You and the target student each use a different colored pen for this game. When the student performs the behavior correctly, he or she is allowed to connect two dots to form one line. If the stu-

REPRODUCIBLE I1.6

I1: What can I do about the students who do not organize or manage assignments, materials, and/or time?

on CD

REPRODUCIBLE
on CD

dent does not follow through on the desired behavior, you or a parent is allowed to draw a line. Once four lines are drawn to complete a box, the person who drew the final line (either the student or teacher/parent) places his or her initials in the box. At the end of the week or month, the student may earn a reward if he or she has more boxes filled in.

This activity can be used with students and teachers in school or students and parents at home.

Source: Pidek, 1993.

MATERIALS PREP

GRADE LEVELS:
3–8

INTERVENTION TYPE:
Behavior—Motivation

REPRODUCIBLE
on CD

NOTE:
The Assignment Initials (I1.6) and Assignment Banking appear on one reproducible on the companion CD and can be used in conjunction with one another.

I1.7 ASSIGNMENT BANKING

Students make bank deposits or withdrawals by placing tally marks on the appropriate side of the bank.

If students remember to record assignments, organize their notebooks, or manage materials, a mark is placed on the deposit side. If students do not remember, a mark is placed on the withdrawal side. If students have more marks on the deposit side at the end of the week, they may earn a reward. Weekly aims for number of deposits and withdrawals can be determined prior to implementation.

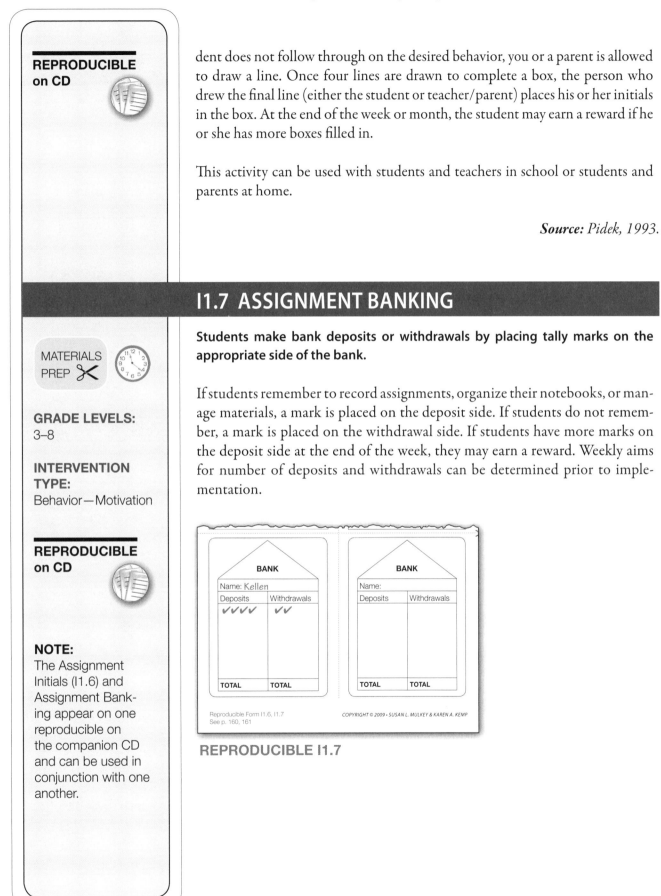

Reproducible Form I1.6, I1.7
See p. 160, 161

COPYRIGHT © 2009 • SUSAN L. MULKEY & KAREN A. KEMP

REPRODUCIBLE I1.7

I1.8 ORGANIZATION CARDS

MATERIALS PREP

GRADE LEVELS:
4–8

INTERVENTION TYPE:
Behavior—Motivation

REPRODUCIBLE on CD

Give each student individual cards to track their organizational skills.

At the end of the class period or day, initial the students' cards in the teacher's initials (T.I.) column. At the end of the week, the point total (P.T.) can be written at the bottom. Reinforce according to performance and improvement.

Teach All, Reach All

Organization Cards

Name: LaWanda
Did I Bring?

	Binder	Book	Material	Teacher's Initials
Mon.	✔	✔	✔	R.B.
Tues.				
Wed.				
Thurs.				
Fri.				
POINT TOTAL				

Name: Paulo
Do I Have?

	Binder	Book	Material	Teacher's Initials
Mon.	✔		✔	R.B.
Tues.				
Wed.				
Thurs.				
Fri.				
POINT TOTAL				

REPRODUCIBLE I1.8

I1.9 ASSIGNMENT LOG

MATERIALS PREP

GRADE LEVELS:
4–8

INTERVENTION TYPE:
Behavior—Motivation

REPRODUCIBLE on CD

Teach students to fill out a daily assignment log.

The students fill in the subject, class assignment, and homework boxes. Materials, if necessary, should be indicated by checking the Yes/No boxes. If the assignment was completed in class, the student checks the appropriate box under the Done column. If the No box was checked, the student writes in the homework assignment in the next column.

Teach All, Reach All

Daily Assignment Log

Name: Ruthie
Date: 11/29

Materials	Subject	Class Assignment	Done	Homework	Done
☐ Yes ☐ No	Math		☑Yes ☐ No	Ch. 2	☐ Yes ☐ No
☐ Yes ☐ No	L.A.		☐ Yes ☑No	p. 95	☐ Yes ☐ No
☐ Yes ☐ No	Spelling		☐ Yes ☑No		☐ Yes ☐ No
☐ Yes ☐ No			☐ Yes ☐ No		☐ Yes ☐ No
☐ Yes ☐ No			☐ Yes ☐ No		☐ Yes ☐ No
TOTALS __Yes __No			**TOTALS** __Yes __No	**TOTALS** __Yes __No	

Reproducible Form I1.9
See p. 162

COPYRIGHT © 2009 · SUSAN L. MULKEY & KAREN A. KEMP

REPRODUCIBLE I1.9

Upon completion or noncompletion of homework, the student marks the appropriate box in the final Done column. Daily and/or weekly rewards can be given for completed work. Yes/No totals can be figured in the bottom row. This self-monitoring technique can be combined with Magic Pens (G2.5, p. 121) and Wild Card Spinner (T3.4, p. 48).

Source: *Fister & Kemp, 1994.*

I1: What can I do about the students who do not organize or manage assignments, materials, and/or time?

I1.10 TIME MANAGEMENT CHARTS

MATERIALS PREP

GRADE LEVELS:
4–8

INTERVENTION TYPE:
Behavior—Social Motivation

REPRODUCIBLE
on CD
(2 versions)

Use daily and weekly time charts to identify the varying responsibilities students have and how much time is needed for homework.

Assist students in making a schedule for study and homework time. Provide students with a chart (see illustration) and have them fill in the times that are committed for sports, family time, chores etc. Help them identify when an appropriate study time would be. Have students keep track of the time they spend daily on homework and make a visual chart so they can follow their progress.

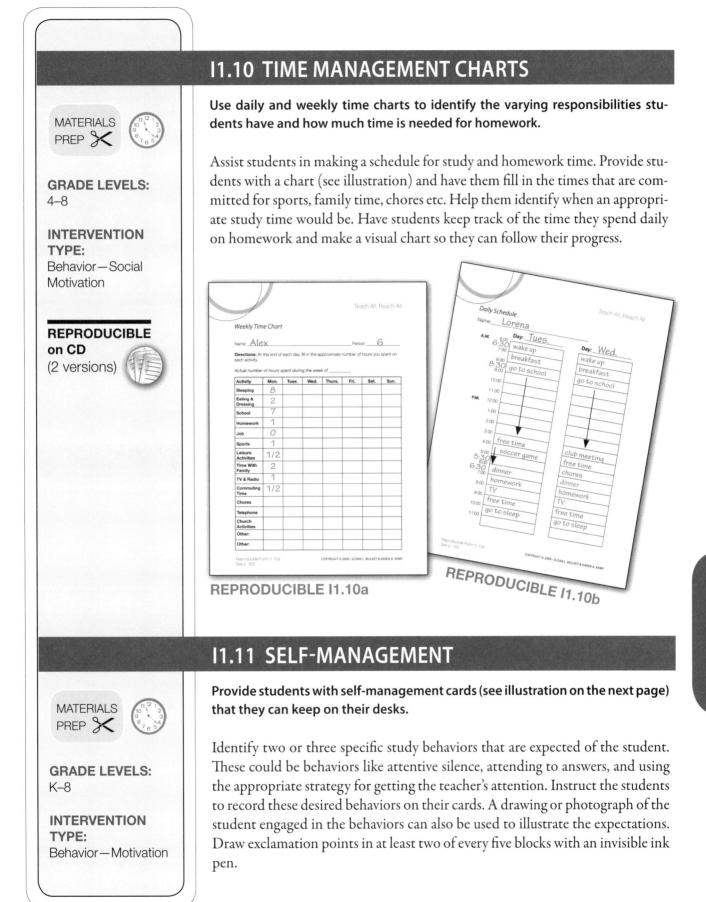

REPRODUCIBLE I1.10a

REPRODUCIBLE I1.10b

I1.11 SELF-MANAGEMENT

MATERIALS PREP

GRADE LEVELS:
K–8

INTERVENTION TYPE:
Behavior—Motivation

Provide students with self-management cards (see illustration on the next page) that they can keep on their desks.

Identify two or three specific study behaviors that are expected of the student. These could be behaviors like attentive silence, attending to answers, and using the appropriate strategy for getting the teacher's attention. Instruct the students to record these desired behaviors on their cards. A drawing or photograph of the student engaged in the behaviors can also be used to illustrate the expectations. Draw exclamation points in at least two of every five blocks with an invisible ink pen.

T
G
I
F

During independent work, set a timer or use an interval tape to sound every three minutes. Tell the students that for every three minutes of appropriate working time, they can use a decoder pen to fill in a block on the study card. If one of the invisible ink exclamation points shows through, the student earns a spin on the Wild Card Spinner (see T3.4, p. 48) or another predetermined reinforcer.

| 1. Writing answers. ✎ | | | | | |
2. Asking questions. ？					
	!		!		
		!	!		
!				!	
		!			!

I1.12 PARENT PARTNERS

MATERIALS PREP ✂

GRADE LEVELS:
K–8

INTERVENTION TYPE:
Behavior—Motivation

REPRODUCIBLE on CD

Invite parents to come to school for an overview of the organizational strategies that will be used with their child.

Obtain parental support by having parents agree to help their child become more organized at home. Information given to parents about the program and strategies used at school will provide consistency for the student in both environments. The sample letter and form at right can be used with parents and students when setting up organization programs.

REPRODUCIBLE I1.12

I1: What can I do about the students who do not organize or manage assignments, materials, and/or time?

I1.13 ASSIGNMENT NOTEBOOKS

Instruct students in how to use notebooks for recording and tracking their assignments.

Assignment notebooks can be made or purchased in a variety of styles. If three-ring binders are used, they should include:

- Calendars for assignment due dates
- A plastic pouch for pencils, erasers, pens, paper punch, etc.
- Folder pockets to hold class assignments, study guides, etc.
- Loose-leaf paper and spiral notebook for each class
- Strategy cards for note-taking and scanning for information (see LITES [T10.5, p. 92] and SR.I.SRV [G3.26, p. 138])

When notebooks are introduced to the classroom, the following sections should be included:

- Subject
- Assignment
- Date
- Things to bring home
- Things to bring to school
- Special projects or long-term assignments
- Upcoming tests

Before students use the assignment notebooks, demonstration, discussion, and practice should be provided on how to use them.

Source: *Pidek, 1991.*

MATERIALS PREP ✂

GRADE LEVELS:
4–8

INTERVENTION TYPE:
Behavior—Motivation

REPRODUCIBLE on CD
(2 versions)

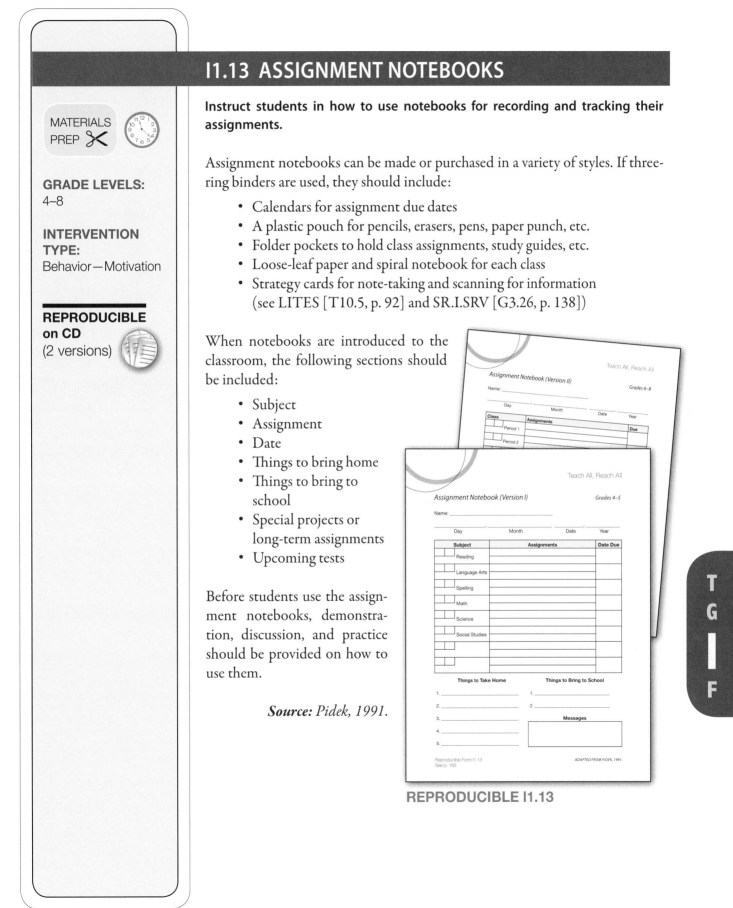

REPRODUCIBLE I1.13

I_2 INDEPENDENT PRACTICE ACTIVITIES

What can I do about the students who do not complete or submit assignments?

I2.1 DAILY CHECKOUT

GRADE LEVELS:
3–8

INTERVENTION TYPE:
Behavior—Motivation

At the end of the class period or the end of the day, have students go through a checkout list. This can be posted in the class or in assignment notebooks.

Items to be checked off might include:

- Did I put all materials away?
- Are my papers turned in?
- What materials do I need for homework?
- Do I understand the work?

You can use the checklist as a ticket out of class, or have students check one another's lists before starting the next activity.

Name:	Mon.	Tues.	Wed.	Thurs.	Fri.
1. All materials put away.					
2. Papers turned in.					
3. Homework materials ready.					
4. Homework instructions clear.					

I2: What can I do about the students who do not complete or submit assignments?

I2.2 STOP/GO FOLDERS

GRADE LEVELS:
K–8

INTERVENTION TYPE:
Behavior—Motivation

Provide students with red and green folders, or folders labeled "Stop" and "Go."

When students complete an assignment, the paper goes in the Stop folder so it can be handed in or corrected. If a paper is incomplete, it goes in the Go folder. Work in the Go folder can be finished at recess, during free time, or at another designated time. Provide students with deadlines for the work that remains in the Go folder.

I2.3 HOME/SCHOOL TALK

MATERIALS PREP

GRADE LEVELS:
K–8

INTERVENTION TYPE:
Behavior—Motivation

REPRODUCIBLE on CD
(3 versions)

Arrange with parents to have students complete a home/school note each day that will be initialed by you and the parent.

Three Progress Report forms appear on the CD. Version I can be customized by subject and behavior. Version III is a more detailed form for older students.

Combine this technique with other motivation systems such as Mystery Motivators (T3.6, p. 50), Wild Card Spinner (T3.4, p. 48), or Behavior Bingo (T2.7, p. 43; G1.14, p. 112).

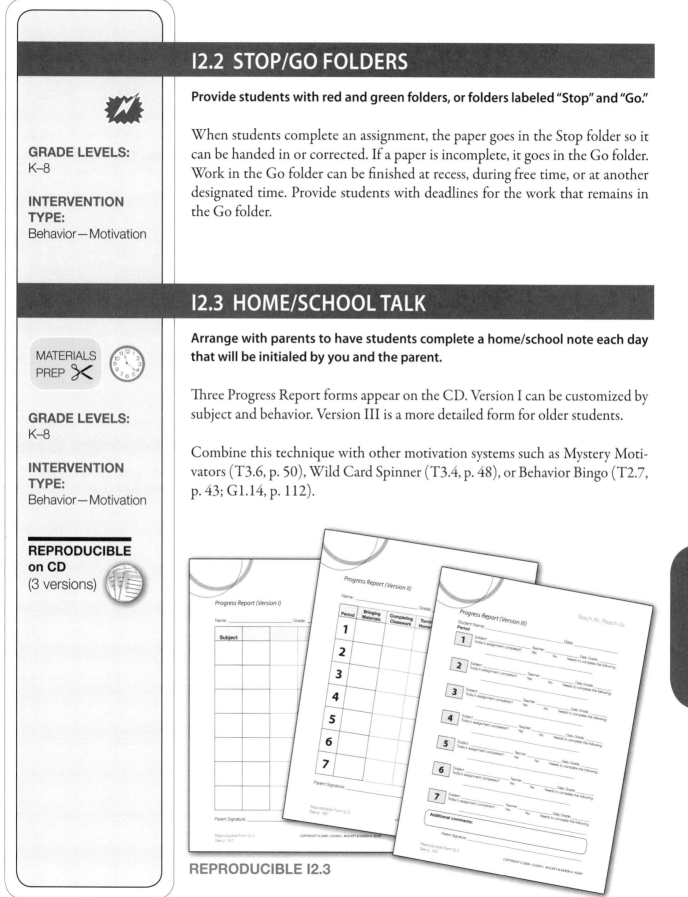

REPRODUCIBLE I2.3

I2.4 HOME/SCHOOL FOLDERS

Provide target students with folders that are sent home each day.

The folders include work that has been completed in class along with assignments that need to be worked on. A log sheet can be attached inside the folder to track the status of assignments. Parents can be kept informed about completed and not-completed assignments along with due dates. Points can be awarded for parent initials, work submitted, and returning the folder each day.

Home/School Log

Name: ___Akeem___

Date	Assignment	Completed	Turned In	Parent Signature
12/22	Division	✔	✔	L.C

REPRODUCIBLE I2.4

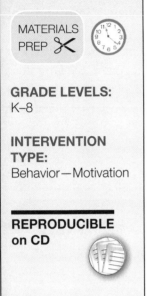

MATERIALS PREP

GRADE LEVELS:
K–8

INTERVENTION TYPE:
Behavior—Motivation

REPRODUCIBLE on CD

MATERIALS PREP

GRADE LEVELS:
3–8

INTERVENTION TYPE:
Behavior—Motivation

REPRODUCIBLE on CD
(2 versions)

I2.5 HOMEWORK TRACKING CHARTS

Keep a class homework tracking chart (see illustration at right) to monitor and assist in the evaluation of the students' homework performance.

The name of each student is listed in the left column. Simply make a mark each time an assignment is turned in. With the chart, you can identify at a glance the status of each student in the class.

Each student can keep a homework tracking chart to self-monitor performance.

Homework Tracking Chart (Student)

Student: ___Laura T.-B.___

Date	Used Note-Book	Completed	Turned In
10/2	✔	✔	✔
10/3	✔		

Homework Tracking Chart (Class)

Name	Week One	Week Two	Week Three	Week Four	Comments
Laura	✔✔✔				
Felipe	✔				talk w/student
Konrad	✔✔✔				
Jiang	✔✔✔				
Mason	✔✔✔				
DeeDee	✔✔				will make up
Doyle	✔✔✔				
Cammie	✔✔✔				

REPRODUCIBLE I2.5

I2.6 HIT THE HOMEWORK TARGET

MATERIALS
PREP ✄

GRADE LEVELS:
3–8

**INTERVENTION
TYPE:**
Behavior—Motivation

**REPRODUCIBLE
on CD**

Homework Target is a procedure that involves peers working together as teams to encourage homework completion.

Step 1. Divide the class into two teams. Pair up students within each team to become homework partners. Explain to students that they will work together to complete their homework target. Each pair needs one copy of the target shown in the illustration.

Step 2. Instruct students in the procedure for using the chart. On the day homework is assigned, the partners receive one point if both students write the information in their assignment notebooks. When the homework is due, the partners receive one point if both students complete the assignment and one point if they both turn in their assignments on time. Each point is entered as a tally mark in the corresponding day and week of the chart.

Step 3. At the end of the week, partners total their points and record them in the weekly total box. At the end of the month, the totals of all partners on each team are added together for the team score. The team with the highest score for the month is recognized. When a new month starts, team members and partners can be rearranged.

Source: *Pidek, 1991.*

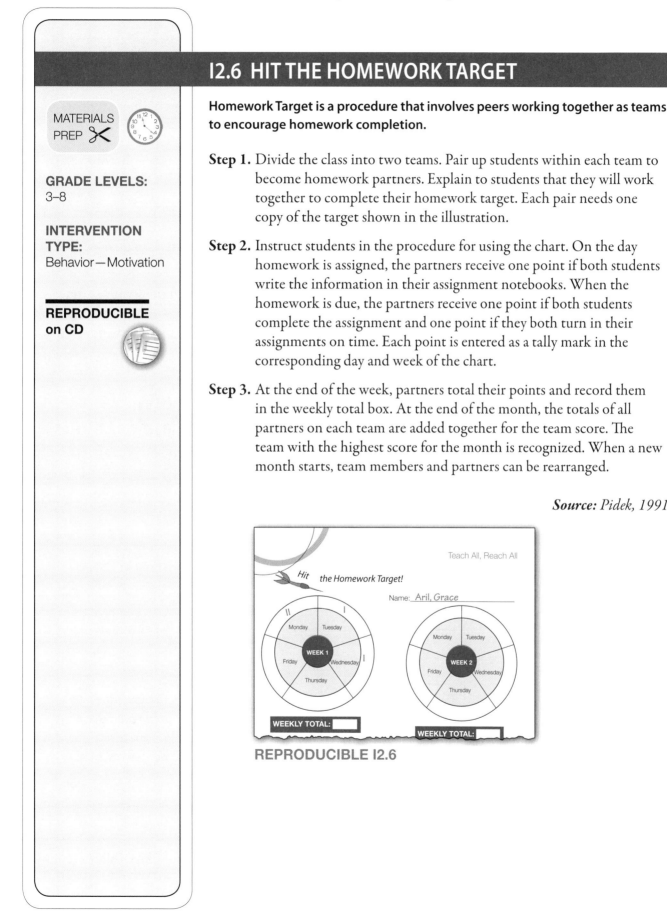

REPRODUCIBLE I2.6

T
G
I
F

12.7 HOMEWORK TEAMS

MATERIALS PREP ✂

GRADE LEVELS:
3–8

INTERVENTION TYPE:
Behavior—Motivation

Homework Teams is a cooperative structure where teams of three students are assigned specific responsibilities for homework completion.

Step 1. Organize students into teams of three and assign the following roles: scorekeeper, manager, and coach.

Step 2. Train the students in the responsibilities of each of the roles (see table below) and explain that the responsibilities are to be carried out each day that homework is assigned. All students should know the responsibilities of their particular role.

Step 3. A daily team scorecard (see page opposite) is used along with a team poster for each team to monitor and record their progress (see illustration below). The daily team scorecard should give the students enough space to account for all the homework sheets returned. The team poster should provide the students with space to post the team's daily scores. Daily scores can be written as team totals or average scores.

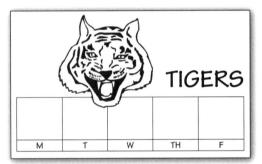

Job Descriptions			
	Scorekeeper	Manager	Coach
1.	Collect all homework assignments.	Correct each assignment again.	Set team goals; pass out peer tutoring folders if needed.
2.	Correct each assignment.	Score each assignment.	Review at least one team strategy for meeting the homework goal.
3.	Give each assignment a score.	Fill out Daily Team Scorecard.	Pass out rewards in the form of "tickets."
4.	Give all materials to the manager.	Write score on Team Poster.	Pass out new homework sheets.

I2: What can I do about the students who do not complete or submit assignments?

Step 4. Reinforcement can be given to both individual students and teams based on performance. Tickets or points can be awarded for meeting specific criteria you set, such as all members returning assignments, perfect scores on assignments, and entire class returning assignments.

Daily Team Scorecard			
Team Name: Tigers			Date: 10/23
Homework Returned	80% or Above Correct	90% or Above Correct	100% Correct
Scott (yes) no	(yes) no	(yes) no	(yes) no
Shayna (yes) no	(yes) no	(yes) no	yes (no)
Chris (yes) no	(yes) no	(yes) no	yes (no)
All returned? Team Ticket: ✔ Yes ___ No	(# of "yes's circled = # of tickets)		All 100% Team Ticket: ___ Yes ✔ No
Individual Tickets: 7	Team Tickets: 0 (1) 2 (circle one)		Total Tickets: 8

Source: *Olympia, Andrews, Valum, & Jenson, 1993.*

T
G
I
F

I2.8 SELF-GRAPHING CHARTS

MATERIALS PREP

GRADE LEVELS:
3–8

INTERVENTION TYPE:
Behavior—Motivation

REPRODUCIBLE on CD

Have students keep track of the number of individual problems completed during a class period or number of assignments completed during the day.

Use a tracking chart (see illustration) and explain to the students that each time a problem or assignment is completed, they are to check a box on the chart. At the end of the class or day, a circle is drawn around the last checkmark to indicate the total number of problems or assignments completed. If the student remembers to turn in the assignment, bonus points can be awarded and added to the total. The circled checkmarks provide a visual display of the student's performance. This technique can be combined with other reinforcement and motivation procedures.

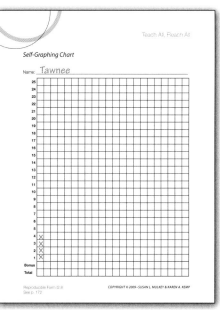

REPRODUCIBLE I2.8

I2.9 ASSIGNMENT CONTRACTS

MATERIALS PREP

GRADE LEVELS:
4–8

INTERVENTION TYPE:
Behavior—Motivation

REPRODUCIBLE on CD

Write a contract with students that specifies what they will complete and turn in during class time or for homework.

Make it a short-term contract to begin with. If students comply with the contracts, they can be extended. Include the following information on the contract:

- Dates
- Target behavior
- Specific reward
- Schedule of reinforcement
- Date for review of progress
- Signatures of everyone involved
- Bonus for exceptional performance
- Penalties if behavior is not performed

REPRODUCIBLE I2.9

I2.10 FILL IN THE DOTS

Encourage students to complete and turn in assignments.

MATERIALS PREP

GRADE LEVELS:
K–6

TYPE:
Behavior—Motivation

**REPRODUCIBLE
on CD**

Provide the target student with an illustration covered with white dots. Each time the student completes an assignment, a dot is punched or filled in with a crayon or marker. When the card has been completely punched or filled in, the student receives a previously negotiated reward. If reinforcement is needed before the card is filled, invisible ink pens (G2.5, p. 121) can be used to mark several of the dots. When a student fills in a dot that has been highlighted, the student receives an interim reward.

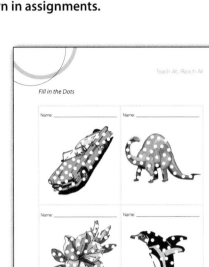

REPRODUCIBLE I2.10

I2.11 ASSIGNMENT CHAMPION NOTEBOOK

Use a sign-in sheet to encourage students to turn in assignments.

MATERIALS PREP

GRADE LEVELS:
3–8

INTERVENTION TYPE:
Behavior—Motivation

**REPRODUCIBLE
on CD**

Display a notebook in the classroom that has a colorful design and cover. At the top of every page, put the date and leave spaces for students to sign their names. If students complete and turn in all assignments, they become Assignment Champions and are allowed to sign the notebook that day. Add additional reinforcers for students who turn in every assignment for the week. This technique can be used as a checkout from the class or for the entire day. Give bonus points for students whose names appear a specified number of times during a unit or quarter.

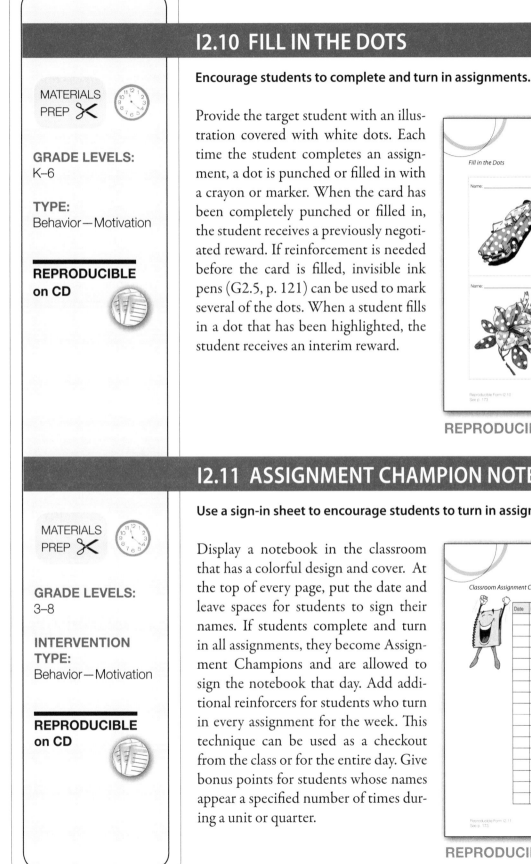

REPRODUCIBLE I2.11

T
G
I
F

MATERIALS PREP ✂ 🕐

GRADE LEVELS:
K–8

INTERVENTION TYPE:
Behavior—Motivation

REPRODUCIBLE
on CD

I2.12 HOW DO I RATE?

Develop recording and evaluating charts that have spaces for number of problems completed, number of problems completed correctly, and rating criteria for performance.

Step 1. Each time students finish a task, they record the total number of problems completed on their chart.

Step 2. The teacher or student then grades the assignment for accuracy, and the number of problems completed correctly is recorded on the chart (e.g., 8/10 reflects that the student answered eight problems correctly out of a possible ten).

Step 3. The students self-evaluate the overall performance of their completion rate. Determine the evaluation criteria based on the student's previous completion rate. For example, if the student completed the following number of problems last week: 28, 26, 25, 22, and 21, the median rate of problem completion is 25. This number is then used as the upper aim for a "1" rating, and the lower point is the median minus 20% (in this case, the lower aim is 20). If the student completes fewer than 20 problems, the rating is 0. If he or she completes 20–25, the rating is 1. If he or she completes more than 25, the rating is 2.

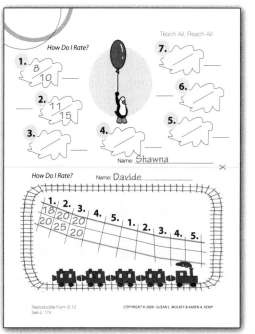

REPRODUCIBLE I2.12

I2: What can I do about the students who do not complete or submit assignments?

Reinforcement can be earned if the student's rating is at 2 for three days in a row. The next week, the median score is refigured, and the student continues to record and self-evaluate until the performance is at the desired level.

Rating Chart	
21	20% of 25 = 5
22	Median (25) – 5 = 20
25 Median (becomes upper aim for next week)	20 (becomes the lower aim for the next week)
26	
28	

Rating Scale for Example
Below 20 = 0
21–25 = 1 point
Above 25 = 2 points

Source: Hughes et al., 1988.

T
G
I
F

I3 INDEPENDENT PRACTICE ACTIVITIES

> What can I do about the students who do not understand the independent assignment?

I3.1 I AM WORKING/I NEED HELP SIGN

MATERIALS
PREP ✂

GRADE LEVELS:
K–6

INTERVENTION TYPE:
Behavior—Motivation

REPRODUCIBLE on CD

NOTE:
The CD contains two versions of the sign—a color one and a black-and-white one that students can color.

The I Am Working/I Need Help Sign consists of a laminated 3″ x 5″ (or larger) card taped to the front edge of the student's desk.

The card is attached with masking tape or strapping tape so that it can be flipped back and forth to lie flat on top of the student's desk or hang off the side of the desk. One side of the card is red and has the words "I Need Help." The other side of the card is green and has the words "I am Working."

During independent work time, the green side of the card is resting on the desk so that it faces the student. When help is needed, the student is instructed to flip the card over so that the red side is hanging off the edge of the desk and the words "I Need Help" are visible.

You can easily scan the classroom to determine which students need help by noticing the position of the red or green side of the card.

After the help has been given, the card is flipped back on top of the student's desk so that the green side is showing.

REPRODUCIBLE I3.1

A grid of boxes can be added to the green side of the card. As you move around the classroom, you can place marks in the boxes to reinforce students for independent working behaviors, using appropriate procedures for getting the teacher's attention, etc.

I3.2 ASK THREE BEFORE ME

GRADE LEVELS:
K–8

INTERVENTION TYPE:
Behavior—Social

Teach students to ask three other students for assistance before they ask you when they need help on independent work.

Before using this procedure, demonstrate and clarify for students the procedure for asking another student for help. This should include examples and non-examples of the appropriate tone of voice, out-of-seat procedures, and the words to use when asking another student for help.

I3.3 THE FOOLER GAME

GRADE LEVELS:
K–8

INTERVENTION TYPE:
Behavior—Motivation

This game reinforces students' understanding of assignments.

Begin by gaining the students' attention. Then say, "We're going to play The Fooler Game." This means that you will read the instructions for the independent work activity and then ask group and/or individual questions about the instructions to see if anyone can be fooled.

When the students give a correct response, award them a point under the YOU side of the Fooler Chart (see illustration) and say something like, "Oh, I can't fool you! You were listening and paying attention to the instructions!"

When the students give an incorrect response, award yourself a point on the ME side of the Fooler Chart and say something like, "I fooled you!" When the students make an error, reread the appropriate part of the instructions that answers the question and then repeat the question to elicit a correct response.

Fooler Chart	
YOU	ME
III	II

T
G
I
F

177

I3.4 EMPHASIZE INSTRUCTIONS

GRADE LEVELS:
3–8

INTERVENTION TYPE:
Behavior—Motivation

Tell the students that you will read aloud the instructions for their independent work assignment and then ask them questions about these instructions.

Emphasize important words in the instructions when reading aloud. Use a signal to elicit group responses after each question is asked.

EXAMPLES

INSTRUCTIONS COULD INCLUDE:

- Listen to these instructions: Find the area of each rectangle.

- Write the multiplication problem and the answer with the unit name. Now, get ready to answer questions about the instructions.

QUESTIONS COULD INCLUDE:

- What is the problem asking you to do? (Find the area of each rectangle.)

- What is the first step? (Write the multiplication problem.)

- What is the next step? (Write the answer with the unit name.)

- Does the problem tell you to find the area or the perimeter? (The area.)

- Will you write the answer, or the problem and the answer? (The problem and the answer.)

- What kind of name needs to be on the answer? (The unit name.)

- Think of one example of a unit name and tell your partner. (Miles, inches, feet . . .)

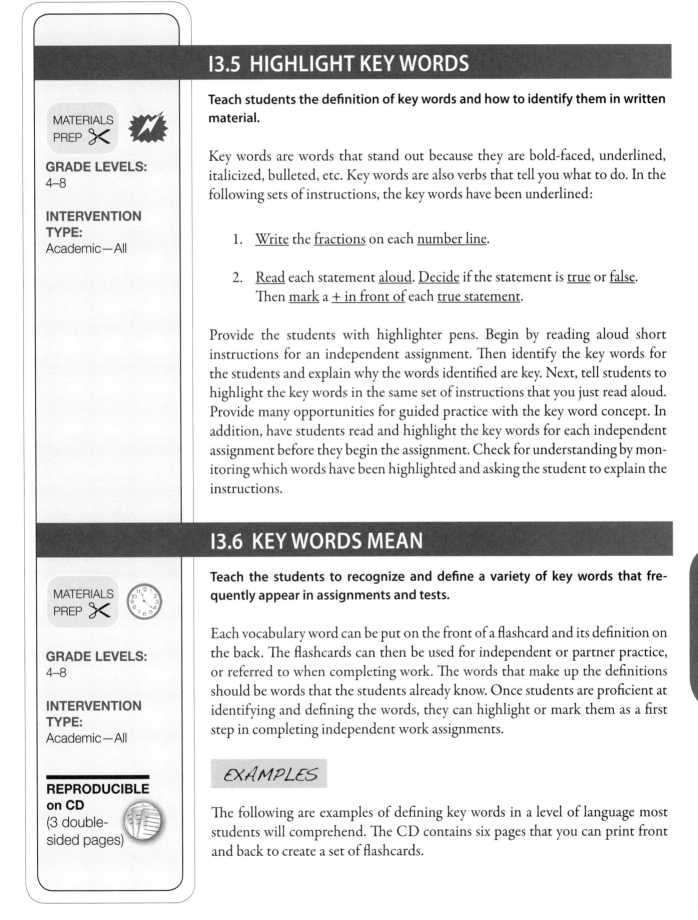

I3.5 HIGHLIGHT KEY WORDS

MATERIALS
PREP ✂

GRADE LEVELS:
4–8

**INTERVENTION
TYPE:**
Academic—All

Teach students the definition of key words and how to identify them in written material.

Key words are words that stand out because they are bold-faced, underlined, italicized, bulleted, etc. Key words are also verbs that tell you what to do. In the following sets of instructions, the key words have been underlined:

1. Write the fractions on each number line.

2. Read each statement aloud. Decide if the statement is true or false. Then mark a + in front of each true statement.

Provide the students with highlighter pens. Begin by reading aloud short instructions for an independent assignment. Then identify the key words for the students and explain why the words identified are key. Next, tell students to highlight the key words in the same set of instructions that you just read aloud. Provide many opportunities for guided practice with the key word concept. In addition, have students read and highlight the key words for each independent assignment before they begin the assignment. Check for understanding by monitoring which words have been highlighted and asking the student to explain the instructions.

I3.6 KEY WORDS MEAN

MATERIALS
PREP ✂

GRADE LEVELS:
4–8

**INTERVENTION
TYPE:**
Academic—All

**REPRODUCIBLE
on CD**
(3 double-
sided pages)

Teach the students to recognize and define a variety of key words that frequently appear in assignments and tests.

Each vocabulary word can be put on the front of a flashcard and its definition on the back. The flashcards can then be used for independent or partner practice, or referred to when completing work. The words that make up the definitions should be words that the students already know. Once students are proficient at identifying and defining the words, they can highlight or mark them as a first step in completing independent work assignments.

EXAMPLES

The following are examples of defining key words in a level of language most students will comprehend. The CD contains six pages that you can print front and back to create a set of flashcards.

T
G
I
F

Front of flashcard	Back of flashcard
apply	Ways in which the information can be used in a particular situation.
cause and effect	Define the events; tell the order and why and how they happened.
classify	Tell how things or topics are alike.
compare	Show how characteristics of a concept are the same.
contrast	Show how characteristics of a concept are the same and different; stress the differences.
criticize	Explain how something was good or poor and how it could be made better.
define	Tell how a word is like the group to which it belongs and then tell how it differs from others in the group.
diagram	Create a drawing, map, chart, or illustration.
discuss	Give an in-depth explanation of the topic with many examples.
evaluate	Identify the most important ideas; tell why they are important. Give facts to support your answer.
explain	Give reasons or causes, discuss the order, and point out problems. Give details and examples to support your answer.
illustrate	Use examples or provide a diagram or picture proving your point.
interpret	Explain and give your own opinions about something.
justify	Give reasons for your answer.
list	Put the words or answers in a series with numbers.
outline	Discuss major topics and show how they are related; identify details and show how they are related.
prove	Give facts to support your answer or argument.
relate	Show the connections between different ideas.
review	Give a summary and comment about the subject.
summarize	Point out the major ideas and tell how they are related.
trace	Tell about the development or progress of a concept or event.

I3: What can I do about the students who do not understand the independent assignment?

I3.7 GETTING THE HELP I NEED

MATERIALS
PREP ✂

GRADE LEVELS:
K–8

**INTERVENTION
TYPE:**
Behavior—Social

Teach students a strategy to use for getting assistance when they are unclear about an assignment or instructions.

Ask for Help (G1.18, p. 114) or Clarification (T12.8, p. 103) can assist students in successfully getting the help they need.

I3.8 MAP THE INSTRUCTIONS

MATERIALS
PREP ✂

GRADE LEVELS:
4–8

**INTERVENTION
TYPE:**
Academic—All

**REPRODUCIBLE
on CD**

Provide the students with a blank graphic organizer (see illustration) or teach them how to design their own for mapping out the steps required when completing longer independent assignments.

Include a section to list points to keep in mind when completing the steps for each topic. There can be as many steps as necessary for each topic according to each student's needs.

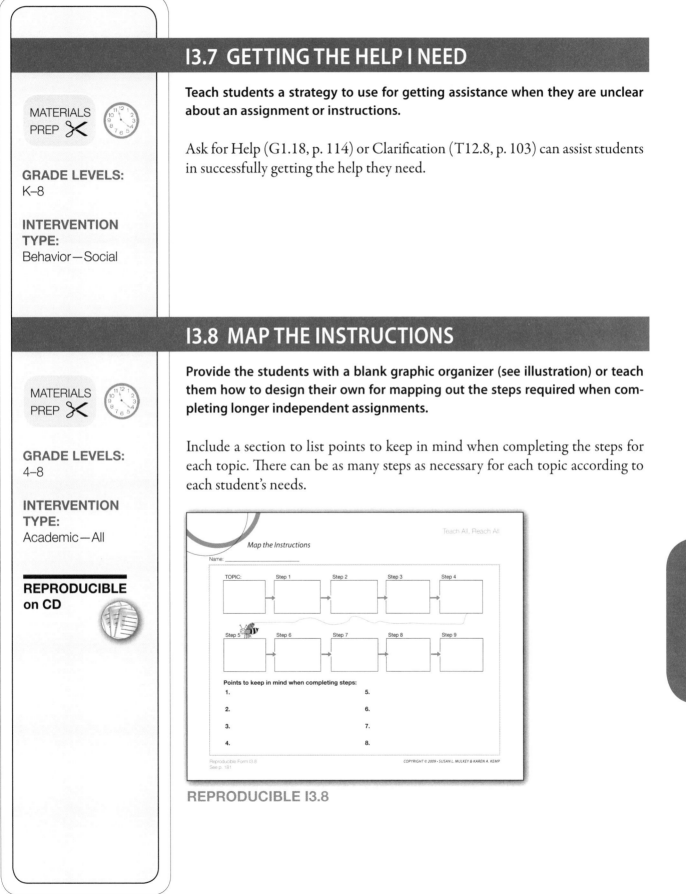

Map the Instructions

Name: _____

| TOPIC: | Step 1 | Step 2 | Step 3 | Step 4 |

| Step 5 | Step 6 | Step 7 | Step 8 | Step 9 |

Points to keep in mind when completing steps:

1.   5.
2.   6.
3.   7.
4.   8.

Reproducible Form I3.8
See p. 181

COPYRIGHT © 2009 · SUSAN L. MULKEY & KAREN A. KEMP

Teach All, Reach All

REPRODUCIBLE I3.8

T
G
I
F

I3.9 INSTRUCTION CARDS (WHAT, HOW, WHEN/WHERE, WHY)

MATERIALS PREP ✂

GRADE LEVELS:
4–8

INTERVENTION TYPE:
Academic—All

REPRODUCIBLE on CD

Instruction cards are useful for students because the assignment is broken down into four basic elements: what, how, when/where, and why. The reasons and benefits of the assignment are clarified for students.

Have them complete a card for each independent assignment by filling in the relevant information for each category.

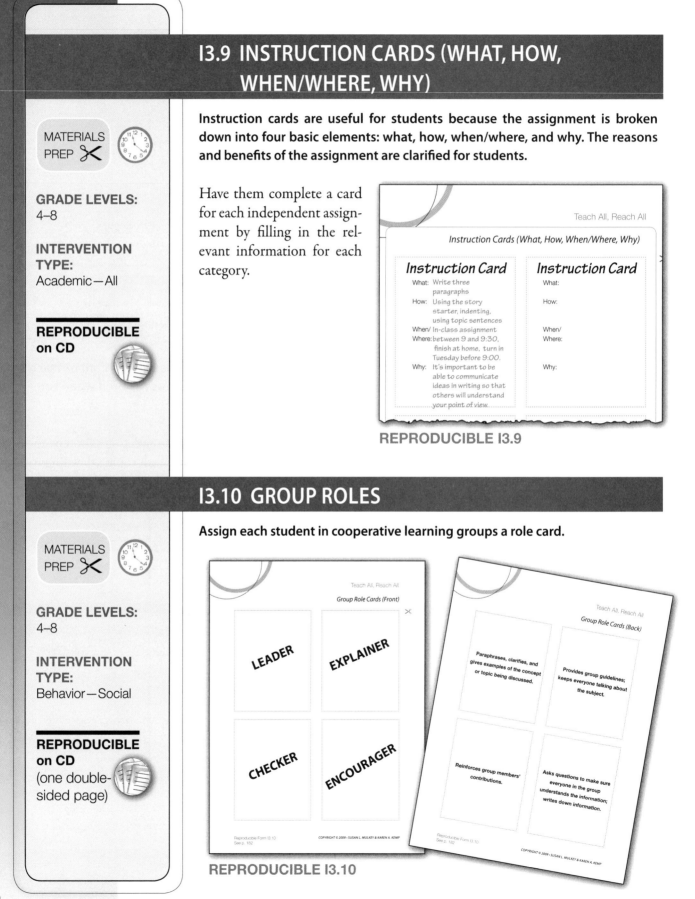

Teach All, Reach All

Instruction Cards (What, How, When/Where, Why)

Instruction Card

What: Write three paragraphs

How: Using the story starter, indenting, using topic sentences

When/ In-class assignment
Where: between 9 and 9:30, finish at home, turn in Tuesday before 9:00.

Why: It's important to be able to communicate ideas in writing so that others will understand your point of view.

Instruction Card

What:

How:

When/
Where:

Why:

REPRODUCIBLE I3.9

I3.10 GROUP ROLES

MATERIALS PREP ✂

GRADE LEVELS:
4–8

INTERVENTION TYPE:
Behavior—Social

REPRODUCIBLE on CD
(one double-sided page)

Assign each student in cooperative learning groups a role card.

Teach All, Reach All

Group Role Cards (Front)

LEADER   EXPLAINER

CHECKER   ENCOURAGER

Reproducible Form I3.10
See p. 182   COPYRIGHT © 2009 • SUSAN L. MULKEY & KAREN A. KEMP

Teach All, Reach All

Group Role Cards (Back)

Paraphrases, clarifies, and gives examples of the concept or topic being discussed.

Provides group guidelines; keeps everyone talking about the subject.

Reinforces group members' contributions.

Asks questions to make sure everyone in the group understands the information; writes down information.

Reproducible Form I3.10
See p. 182   COPYRIGHT © 2009 • SUSAN L. MULKEY & KAREN A. KEMP

REPRODUCIBLE I3.10

I3: What can I do about the students who do not understand the independent assignment?

The role cards can be duplicated (one page per group of four) and cut up. Each student takes a role card for the independent work assignment. The responsibilities for each role need to be clearly defined and modeled for the students and should be clearly defined on the back of the role card. Have students switch cards and roles each new day.

I3.11 INDEPENDENT WORK BUDDIES

Arrange students in dyads for completing independent work assignments.

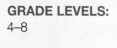

MATERIALS PREP ✂

GRADE LEVELS:
4–8

INTERVENTION TYPE:
Behavior—Motivation

REPRODUCIBLE on CD

Provide each dyad with one Work Buddies Scorecard (see illustration). You can use the card with the pre-identified behaviors or choose your own expected behaviors and write them on the blank card. Points are awarded to dyads at the end of the activity for productive and attentive work. The points can be totaled each day and publicly posted. The scorecards can be recycled or disposed of after one day or, if they are laminated, wiped off for reuse. Students can remain in their same dyads for one or more days.

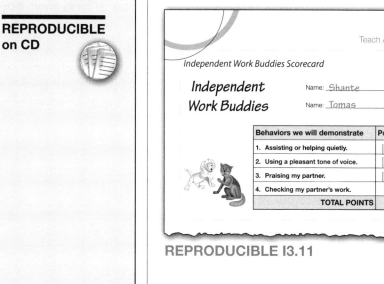

REPRODUCIBLE I3.11

T
G
I
F

I4 INDEPENDENT PRACTICE ACTIVITIES

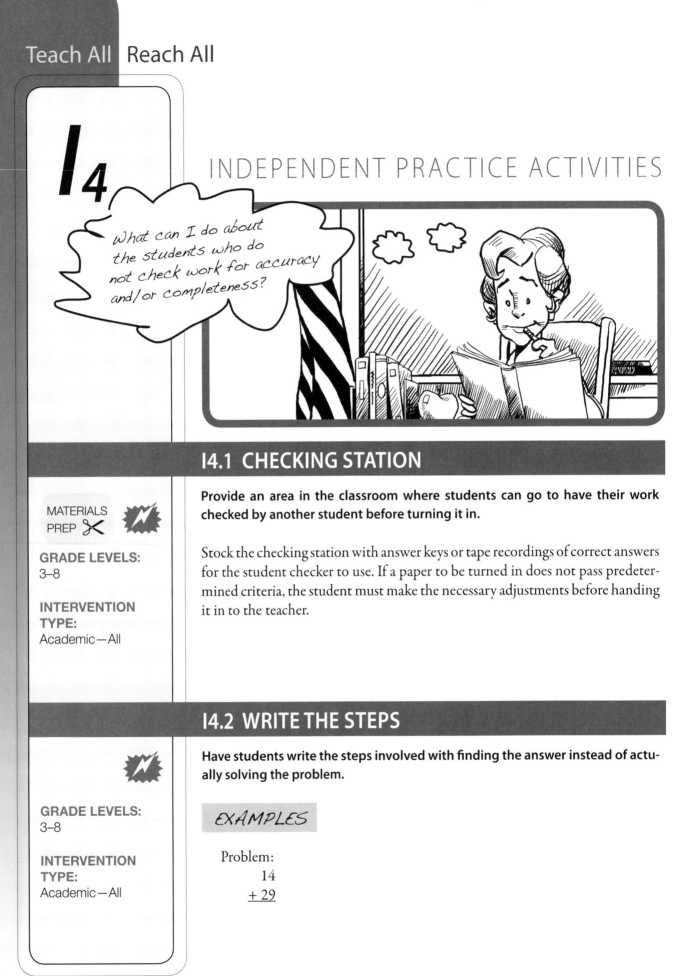

What can I do about the students who do not check work for accuracy and/or completeness?

I4.1 CHECKING STATION

MATERIALS
PREP ✂

GRADE LEVELS:
3–8

INTERVENTION TYPE:
Academic—All

Provide an area in the classroom where students can go to have their work checked by another student before turning it in.

Stock the checking station with answer keys or tape recordings of correct answers for the student checker to use. If a paper to be turned in does not pass predetermined criteria, the student must make the necessary adjustments before handing it in to the teacher.

I4.2 WRITE THE STEPS

GRADE LEVELS:
3–8

INTERVENTION TYPE:
Academic—All

Have students write the steps involved with finding the answer instead of actually solving the problem.

EXAMPLES

Problem:
$$14$$
$$+\ 29$$

I4: What can I do about the students who do not check work for accuracy and/or completeness?

The student writes:

1. Add the ones column: 9 + 4.
2. Write down the 3 and carry the 1.
3. Add the tens column: 1 + 2 and the 1 that was carried.

Instead of answering a question from a book, the student writes the steps to finding the answer:

1. Read the question and identify the key words.
2. Turn to page 15 where it talks about the main idea.
3. Scan the page and locate the key words.
4. Read the sentences that fall before and after the key words.
5. Formulate an answer.

I4.3 CHECKING AND COMPLETING

Describe and model the steps for completing work and checking accuracy.

The following steps can be used to improve students' overall performance and follow-through.

Step 1. Focus on the task.

Step 2. Read all directions and circle key words.

Step 3. Explain to yourself what you need to do, and do it all.

Step 4. Ask for help if necessary.

Step 5. Check for completeness and correctness when proofing your work (see Proofing Skills, I4.4).

Step 6. Turn your assignment in.

I4.4 PROOFING SKILLS

Describe and model examples of what proofing entails for different assignments.

Students can utilize their proofing skills when checking for errors in a completed assignment or when returning to a previous assignment to correct mistakes made. Provide many practice opportunities for students and use visual charts of the steps as reminders. If the student is not familiar with a particular step in a proofing strategy, instruction on that step must take place prior to teaching the entire strategy.

GRADE LEVELS:
3–8

INTERVENTION TYPE:
Academic—All

GRADE LEVELS:
3–8

INTERVENTION TYPE:
Academic—All

T
G
I
F

EXAMPLES

The following proofing strategy can be used for math problems.

- Reread the problem.
- Reexamine the question.
- Check selection of operation.
- Recalculate and compare answers.

Source: *Gable & Evans, 1993.*

The following proofing strategy can be used when answering comprehension questions.

- Reread the question and circle the words that tell you how to answer the question, such as: list, define, compare, or explain.
- Next, underline what the question is talking about (i.e., the main idea). Examples might be rocks, presidents, story characters, etc.
- Check your answer to see how well it was done and if the main idea has been included.

For writing assignments, students can use the following mnemonic (COPS) for proofing.

Capitalization

Overall appearance

Punctuation

Spelling

Source: *Schumaker et al., 1985.*

Teach students editing symbols along with the proofing strategy so they can revise their own work.

Proofreading Marks	
⬭	Circle words spelled incorrectly.
/	Change a capital letter to a small letter.
≡	Change a small letter to a capital letter.
⋁	Add letters, words, or sentences.

I4: What can I do about the students who do not check work for accuracy and/or completeness?

$\odot$	Add a period.
$\wp$	Take out letters, words, or punctuation.
$\wedge$,	Add a comma.
?	Anything you are unclear about.

These strategies work well in partner situations where students can proof one another's work after they have proofed their own.

I4.5 COUNT CORRECTS AND ERRORS

After completing an assignment, have students check their work and put a ✓ over the errors made and a + over the correct responses.

Count up the total number of responses possible, the number of corrects, and the number of errors (see sample). Have students set an error limit for their assignment.

GRADE LEVELS:
3–8

INTERVENTION TYPE:
Academic — All

Worksheet

| 1. ⁴
28
x 15
+ + +
140
+ + +
280
+ + +
420 | 2. 10
x 10
+ + +
100 |
| 3. 9
x 8
+ +
72 | 4. 19
x 20
+ +
00
✓ ✓
38
✓ ✓
38 |

Name: Margaret S.				
Date	Total Possible	Corrects	Errors	Error Limit
5/2	19	15	4	29%

T
G
I
F

I4.6 ACCURACY AIMS

MATERIALS
PREP ✂

GRADE LEVELS:
3–8

INTERVENTION TYPE:
Academic—All

Set aims ahead of time for the number of problems to be completed accurately.

If students complete that number without error, provide reinforcement and increase the aim by one. Have students keep track of progress made by using a tracker card or chart.

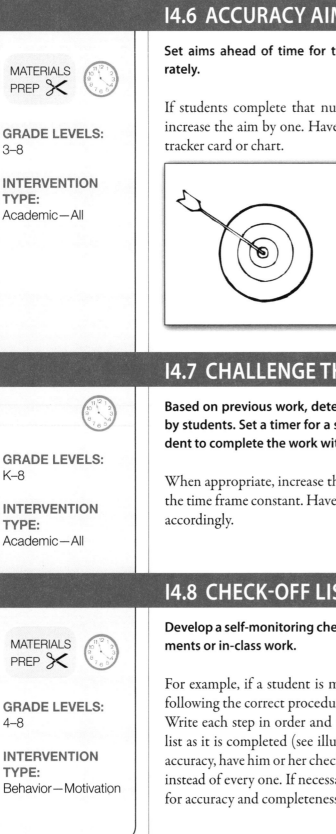

Name: _Leroy_

Beg. Date: _11/26_

End Date: _12/3_

Aim: _56_

I4.7 CHALLENGE THE TIME

GRADE LEVELS:
K–8

INTERVENTION TYPE:
Academic—All

Based on previous work, determine the number of problems to be completed by students. Set a timer for a specified amount of time and challenge each student to complete the work within that time frame.

When appropriate, increase the number of problems to be completed, but keep the time frame constant. Have students keep track of performance and reinforce accordingly.

I4.8 CHECK-OFF LIST

MATERIALS
PREP ✂

GRADE LEVELS:
4–8

INTERVENTION TYPE:
Behavior—Motivation

Develop a self-monitoring checklist for students to use as they complete assignments or in-class work.

For example, if a student is making errors because he or she is rushing or not following the correct procedures, identify the steps the student needs to follow. Write each step in order and then have the student check off each step on the list as it is completed (see illustration). As the student becomes more aware of accuracy, have him or her check the steps after completing two or three problems instead of every one. If necessary, combine this technique with a reinforcement for accuracy and completeness.

I4: What can I do about the students who do not check work for accuracy and/or completeness?

Step	Problem Number									
	1	2	3	4	5	6	7	8	9	10
1. I copied the problem correctly.	✕	✕								
2. I divided the small number into the larger number.	✕	✕								
3. I multiplied the two numbers.	✕	✕								
4. I subtracted the correct numbers.	✕	✕								
5. I brought down the next number.	✕									
6. I started the process over.	✕									

I4.9 PARTNERS PLUS

MATERIALS PREP

GRADE LEVELS:
3–8

INTERVENTION TYPE:
Academic—All

REPRODUCIBLE on CD

During independent work time, set a timer to sound at predetermined intervals. When the timer goes off, the students switch papers with their partners and correct the work completed.

A plus (+) is awarded for every correct answer. The partners total the number of +'s they have earned for that interval and record it on their Partner Scorecard. At the end of the activity, the total number of +'s earned is tallied. Partners are awarded bonus points for their assignment by trading in +'s earned. Bonus points can be added to assignment or quiz scores.

REPRODUCIBLE I4.9

T
G
I
F

INDEPENDENT PRACTICE ACTIVITIES

I5

What can I do about the students who do not know how to prepare for and/or study for a test?

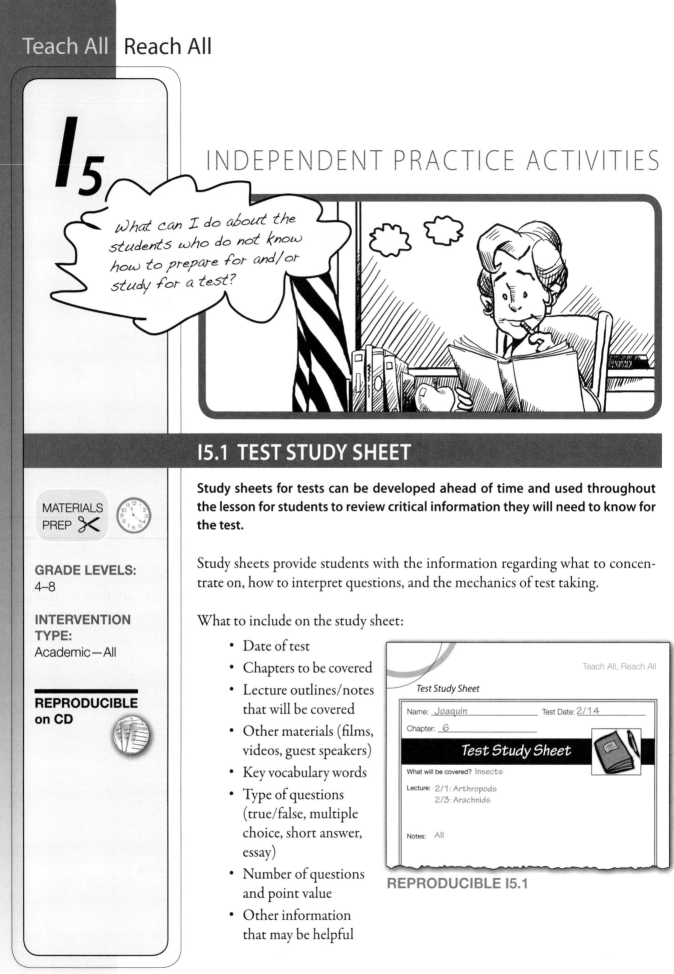

I5.1 TEST STUDY SHEET

MATERIALS
PREP ✂

GRADE LEVELS:
4–8

INTERVENTION
TYPE:
Academic—All

REPRODUCIBLE
on CD

Study sheets for tests can be developed ahead of time and used throughout the lesson for students to review critical information they will need to know for the test.

Study sheets provide students with the information regarding what to concentrate on, how to interpret questions, and the mechanics of test taking.

What to include on the study sheet:

- Date of test
- Chapters to be covered
- Lecture outlines/notes that will be covered
- Other materials (films, videos, guest speakers)
- Key vocabulary words
- Type of questions (true/false, multiple choice, short answer, essay)
- Number of questions and point value
- Other information that may be helpful

Teach All, Reach All

Test Study Sheet

Name: Joaquin   Test Date: 2/14

Chapter: 6

Test Study Sheet

What will be covered? Insects

Lecture: 2/1: Arthropods
         2/3: Arachnids

Notes: All

REPRODUCIBLE I5.1

I5: What can I do about the students who do not know how to prepare for and/or study for a test?

I5.2 TERM

MATERIALS
PREP ✂

GRADE LEVELS:
4–8

**INTERVENTION
TYPE:**
Academic—All

Model each of the steps listed for the TERM strategy.

Help to illustrate the concept by using a variety of examples. Provide students with practice opportunities both in class and out of class to aid in generalization. Award points when students use the TERM studying strategy.

Take materials home (notes, book, assignments).

Examine and highlight what you know.

> **Q**uestion what you do not know.
>
> **U**nderline what you think might be on the test.
>
> **E**mphasize and mark what you already know.
>
> **S**kim all reading material.
>
> **T**ime schedule for studying.
>
> **I**nvent test questions.
>
> **O**rganize yourself.
>
> **N**ever give up!

Review known material (anticipate possible questions).

Memorize new material (this is where to spend the bulk of your time).

Source: Frost, 1987.

I5.3 STUDY SCHEDULING

MATERIALS
PREP ✂

GRADE LEVELS:
3–8

**INTERVENTION
TYPE:**
Academic—All

Provide students with a copy of a weekly schedule broken into hour or half-hour blocks of time.

Students complete the schedule by writing in their weekly activities as well as their study schedule. Share with students the following suggestions for setting up a study schedule.

- Plan regular study times.

- Plan at least a half-hour (younger students) or hour (older students) block of time in which to study.

- Plan which assignments you are going to work on during the study time.

T
G
I
F

- Take the first five minutes of each study activity to review what you have already learned and to plan what you are going to accomplish today. This helps promote long-term learning and a sense of accomplishment.

- Plan breaks when studying for longer than one hour and stick to the allotted time.

- Use daytime or early evening for study, if possible. Most people are less efficient at night.

- Work on the most difficult subjects when you are most alert.

- Distribute your studying for a test over time rather than cram at the last minute.

- Balance your activities between studying and other things. Allow time for recreational activities.

- Reward yourself by crossing off items you complete on your schedule each time you meet a commitment.

Source: Bos & Vaughn, 1988.

I5.4 REVIEW GUIDES

MATERIALS PREP ✂

GRADE LEVELS:
3–8

INTERVENTION TYPE:
Academic—All

You can prepare a review guide beforehand, or the students can prepare one as they review for a test.

Information that will assist students in preparing for an exam should be included.

EXAMPLES

MATH

1. **Topic:** Story Problems.

2. **Terms:** All together, remaining.

3. **Definitions:** All together—add the numbers; Remaining—subtract the smaller number from the larger.

I5: What can I do about the students who do not know how to prepare for and/or study for a test?

4. **Examples:**

- Tom had three balls, and Joe had two. How many were there all together?

- Mary had nine cookies. She ate two. How many cookies were remaining?

GEOLOGY

1. **Title/Subject:** Rocks and Minerals.

2. **Purpose:** Describe differences between rocks and minerals.

3. **Key vocabulary and definitions:** igneous, metamorphic, sedimentary.

4. **Brief outline**

5. **Questions:** What are three types of rocks?

6. **Text references:** Pages 451–470.

I5.5 STUDY CHECKLISTS

Distribute a checklist to students that includes important information about studying for an upcoming test.

Teach and review the steps with students. Encourage students to share the checklist with parents and request assistance in using it while studying for a test. Points can be awarded to students for using the study checklist prior to a test.

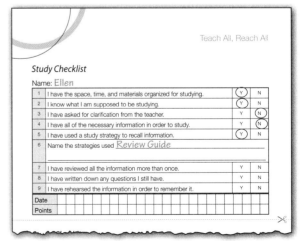

REPRODUCIBLE I5.5

MATERIALS PREP

GRADE LEVELS:
3–8

INTERVENTION TYPE:
Academic — All

REPRODUCIBLE on CD

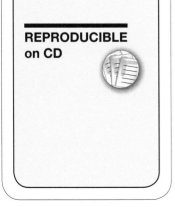

T
G
I
F

I5.6 ACTIVE READING

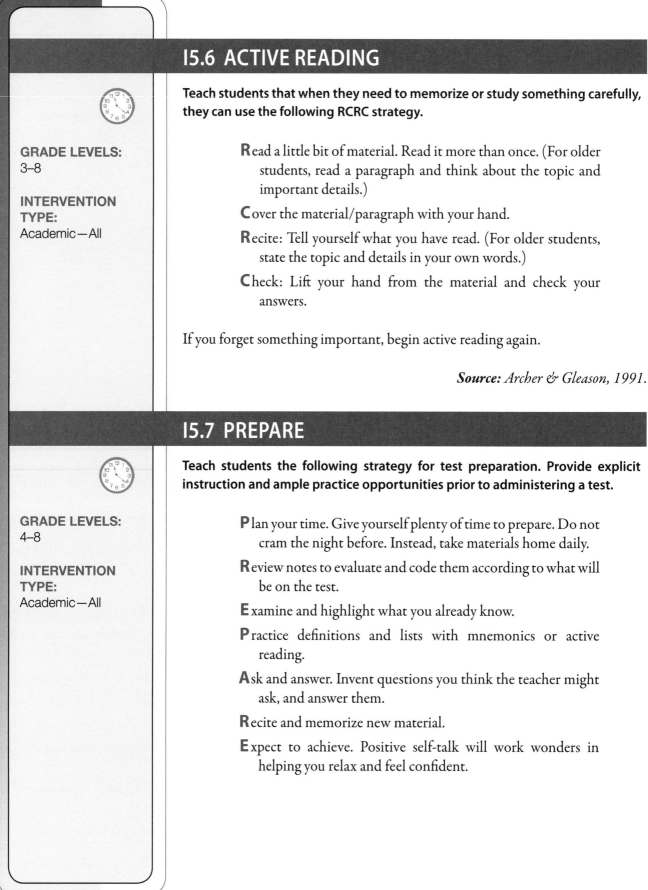

GRADE LEVELS:
3–8

INTERVENTION TYPE:
Academic—All

Teach students that when they need to memorize or study something carefully, they can use the following RCRC strategy.

Read a little bit of material. Read it more than once. (For older students, read a paragraph and think about the topic and important details.)

Cover the material/paragraph with your hand.

Recite: Tell yourself what you have read. (For older students, state the topic and details in your own words.)

Check: Lift your hand from the material and check your answers.

If you forget something important, begin active reading again.

Source: *Archer & Gleason, 1991.*

I5.7 PREPARE

GRADE LEVELS:
4–8

INTERVENTION TYPE:
Academic—All

Teach students the following strategy for test preparation. Provide explicit instruction and ample practice opportunities prior to administering a test.

Plan your time. Give yourself plenty of time to prepare. Do not cram the night before. Instead, take materials home daily.

Review notes to evaluate and code them according to what will be on the test.

Examine and highlight what you already know.

Practice definitions and lists with mnemonics or active reading.

Ask and answer. Invent questions you think the teacher might ask, and answer them.

Recite and memorize new material.

Expect to achieve. Positive self-talk will work wonders in helping you relax and feel confident.

I5.8 WRITE ABOUT

MATERIALS
PREP ✂

GRADE LEVELS:
3–8

**INTERVENTION
TYPE:**
Academic—All

Have students spend five minutes after a lesson writing about what took place during the lesson and what important information they learned.

They can write in a daily log or in their notebooks. The following can be used as prompts for this exercise:

- What were the key concepts covered?
- Develop a mnemonic for one piece of information.
- Pick one concept and explain it in your own words.
- Draw a graphic organizer relating the concepts of the chapter.
- Choose three vocabulary words, identify the key words, and create practice cards.

After students have written their information individually, time can be spent sharing the information in groups or with partners. Allow time prior to the test to review what students included in their Write Abouts.

I5.9 INFORMATION CODING

MATERIALS
PREP ✂

GRADE LEVELS:
4–8

**INTERVENTION
TYPE:**
Academic—All

Teach students a method for coding notes, worksheets, and handouts that will assist them in recalling information for tests.

Highlighter pens and/or symbols can be used for the coding. Provide students with suggestions for the codes or let them generate their own.

EXAMPLES

Key concept	*
Vocabulary word	✓
Need more information?	?
Will be on test	+++
Dates to remember	#
Possible essay	E

After students have completed a daily lesson, give them a few minutes to review and code their notes, handouts, etc. They can do this individually or with a partner.

T
G
I
F

GRADE LEVELS:
3–8

INTERVENTION TYPE:
Academic—All

I5.10 MAP IT OUT

After providing the students with information on a topic, have them map it out (see illustration) for review as a class or individually.

The maps can be kept in a folder to use when preparing for a test. The following mapping steps can be demonstrated to the class.

Step 1. Find the topic.

Step 2. Identify the key concepts related to the topic (subtopics).

Step 3. Determine the supporting details for each key concept.

Step 4. Use the map to recall the important information from the lesson.

Step 5. Combine lesson maps to connect related topics covered in the entire unit.

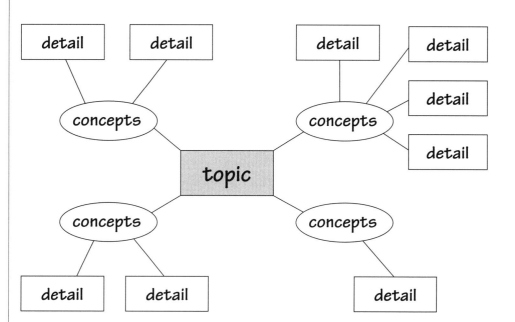

I5: What can I do about the students who do not know how to prepare for and/or study for a test?

I5.11 PRACTICE SHEETS

MATERIALS PREP ✂

GRADE LEVELS:
3–8

INTERVENTION TYPE:
Academic—All

Teach students how to develop vocabulary practice sheets to review key vocabulary and concepts related to the unit of instruction.

After each new concept is introduced, have students write the information on a split sheet of paper or an index card. Fold the sheet down the middle so the vocabulary words are on one side and the definitions on the other. Students can quiz themselves or work with partners. Use the practice sheets for review on a daily basis as well as at the end of the unit.

Entering the World of Work Chapter 2—Finding Jobs	
SEE/SAY FACTS	
1. Listing of businesses in the phone book.	1. Yellow Pages
2. A person or company that hires workers.	2. Employer
3. Shortened words.	3. Abbreviations
4. Money people receive after they no longer work.	4. Social Security
5. An office that matches workers with jobs.	5. Employment Agency
6. A meeting between an employer and a job applicant.	6. Interview
7. Working 40 or more hours per week.	7. Full-time Job
8. Working fewer than 40 hours per week.	8. Part-time Job
9. Shortened words.	9. Abbreviations
10. A meeting between an employer and a job applicant.	10. Interview
11. Working 40 or more hours per week.	11. Full-time Job

T G I F

12. Money people receive after they no longer work.	12. Social Security
13. An office that matches workers with jobs.	13. Employment Agency
14. Working fewer than 40 hours per week.	14. Part-Time Job
15. Listing of businesses in the phone book.	15. Yellow Pages
16. A person or company that hires workers.	16. Employer
17. A meeting between an employer and a job applicant.	17. Interview
(Fold along the middle line.)	

Source: Lovitt et al., 1992.

Throughout **F**, the teacher designs end-of-unit performance assessments that reflect the objectives identified in a unit of curriculum. The measurement tool is administered repeatedly to determine whether students are progressing toward the objectives.

FINAL MEASUREMENT

F₁

FINAL MEASUREMENT

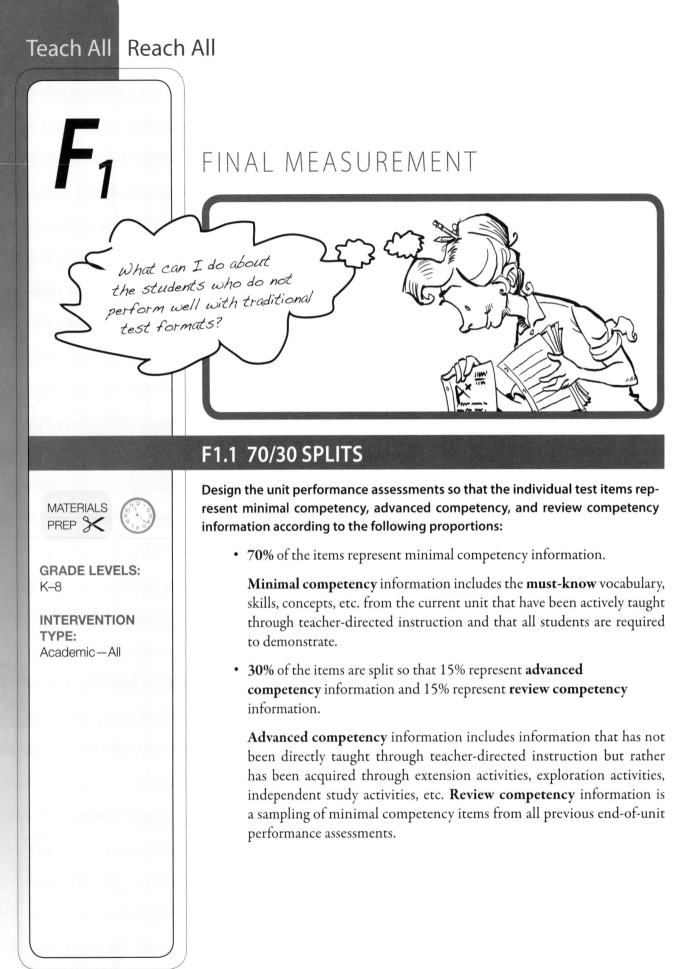

What can I do about the students who do not perform well with traditional test formats?

F1.1 70/30 SPLITS

MATERIALS
PREP ✂

GRADE LEVELS:
K–8

INTERVENTION TYPE:
Academic—All

Design the unit performance assessments so that the individual test items represent minimal competency, advanced competency, and review competency information according to the following proportions:

- **70%** of the items represent minimal competency information.

  Minimal competency information includes the **must-know** vocabulary, skills, concepts, etc. from the current unit that have been actively taught through teacher-directed instruction and that all students are required to demonstrate.

- **30%** of the items are split so that 15% represent **advanced competency** information and 15% represent **review competency** information.

  Advanced competency information includes information that has not been directly taught through teacher-directed instruction but rather has been acquired through extension activities, exploration activities, independent study activities, etc. **Review competency** information is a sampling of minimal competency items from all previous end-of-unit performance assessments.

This type of arrangement allows certain students the opportunity to be successful on minimal competency information from the current unit and previous units and achieve a passing grade on the test without being accountable for advanced competency information. In addition, more sophisticated students still have the opportunity to perform on advanced competency items.

Source: Sprick, 1985.

Introduction to Using Probes

The following seven examples describe quick ways to measure student progress. Each activity involves the use of your own classroom curriculum.

After spending some time each day teaching skills to students, you can use one of the following ideas for quickly measuring their progress.

These quick progress measures are called *probes*. Probes are somewhat like an end-of-unit assessment, but are less time consuming. Probes, unlike unit assessments, are given as often as possible (daily or several times a week) during the unit instead of just at the end of the unit. It is not a problem for students to see a sampling of information from the entire unit on the probe. This focuses their attention on what is going to be coming up throughout the unit. Actually, students who use these probes repeatedly do better than students who are just given an end-of-unit assessment. Probes are manageable because they are usually given for only one or two minutes each day.

Track students' scores on a chart so they can judge their performance frequently; it is almost like a daily report card. If things are not going too well, changes can be made immediately instead of waiting for six or eight weeks. In addition, the daily feedback that students receive on their progress is extremely motivating.

When students attain the mastery level for a probe, you can:

- Give a more traditional unit assessment.

- Move on to the next unit probe.

- Involve the student in extension activities until the rest of the class passes the probe.

- Have the student take review timings on probes that were already passed.

Probes are fun and should not create anxiety for students. They are like taking quick snapshots of student performance each day to see whether learning is occurring. It is important to create a relaxed measurement environment by carefully introducing the idea of probes to students. Consider the following script as a way to introduce probes to the classroom:

"Each day you will have an opportunity to take a picture of yourself during math. It is called a math probe. Instead of giving you a checkout at the end of the unit, I am going to give you the end-of-unit checkout every day. You should not be able to answer (write, say) any of the problems today because I haven't taught you these things yet. Each day I will teach you, and then you will be able to answer more problems the next time we have our math probe. It will also be a check of my teaching. If you are not answering more questions each time we have our math probe, it tells me I need to change something in my teaching. At the end of the unit (six to eight weeks from now), you will ace the math probe! That means you will know all of the answers. Now we will practice what I am talking about."

Teachers should answer these questions when creating any probe:

- What should I measure?

- How long do I measure?

- What materials do I need?

- How do I administer the probe?

- What should I expect students to be able to do?

F1.2 WORD PROBES

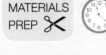

MATERIALS PREP

GRADE LEVELS:
K–6

INTERVENTION TYPE:
Academic—All

WHAT SHOULD I MEASURE?
Reading individual words (30 or more words) aloud. The words to be inserted on the reproducible (F1.2) can be selected from a list of unknown words from a reading unit, book, or novel. They should represent vocabulary that will appear in the unit of instruction.

HOW LONG DO I MEASURE?
One minute.

WHAT MATERIALS DO I NEED?
Two copies of the word list (one for the student and one for the recorder), one transparency to be placed over the recorder's (teacher's) copy so the word list can be reused, transparency pen, and accurate timer, preferably with an auditory signal.

F1: What can I do about the students who do not perform well with traditional test formats?

REPRODUCIBLE
on CD

NOTE:
See Introduction to Using Probes starting on p. 201 for more information on probes.

HOW DO I ADMINISTER THE PROBE?

Step 1. Administer individually.

Step 2. Say, "Please read these words aloud to me, starting here. When you say the first word, I will start the timer and listen to you read for one minute."
(Demonstrate, if necessary, using a separate word list.)
"Try to say each word. If you get stuck on a word for too long, I will tell you the word. You can skip words you do not know. Ready? Please begin."

Step 3. Have the student read for one minute.

Step 4. Put the word list under the transparency and place a slash on the copy to indicate where the student started reading.

Step 5. As the student reads, place a mark (x) over any errors (mispronunciations, words skipped, and words given). If the student hesitates for two or three seconds, provide the word. Do not count an error if the student inserts words, self-corrects, sounds out, or repeats words.

Step 6. At the end of the minute, place a slash on your copy to indicate the last word read by the student during the timing. Allow the student to finish reading the words rather than stopping after one minute.

Step 7. Count the total number of words read correctly in one minute. Teach or assist the student to chart the correct and error information each time a probe is given. Discuss the student's current performance and expectations for future performance. Provide praise for daily improvements in the student's score.

WHAT SHOULD I EXPECT STUDENTS TO BE ABLE TO DO?

By the end of the school year, students should be able to say 60 to 80 correct words per minute with zero to one error per minute on two separate occasions.

Teach All, Reach All

Word Probes

Name: Li-Yuan   Date: 4/7   Grade: 2
Count: correct 20 errors 3   Time: 1 min.

explain	famous	~~field~~	stone
plain	allow	leaves	melt
~~community~~	rescue	extinct	swamp
~~erupt~~	dinosaur	clues	avoid
~~fossil~~	tracks	amazing	protect
survive	dig	imagine /	flying
eggs	scientist	buried	fierce
camp	disappear	dirt	river

Reproducible Form F1.2
See p. 202

COPYRIGHT © 2009 • SUSAN L. MULKEY & KAREN A. KEMP

REPRODUCIBLE F1.2

MATERIALS PREP ✂

GRADE LEVELS:
3–8

INTERVENTION TYPE:
Academic—All

NOTE:
See Introduction to Using Probes starting on p. 201 for more information on probes.

F1.3 ORAL PASSAGE PROBES

WHAT SHOULD I MEASURE?

Reading aloud from a passage at the student's instructional level selected from a reader, textbook, library book, or functional reading materials such as newspapers and magazines. The passage should represent material that will be taught in class.

HOW LONG DO I MEASURE?

One minute.

WHAT MATERIALS DO I NEED?

Two copies of the passage (one for the student and one for the recorder with cumulative word counts at the end of each line—see illustration), one transparency to be placed over the recorder's (teacher's) copy so the passage can be reused, transparency pen, and accurate timer, preferably with an auditory signal.

HOW DO I ADMINISTER THE PROBE?

Step 1. Administer individually.

Step 2. Say, "Starting here, please read this passage out loud to me. When you say the first word, I will start the timer and listen to you read for one minute."
(Demonstrate, if necessary, using a separate passage).
"Try to say each word. If you get stuck on a word for too long, I will tell you the word. You can skip words you do not know. Ready? Please begin."

Step 3. Have the student read for one minute.

Step 4. With the passage under the transparency, place a slash on the copy to indicate where the student started reading.

Step 5. As the student reads, place a mark (x) over any errors (mispronunciations, words skipped, and words given). If the student hesitates for two to three seconds provide the word (see illustration). Do not count an error if the student inserts words, self-corrects, sounds out, or repeats words.

Step 6. At the end of the minute, place a slash on the copy to indicate the last word read by the student in one minute. Allow the student to finish reading the passage rather than stopping after one minute.

Step 7. Count the total number of words read correctly and incorrectly in one minute. Teach or assist the student to chart the correct and error information each time the oral reading probe is given. Discuss the student's current performance and expectations for future performance. Provide praise for daily improvements in the student's score.

WHAT SHOULD I EXPECT STUDENTS TO BE ABLE TO DO?

By the end of grade 3, students should be able to read 150 to 250 correct words per minute with five or fewer errors per minute on two separate occasions.

NOTE:
See chart on page 213 for additional grade levels and performance standards.

Name: Heather   Date: 5/22   Grade: 1

Count: correct   35   error   2   Time: min.

The See-Saw

Jane was going to the store. She went down the street. She	(12)
saw a boy and a little dog.	(19)
The boy said, "Come and play with me. You may play with my	(32)
dog."	(33)
Jane said, "I will play with you. What can the dog do? He	(46)
is not very big."	(50)
"He is a good dog," said the boy. "He can run and jump. And	(64)
he can ride a see-saw."	(70)
"Oh, I want to see him ride," said Jane. "Where is it?"	(82)
"I have it in here," the boy said.	(90)
He said to the dog, "Go find the see-saw. We will have a	(104)
ride."	(105)
The dog ran to the see-saw.	(112)
"Do you like to ride?" said the boy. "What do you say?"	(124)
The dog said, "Bow-wow!"	(129)
"Look at this," said the boy. "I am up and he is down.	(142)
Now he is up and I am down."	(150)
"What a funny ride for a dog!" said Jane.	(159)

T G I F

F1.4 COMPREHENSION PROBES

MATERIALS PREP ✂

GRADE LEVELS:
3–8

INTERVENTION TYPE:
Academic—All

REPRODUCIBLE on CD

NOTE:
See Introduction to Using Probes starting on p. 201 for more information on probes.

NOTE:
Count each idea and detail about ideas. For instance, the "purple dress" counts as two pieces of information. See chart on page 213 for performance standards at different grade levels.

WHAT SHOULD I MEASURE?
Information summarized in the student's own words based on free recall, pictures, listening, and silent or oral reading.

HOW LONG DO I MEASURE?
One minute.

WHAT MATERIALS DO I NEED?
Comprehension record sheet (see illustration), pencil, and accurate timer, preferably with an auditory signal.

Teach All, Reach All
Comprehension Probes

Rafe

Name:	Day/Date				
Example Elements	1	2	3	4	5
States title or author					
Lists character names: who?					
Describes details about character appearance/personalities/feelings	‖				
Describes setting: when/where?					
Recalls events in sequence					
Identifies main idea					
Draws conclusions					
Clarifies fact or fantasy					
Makes predictions					
Gives opinions					
Makes personal connections					
Infers					
Interprets					
TOTAL					

REPRODUCIBLE F1.4

HOW DO I ADMINISTER THE PROBE?

Step 1. Administer individually.

Step 2. Say to the student, "When I say 'please begin,' tell me about the (experience, picture, story you listened to, material you read)."
It may be necessary to demonstrate the summarizing procedure. "Keep telling me about [*insert topic*] until I ask you to stop. I will keep track of what you tell me on this record sheet. Ready? Please begin."
Provide prompts if the student stops summarizing before the minute elapses, such as:
• Keep talking.
• Tell me more.
• What else?

Step 3. Mark correct and error responses using a comprehension record sheet (see illustration).

Step 4. Stop recording after one minute, but allow the student to continue telling thoughts.

Step 5. Teach or assist the student to chart the correct and error information each time a comprehension probe is given. Discuss the student's current performance and expectations for future performance. Provide praise for daily improvements in the student's score.

WHAT SHOULD I EXPECT STUDENTS TO BE ABLE TO DO?
By the end of grade 3, students should be able to retell 15 to 30 ideas or facts per minute with two or fewer incorrect responses per minute on two separate occasions.

F1.5 WRITTEN EXPRESSION PROBES

WHAT SHOULD I MEASURE?
Words written in prose as a response to a story starter.

HOW LONG DO I MEASURE?
One minute think time; three minutes writing time.

WHAT MATERIALS DO I NEED?
Lined paper with story starter, pencils, transparency, transparency pen, overhead projector, and accurate timer, preferably with an auditory signal.

MATERIALS PREP

GRADE LEVELS:
4–8

INTERVENTION TYPE:
Academic—All

NOTE:
See Introduction to Using Probes starting on p. 201 for more information on probes.

Name: *Erica*   Date: *2/24*   Time: *3 minutes*

Last weekend my friend and I went skiing and . . .

We were so excited to finally be cruising down the powdery, free slopes--there wasn't enough time in the world. As we were preparing to get off the lift and continue skiing, I felt a tugging at my pants. I didn't think much of it until I stood up to ski off. The suspenders of my outfit had caught onto the bars of the chairlift and before I knew it, I was hanging upside down. The unknowing chairlift operator kept going until it went all the way around. How emberrassing.

Correct Words = *89*
    Incorrect = *1*

T
G
I
F

HOW DO I ADMINISTER THE PROBE?

Step 1. Administer individually or with entire group.

Step 2. Say, "Today I want you to write a story on the lined paper. I will read the sentence to you at the top of the page, then you will write your story about what happens next." (Use the overhead transparency to demonstrate the procedure for the students.)

Step 3. Then say, "I will give you one minute to think about what you want to write, and then I will give you three minutes to write. Please begin thinking."

Step 4. After the thinking time has elapsed, say, "Please start writing."

Step 5. After the three minutes, say, "Please stop. Put your pencils down. Thank you."

Step 6. Teach or assist the student to count the number of words that were written. Correct words include intelligible words that make sense in the story. Words do not need to be spelled correctly unless included as part of the criteria for mastery.

Step 7. Teach or assist the student to chart the total number of correct and error words. Discuss the student's current performance and expectations for future performance. Provide praise for daily improvements in the student's score.

WHAT SHOULD I EXPECT STUDENTS TO BE ABLE TO DO?

30 to 40 correct words per minute with two or fewer errors (e.g., punctuation, spelling, capitalization, verb agreement, etc.) per minute on two separate occasions.

F1.6 MATH PROBES

GRADE LEVELS:
3–8

INTERVENTION TYPE:
Academic—All

WHAT SHOULD I MEASURE?

Digits written when computing math problems.

HOW LONG DO I MEASURE?

One minute.

WHAT MATERIALS DO I NEED?

Response sheet, pencils, answer key, transparency demonstration sheet, transparency pen, overhead projector, and accurate timing device, preferably with an auditory signal.

F1: What can I do about the students who do not perform well with traditional test formats?

NOTE:
See Introduction to
Using Probes starting
on p. 201 for more in-
formation on probes.

HOW DO I ADMINISTER THE PROBE?

Step 1. Administer to an individual student or the entire group.

Step 2. Say: "When I say, 'Please begin,' you will write the answers to these math problems as quickly and as carefully as you can." The response sheet can be put in a folder under an acetate sheet taped inside the folder. Students can use a transparency pen to write their answers. Using this procedure, the response sheet does not need to be duplicated each time the student takes the probe. This procedure can be demonstrated using an overhead transparency, also.

Step 3. If the response sheet includes problems with different operation signs, point this out to the students. For students with less-developed skills, the response sheet can include only one type of problem, or have them simply write numbers.

Step 4. Next, say, "If you have trouble with a problem, try it, write something, and then move on to the next problem. Do not erase. Ready? Please begin."

Step 5. After one minute has elapsed, say, "Please stop. Put your pencils down. Thank you."

Step 6. Provide answer keys for correction and counting. (If you are using acetate sheets, the answer key can be duplicated on the back side of the response sheet and placed under the acetate for easy correction.) Teach or assist students to count the number of correct digits (not answers) written. For example: 7 + 6 = 13 would be counted as two digits correct (1 and 3); 9 x 4 = 35 would be counted as one digit correct (3) and one error (5). For more involved problems, points can be given for equal and operation signs, lines, numbers carried, proper alignment of numbers, or commas (see illustration).

$$249 \times 86$$
$$1494$$
$$1992$$
$$21{,}414$$

Count 20

(13 digits, 1 alignment, 4 digits carried, 1 line to separate answer, 1 comma)

$$1 \tfrac{1}{4} = 1 \tfrac{3}{12}$$
$$+ 3 \tfrac{2}{3} = 3 \tfrac{8}{12}$$
$$4 \tfrac{11}{12}$$

Count 19

(2 equal signs, 13 digits, 3 fraction lines, 1 line to separate answer)

NOTE:
See chart on page
213 for additional
grade levels and per-
formance standards.

T G I F

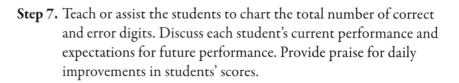

Step 7. Teach or assist the students to chart the total number of correct and error digits. Discuss each student's current performance and expectations for future performance. Provide praise for daily improvements in students' scores.

WHAT SHOULD I EXPECT STUDENTS TO BE ABLE TO DO?

By the end of grade 3, students should be able to figure 70 to 90 correct digits per minute with no more than one error per minute on two separate occasions.

F1.7 SOCIAL SKILLS PROBES

MATERIALS PREP

GRADE LEVELS:
K–8

INTERVENTION TYPE:
Academic—All

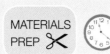

REPRODUCIBLE on CD
(2 pages)

NOTE:
See Introduction to Using Probes starting on p. 201 for more information on probes.

WHAT SHOULD I MEASURE?

Demonstration of socially appropriate/inappropriate behavior in school, home, and community settings. For example:

- Following Instructions
- Accepting Feedback
- Making a Greeting
- Making a Request
- Getting the Teacher's Attention
- Disagreeing Appropriately
- Apologizing
- Engaging in a Conversation
- Giving a Compliment

HOW LONG DO I MEASURE?

Varies depending on the social skill being measured.

WHAT MATERIALS DO I NEED?

If self-recording, a tracker card, a counting device, and a timing device.

HOW DO I ADMINISTER?

Step 1. Determine the social skill to be observed. Whenever possible, teach the students to observe and record their own behavior.

Step 2. Determine a setting for observation and recording, such as during role play, in the classroom, on the playground, at home, or at a work setting.

Step 3. Determine an appropriate length of time for observation. This should ideally be a standard time for each observation period. This could be 30 minutes for Getting the Teacher's Attention, one hour

F1: What can I do about the students who do not perform well with traditional test formats?

for Following Instructions, or an entire school day for Engaging in Conversations.

Step 4. Define the behavioral components for the social skill so that it can be easily counted. (See the pocket tracker card illustration.) For example, Engaging in a Conversation can be defined as:

- Look at the person.
- Use a pleasant tone of voice.
- Ask the person questions.
- Don't interrupt.
- After the person's answer, make a comment without changing the subject.

Step 5. Teach or assist students to count the number of occurrences of the behavior during the observation time. (See the Behavior Components illustration.) Teach or assist students to chart the number of occurrences of appropriate and inappropriate behavior. While referring to the chart, discuss each student's current performance and expectations for future performance. Provide praise for daily improvements in each student's performance.

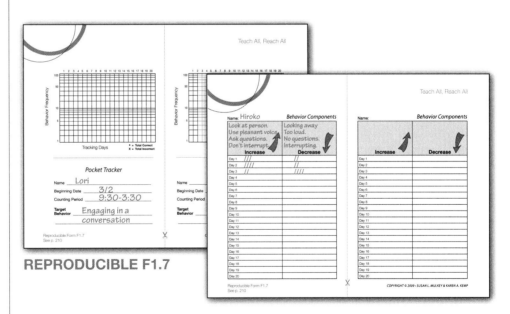

REPRODUCIBLE F1.7

WHAT SHOULD I EXPECT STUDENTS TO BE ABLE TO DO?

Students should display 99% or more appropriate social behaviors during socially engaged time in school, home, leisure, or work environments on two separate occasions.

T
G
I
F

F1.8 CONTENT AREA/FUNCTIONAL SKILLS PROBES

MATERIALS PREP ✂

GRADE LEVELS:
K–8

INTERVENTION TYPE:
Academic—All

When teaching in the content areas (e.g., social studies, science, English literature, biology, current events, community awareness, health and safety, etc.), it is effective to individually measure a student's ability to:

1. **Communicate** (talk or write about the subject matter so as to be understood and understand others).

2. **Clarify Values or Opinions** (be able to provide a range of opinions related to the topic/issue).

3. **Problem Solve/Make Decisions/ Determine Consequences** (interpret content area information to solve problems, make decisions, and predict results).

EXAMPLES

The measurement for a Science/Cell Biology objective where students will correctly use 18 of the 20 critical ("must know") vocabulary and 15 of the 17 critical ("must know") concepts in cell biology might be:

- A ten-minute written narrative summary
- A two-minute paraphrasing summary
- A one-minute oral summary

The measurement for a History/Economic Depressions objective where students will evaluate government programs for stimulating prosperity and compare and contrast unemployment problems of the 1930s and the 1990s might be:

- A ten-minute oral summary
- A five-minute debate
- A ten-minute written comparison

The measurement for a Drug and Alcohol objective where students will describe ideas for nurturing themselves might be:

- A one-minute written summary
- A 30-second commercial
- A 30-second recap of an illustrated magazine advertisement

***Source:** Starlin, 1989.*

F1: What can I do about the students who do not perform well with traditional test formats?

Suggested Performance Standards (Guidelines to Use With Probes)	
Pinpoint	Standard
Reading	
See/Say Isolated Sounds	60–80 sounds/minute
See/Say Phonetic Words	60–80 words/minute
Think/Say Alphabet (forward or back)	400+ letters/minute
See/Say Letter Names	80–100 letters/minute
See/Say Sight Words	80–100 words/minute
See/Say Words in Context (oral reading)	200+ words/minute
See/Think Words in Context (silent reading)	400+ words/minute
Think/Say Ideas or Facts	15–30 ideas/minute
Handwriting	
Emphasizing Speed	
See/Write Slashes	200–400 slashes/minute
See/Write Circles	100–150 circles/minute
Think/Write Alphabet	80–100 letters/minute
Emphasizing Accuracy	
See/Write Letters (count three per letter)	75 correct/minute
See/Write Cursive Letters Connected (count three per letter)	125 correct/minute
Spelling	
Hear/Write Dictated Words	80–100 letters/minute
Hear/Write Dictated Words	15–25 words/minute
Math	
See/Write Numbers Random	100–120 digits/minute
Think/Write Numbers (zero through nine serial)	120–160 digits/minute
See/Say Numbers	80–100 numbers/minute
Think/Say Numbers in Sequence (count-by)	150–200+ numbers/minute
See/Write Math Facts	70–90 digits/minute

Source: Beck, 1976.

F₂

FINAL MEASUREMENT

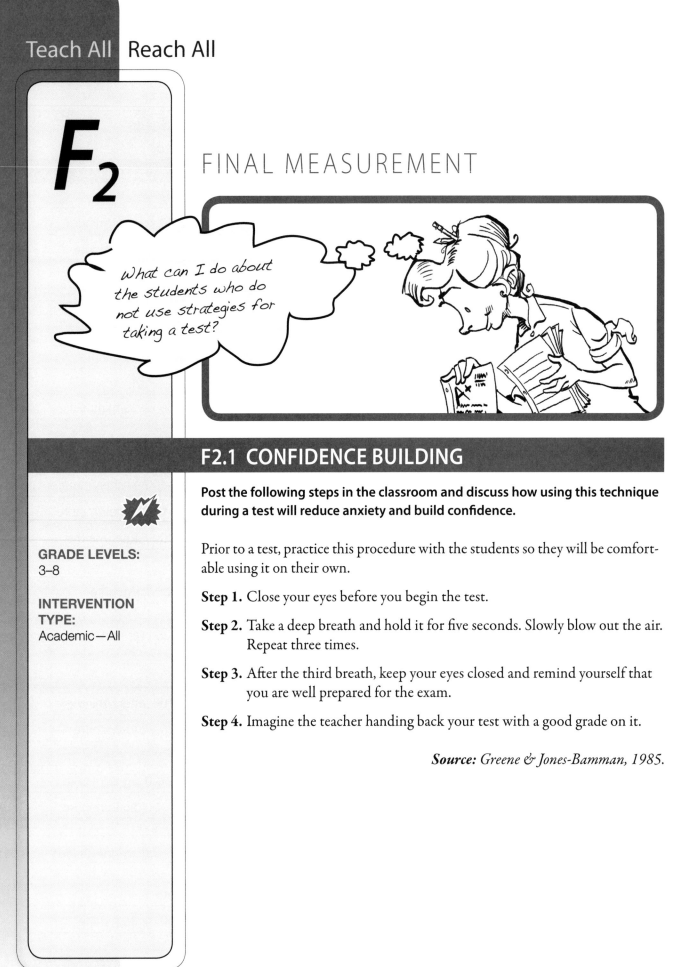

What can I do about the students who do not use strategies for taking a test?

F2.1 CONFIDENCE BUILDING

GRADE LEVELS:
3–8

INTERVENTION TYPE:
Academic—All

Post the following steps in the classroom and discuss how using this technique during a test will reduce anxiety and build confidence.

Prior to a test, practice this procedure with the students so they will be comfortable using it on their own.

Step 1. Close your eyes before you begin the test.

Step 2. Take a deep breath and hold it for five seconds. Slowly blow out the air. Repeat three times.

Step 3. After the third breath, keep your eyes closed and remind yourself that you are well prepared for the exam.

Step 4. Imagine the teacher handing back your test with a good grade on it.

Source: *Greene & Jones-Bamman, 1985.*

F2.2 TEST-TAKING AWARENESS

GRADE LEVELS:
3–8

**INTERVENTION
TYPE:**
Academic — All

Instruct the students in the general techniques used to prepare for any test.

Explain and demonstrate each of the following tips by providing students with examples and non-examples.

1. Review the entire test.

2. Know the allotted time for the test.

3. Know the point value for each question.

4. Read and follow directions carefully.

5. Underline key words in directions.

6. Answer questions you are sure of first.

7. Mark the questions you need to come back to later.

8. Return to questions that are marked.

9. Review all questions to be sure they are completed.

F2.3 KNOWING THE QUESTION

GRADE LEVELS:
3–8

**INTERVENTION
TYPE:**
Academic — All

Teach the student specific methods for answering a wide range of test questions.

EXAMPLES

TRUE/FALSE ITEMS

- To be true, everything in the question must be true; only one detail needs to be false for the answer to be false.

- Be sure qualifiers are understood. Words such as *always*, *none*, *only*, and *all* are likely to be found in false statements. Words such as *usually*, *generally*, *sometimes*, and *certain* tend to make statements true.

- Simplify questions by crossing out double negatives, then answer the question.

- First impressions are usually correct.

T
G
I
F

MULTIPLE-CHOICE ITEMS

- Determine how the question is to be answered (circle the response or write the number next to the question).

- Use the process of elimination—cross out the answers you know are wrong.

- Look for exact answers.

- The longest answer is often correct because more information is usually necessary to make a correct statement.

- Answers with qualifiers are often correct.

MATCHING ITEMS

- Determine if there are an equal number of items in each column.

- Begin with the easiest items and individually focus on each and its match.

- Cross out items as they are matched to avoid confusion.

SHORT ANSWER/COMPLETION ITEMS

- Read the question carefully to determine what is being asked.

- Use cues such as the number of blank spaces.

- Be sure the answer is logical and grammatically correct.

ESSAY QUESTIONS

- Read the question carefully and identify key words to help determine how to set up your answer.

- Plan time for organizing, writing, and proofreading.

- Organize your answer by jotting down your ideas or outlining them using a web or map.

- Write on every other line to make changes easier.

- Respond to all the information in the question.

MATERIALS
PREP

GRADE LEVELS:
4–8

INTERVENTION
TYPE:
Academic—All

REPRODUCIBLE
on CD

F2.4 POST-TEST CHECKLIST

After students have taken a test and it has been returned, have them respond to a list of questions related to successful test-taking procedures.

Have students determine what areas they need to concentrate on for the next test. Use the information on the checklist to conference with students and provide additional strategies for test taking.

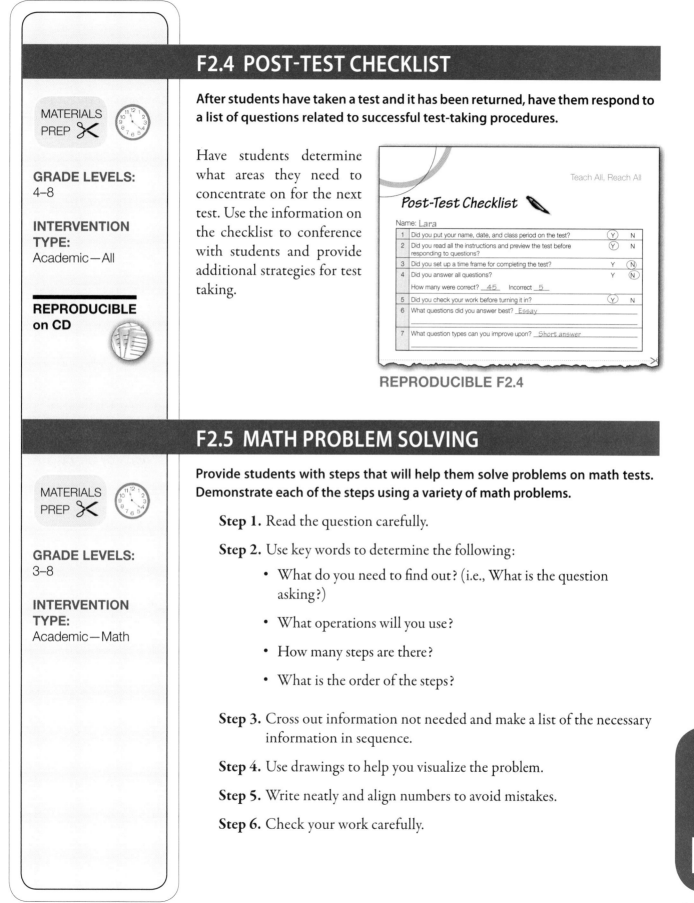

Teach All, Reach All

Post-Test Checklist

Name: Lara

1	Did you put your name, date, and class period on the test?	(Y)	N
2	Did you read all the instructions and preview the test before responding to questions?	(Y)	N
3	Did you set up a time frame for completing the test?	Y	(N)
4	Did you answer all questions?	Y	(N)
	How many were correct? __45__ Incorrect __5__		
5	Did you check your work before turning it in?	(Y)	N
6	What questions did you answer best? _Essay_		
7	What question types can you improve upon? _Short answer_		

REPRODUCIBLE F2.4

F2.5 MATH PROBLEM SOLVING

MATERIALS
PREP

GRADE LEVELS:
3–8

INTERVENTION
TYPE:
Academic—Math

Provide students with steps that will help them solve problems on math tests. Demonstrate each of the steps using a variety of math problems.

Step 1. Read the question carefully.

Step 2. Use key words to determine the following:

- What do you need to find out? (i.e., What is the question asking?)

- What operations will you use?

- How many steps are there?

- What is the order of the steps?

Step 3. Cross out information not needed and make a list of the necessary information in sequence.

Step 4. Use drawings to help you visualize the problem.

Step 5. Write neatly and align numbers to avoid mistakes.

Step 6. Check your work carefully.

T
G
I
F

GRADE LEVELS:
4–8

INTERVENTION TYPE:
Academic—Math

F2.6 RIDGES

Teach students the following mnemonic to facilitate understanding and organization of mathematical word problems.

Examples and non-examples of each step should be demonstrated and practiced prior to using the strategy.

Read the problem. Be sure you understand what the problem is asking. Reread if necessary.

I Know statements. List all the information in the problem.

Draw a picture. Include all the information from the "I Know" statements.

Goal statement. Write "I want to know." This assists students with clues for the next step.

Equation development. Write an equation to solve the problem.

Solve the equation. Plug in the necessary information to reach the goal and solve the problem.

Source: Snyder, 1987.

F2: What can I do about the students who do not use strategies for taking a test?

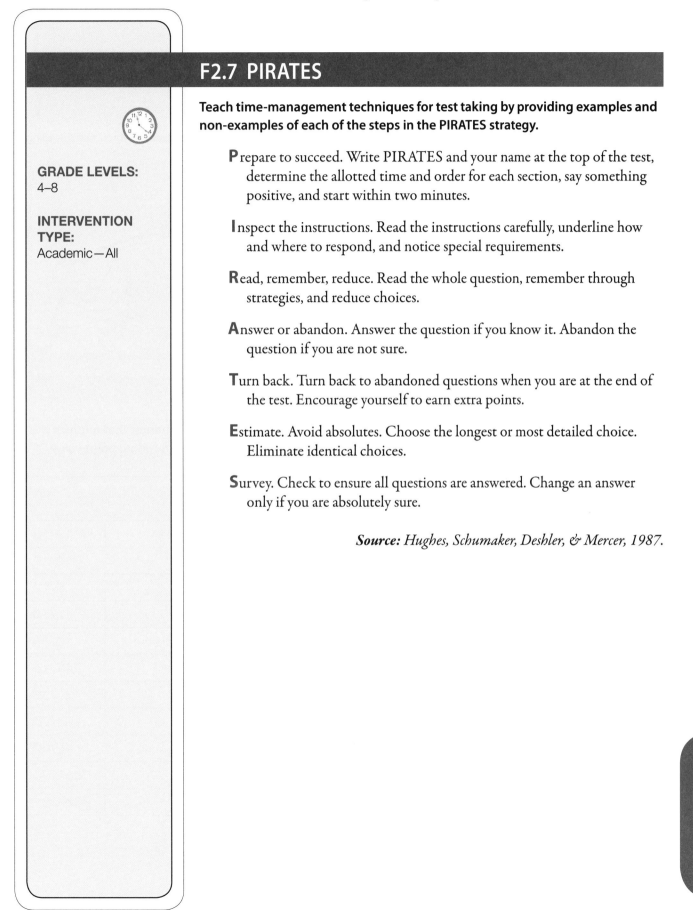

F2.7 PIRATES

GRADE LEVELS:
4–8

INTERVENTION TYPE:
Academic—All

Teach time-management techniques for test taking by providing examples and non-examples of each of the steps in the PIRATES strategy.

Prepare to succeed. Write PIRATES and your name at the top of the test, determine the allotted time and order for each section, say something positive, and start within two minutes.

Inspect the instructions. Read the instructions carefully, underline how and where to respond, and notice special requirements.

Read, remember, reduce. Read the whole question, remember through strategies, and reduce choices.

Answer or abandon. Answer the question if you know it. Abandon the question if you are not sure.

Turn back. Turn back to abandoned questions when you are at the end of the test. Encourage yourself to earn extra points.

Estimate. Avoid absolutes. Choose the longest or most detailed choice. Eliminate identical choices.

Survey. Check to ensure all questions are answered. Change an answer only if you are absolutely sure.

Source: Hughes, Schumaker, Deshler, & Mercer, 1987.

T G I **F**

F₃

FINAL MEASUREMENT

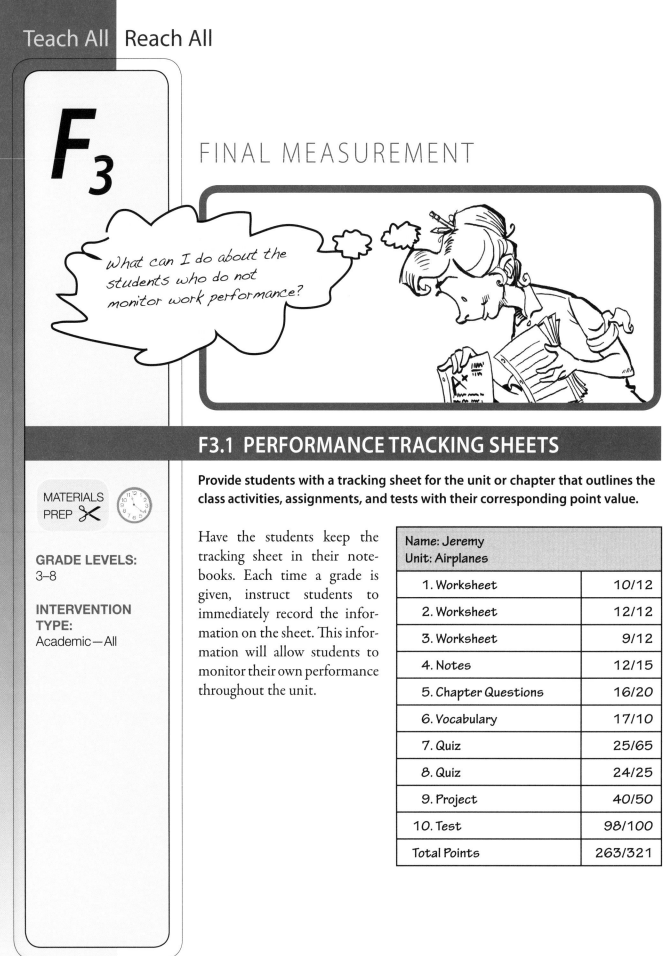

What can I do about the students who do not monitor work performance?

F3.1 PERFORMANCE TRACKING SHEETS

Provide students with a tracking sheet for the unit or chapter that outlines the class activities, assignments, and tests with their corresponding point value.

MATERIALS
PREP ✂

GRADE LEVELS:
3–8

INTERVENTION TYPE:
Academic—All

Have the students keep the tracking sheet in their notebooks. Each time a grade is given, instruct students to immediately record the information on the sheet. This information will allow students to monitor their own performance throughout the unit.

Name: Jeremy Unit: Airplanes	
1. Worksheet	10/12
2. Worksheet	12/12
3. Worksheet	9/12
4. Notes	12/15
5. Chapter Questions	16/20
6. Vocabulary	17/10
7. Quiz	25/65
8. Quiz	24/25
9. Project	40/50
10. Test	98/100
Total Points	263/321

F3: What can I do about the students who do not monitor work performance?

F3.2 PERFORMANCE CONFERENCE

MATERIALS PREP

GRADE LEVELS:
3–8

INTERVENTION TYPE:
Academic—All

Set up a five-minute meeting with each student in the class during independent work. These meetings should occur on a weekly basis to review the student's performance in the class.

Information related to the student's assignments, class participation, test scores, and/or behavior can be discussed at the conference. You or the student should keep anecdotal records on the outcome of the meetings and include them in the student's folder or portfolio. This technique can be combined with Performance Choices (F3.7), Performance Checkouts (F3.3), or Performance Tracking Sheets (F3.1).

F3.3 PERFORMANCE CHECKOUTS

MATERIALS PREP

GRADE LEVELS:
3–8

INTERVENTION TYPE:
Academic—All

REPRODUCIBLE on CD

Have students keep records of their daily or weekly performance in class.

A chart (see illustration) can be used to assist students in monitoring progress throughout the entire unit of instruction. At the end of the week, students check off each assignment or activity they have worked on during the week by placing a checkmark in the corresponding column. In the grade column (G), students determine their own performance grade for the week in each area. A simple system such as **E** (Excellent), **S** (Satisfactory) and **N** (Needs Improvement) can be used.

Review each student's sheet and write feedback statements about their performance on each assignment. The students then write a goal for the next week based on both their own evaluation of the work done and your feedback. The sheet is initialed by both you and the student and kept in a portfolio or notebook.

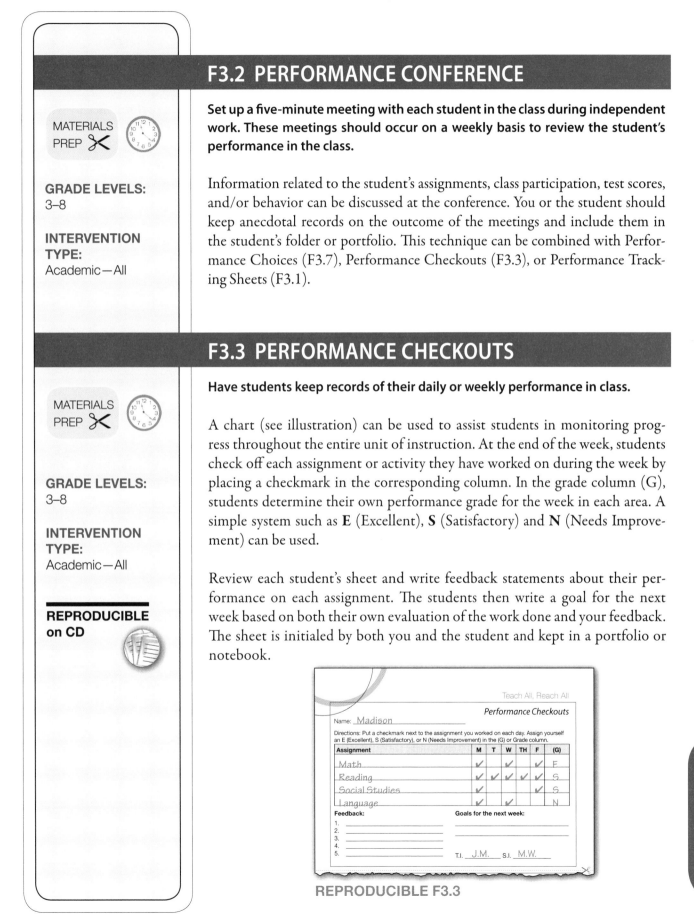

REPRODUCIBLE F3.3

T
G
I
F

F3.4 PERFORMANCE JOURNAL

Have students respond to questions related to their class performance by writing in a journal on a regular basis.

This information can be included in students' portfolios or can be incorporated into the grading system. The following are some statements related to student performance that might be included in a performance journal.

EXAMPLES

- I think I am earning a grade of _____ in this class because . . .

- If I had to describe my performance in this class, I would say . . .

- I would compare my performance in this class with . . .

- Another classmate would describe me as a _____ worker because . . .

- I am doing great, OK, or poorly in this class because . . .

MATERIALS PREP

GRADE LEVELS:
4–8

INTERVENTION TYPE:
Academic—All

F3.5 CHARTING

MATERIALS PREP

GRADE LEVELS:
3–8

INTERVENTION TYPE:
Academic—All

REPRODUCIBLE on CD

Use Probes as described in F1.3–F1.9 to measure student performance on a frequent basis.

Students can be taught how to keep track of their scores by recording them on a chart. Displaying the scores on a chart provides students with immediate feedback and a picture of their ongoing performance. After several scores (five to eight) have been recorded on the chart, each student, with assistance from the teacher, can make important decisions about his or her progress. The tracking chart should have the following features:

1. The extended curved line is drawn just before the day measurement begins. The specific objective is written along the curved line to show what is being measured (e.g., Say Unit One Words).

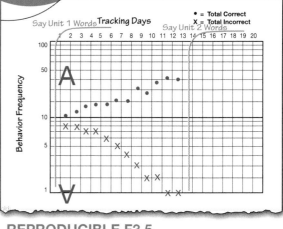

REPRODUCIBLE F3.5

NOTE:
Certain circumstances may warrant a decision to move on to another unit objective before the student has achieved the current one.

2. A large capital A (representing the aim or goal) is drawn on the chart. The bar of the A crosses at the level at which you expect the student to be performing (i.e., correct responses) after several weeks of instruction. An inverted A can also be placed on the chart to show the level of incorrect responses at which you expect the student to be performing after several weeks of instruction.

3. Students record their performance after each probe by marking their correct/appropriate score with a ● and their incorrect/inappropriate score with an **X**.

4. When the student's ●'s and **X**'s reach the goal level for at least two consecutive days, another curved line can be drawn on the chart to show that measurement begins for a new objective.

Source: *Beck, 1976.*

F3.6 GOAL SETTING

MATERIALS PREP ✂

GRADE LEVELS:
3–8

INTERVENTION TYPE:
Academic—All

REPRODUCIBLE on CD

Assist students in setting performance goals for themselves that are beyond their present level of performance.

Do this by letting them know how they are currently doing and explaining how to select a reasonable goal. Help students decide if they need to work on daily, weekly, or monthly goals. Then have students write goals and action steps that will help them to achieve each goal. In addition, discuss how the students can be rewarded if the goal is met. Require students to complete periodic progress reports related to their goal by charting the information or keeping anecdotal reports.

REPRODUCIBLE F3.6

T G I F

F3.7 PERFORMANCE CHOICES

MATERIALS PREP ✂

GRADE LEVELS:
4–8

INTERVENTION TYPE:
Academic—All

This choice sheet allows students to make choices about the work they will do and provides feedback on their progress throughout the unit.

At the beginning of every unit, pass out a sheet similar to the one in the illustration. Have each student fill out the sheet and turn it in for approval. Have students review the sheet throughout the unit to monitor the completion of activities and their performance.

Name Latrice   **Date** 5/16

I will do five of following to show I understand the material in Chapter <u>14</u>
(Everyone must complete the circled items.)

_____ 1. Design a PowerPoint presentation of the key concepts.

✔ 2. Write a summary of each of the major points and answer the questions at the end of the chapter.

_____ 3. Give a five-minute oral report on _____

✔ 4. Discuss the major points with two peers over a voice recorder.

✔ 5. Complete <u>4</u> out of <u>5</u> worksheets.

✔ 6. Take the final test.

✔ 7. Complete a notebook of major facts.

_____ 8. Another option approved by the teacher.

F₄

FINAL MEASUREMENT

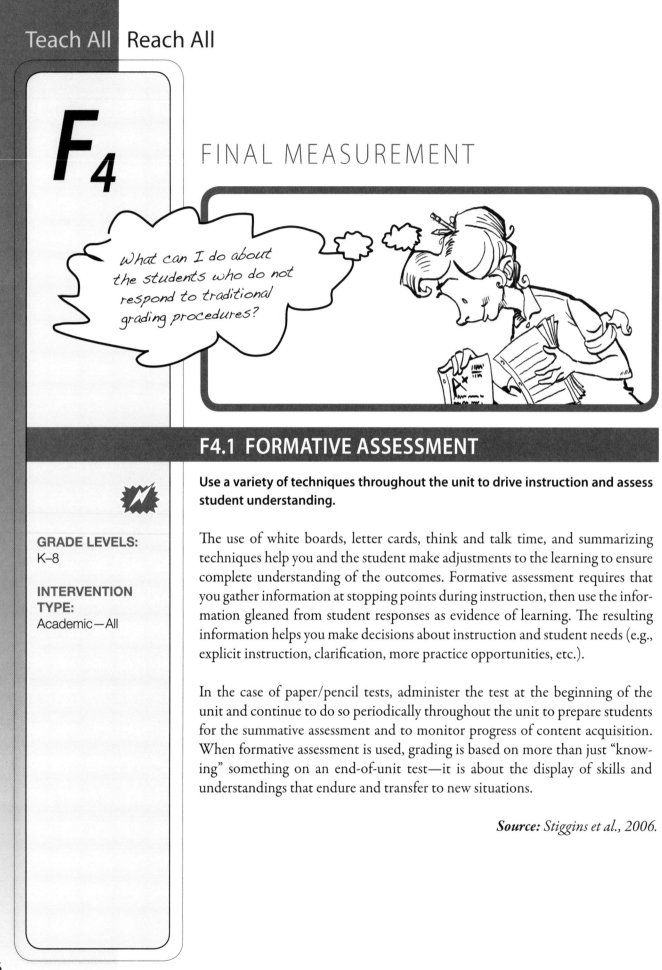

What can I do about the students who do not respond to traditional grading procedures?

F4.1 FORMATIVE ASSESSMENT

GRADE LEVELS:
K–8

INTERVENTION TYPE:
Academic—All

Use a variety of techniques throughout the unit to drive instruction and assess student understanding.

The use of white boards, letter cards, think and talk time, and summarizing techniques help you and the student make adjustments to the learning to ensure complete understanding of the outcomes. Formative assessment requires that you gather information at stopping points during instruction, then use the information gleaned from student responses as evidence of learning. The resulting information helps you make decisions about instruction and student needs (e.g., explicit instruction, clarification, more practice opportunities, etc.).

In the case of paper/pencil tests, administer the test at the beginning of the unit and continue to do so periodically throughout the unit to prepare students for the summative assessment and to monitor progress of content acquisition. When formative assessment is used, grading is based on more than just "knowing" something on an end-of-unit test—it is about the display of skills and understandings that endure and transfer to new situations.

Source: *Stiggins et al., 2006.*

F4.2 CODED GRADING

GRADE LEVELS:
3–8

INTERVENTION TYPE:
Academic—All

Coded grading uses three levels (A1, A2, A3, B1, B2, B3, etc.) within each of the standard letter grades.

The numbers assigned to each letter grade could represent the following:

1 = based on use of **above** grade-level material or **advanced** competencies.

2 = based on use of **on** grade-level material or **minimal** competencies.

3 = based on use of **below** grade-level material or **adapted** competencies.

EXAMPLE

Awarding a student an A1 indicates that the student earned a standard grade of A using material above the student's actual grade-level placement. A grade of C3 would indicate that the student earned a standard grade of C using material below the student's actual grade level.

Source: DeBoer, 1994.

F4.3 ASTERISK GRADING

GRADE LEVELS:
K–8

INTERVENTION TYPE:
Academic—All

Letter grades are awarded to students and may include an asterisk. An asterisk indicates that certain accommodations were made in order to meet the needs of that student.

The specific accommodations used for a particular student are indicated by marking the appropriate items on a checklist (see illustration below for example) that is attached to the report card.

Accommodation Checklist	
✔	Test read to the student.
	Student dictated answers to teacher/another student.
	Tests explained in detail/reviewed prior to taking them.
	Materials audiotaped for the student.

T
G
I
F

	Materials videotaped for the student.
	Study guides/graphic organizers provided during lecture.
✔	Additional time provided for work/test completion.
	Instructional objectives prioritized and reduced.
	Instructional objectives adapted.

Source: Adapted from DeBoer, 1994.

F4.4 A/B/C/NOT YET

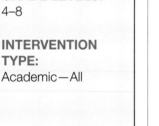

GRADE LEVELS:
4–8

INTERVENTION TYPE:
Academic—All

A/B/C/Not Yet (or Incomplete) is based on a mastery learning premise that all students will succeed.

If a student does not demonstrate minimal competency performance or above, a **Not Yet** is given and re-teaching is provided.

Source: DeBoer, 1994.

F4.5 DOUBLE GRADING

GRADE LEVELS:
3–8

INTERVENTION TYPE:
Academic—All

Double grading involves giving the student two grades, such as A/C or C/C. The first grade represents the student's learning over the instructional time period compared with their beginning performance. The second grade represents the student's performance compared with the performance of the entire class.

Source: DeBoer, 1994.

F4: What can I do about the students who do not respond to traditional grading procedures?

MATERIALS
PREP

GRADE LEVELS:
4–8

INTERVENTION TYPE:
Academic—All

F4.6 CHALLENGE GRADING

Challenge grading involves the assignment of differing point values on test questions (or other performance measures such as demonstrations, interviews, projects, portfolios, exhibits, etc.) based on their difficulty level.

EXAMPLES

The student has the option of answering:

- A group of ten easier questions/tasks valued at ten points each (total 100).

- A group of five slightly more difficult questions/tasks valued at 20 points each (total 100).

- A group of four more difficult questions/tasks valued at 25 points each (total 100).

- Two even more difficult questions/tasks valued at 50 points each (total 100).

- One very difficult question/task valued at 100 points.

The difficulty level of questions can be varied by modifying the question type (e.g., true/false, multiple choice, fill in the blank, short answer, essay, projects, etc.) and/or the level of cognition that is expected (e.g., list, define, compare, contrast, develop, evaluate, critique, etc.).

Source: DeBoer, 1994.

T
G
I
F

F4.7 CONTRACT GRADING

Grade contracts are formal arrangements that are negotiated between individual students and the teacher.

The students can be offered different options for demonstrating performance on the stated objectives or adapted objectives. Performance measures can include tests, demonstrations, interviews, projects, portfolios, exhibits, etc. An agreement should be reached that is acceptable to both you and the student (see illustration). A grading contract should include the following components:

1. The type of work to be completed by the student.

2. The quantity and quality of work to be completed.

3. The signatures of the teacher, student, and parent (when appropriate).

4. Timelines for the completion of work.

MATERIALS PREP

GRADE LEVELS:
4–8

INTERVENTION TYPE:
Academic—All

REPRODUCIBLE on CD

Teach All, Reach All

Contract Grading   Name: __Melinda_____

1. _Complete reading assignments_____

2. _____

3. _____

I agree to complete the following activities to demonstrate mastery of the above-stated objectives:

1. _Start homework with plenty of time._____

2. _Review regularly._____

3. _____

4. _____

REPRODUCIBLE F4.7

Teacher-Directed Instruction

T1 What can I do about the students who do not achieve the classroom goals and objectives?

T2 What can I do about the students who do not respond to my instructions?

T3 What can I do about the students who do not participate during my instruction?

T4 What can I do about the students who disrupt during my instruction?

T5 What can I do about the students who forget information that I presented yesterday, or a few hours ago?

T6 What can I do about the students who fail to see the relevance of my instruction?

T7 What can I do about the students who, following my instruction, do not understand or misgeneralize the concept?

T8 What can I do about the students who do not volunteer during my instruction?

T9 What can I do about the students who make hesitant responses or frequent errors during my instruction?

T10 What can I do about the students who have difficulty taking notes during my instruction?

T11 What can I do about the students who have a difficult time determining the critical information from my instruction?

T12 What can I do about the students who do not respond to my questions?

Guided Practice Activities

G1 What can I do about the students who do not begin or complete practice/seatwork activities?

G2 What can I do about the students who make careless errors when completing practice/seatwork activities?

G3 What can I do about the students who do not comprehend and/or respond to written material during practice/seatwork activities?

G4 What can I do about the students who do not work cooperatively, or rely on others to do the practice/seatwork activities?

G5 What can I do about the students who do not contribute to class discussions during practice activities?

Independent Practice Activities

I1 What can I do about the students who do not organize or manage assignments, materials, and/or time?

I2 What can I do about the students who do not complete or submit assignments?

I3 What can I do about the students who do not understand the independent assignment?

I4 What can I do about the students who do not check work for accuracy and/or completeness?

I5 What can I do about the students who do not know how to prepare for and/or study for a test?

Final Measurement

F1 What can I do about the students who do not perform well with traditional test formats?

F2 What can I do about the students who do not use strategies for taking a test?

F3 What can I do about the students who do not monitor work performance?

F4 What can I do about the students who do not respond to traditional grading procedures?

QUICK REFERENCE GUIDE

PREPARATION TIME

 Little Preparation Time

T1.1   Essential Questions......... 34
T1.2   Condition Shift 35
T1.3   Proficiency Shift 35
T1.4   Product Shift 36
T1.5   Ticket Out the Door 36
T2.1   Get Ready 40
T2.2   Listening Cues 41
T2.3   You-Me Game 41
T2.4   I Can Say It.............. 41
T3.1   Participation Board 46
T3.2   Participation Buddies 47
T4.1   Everybody Say 52
T4.2   Frequent Questions 53
T4.3   On-Task Chart 53
T4.4   Name's Up Listening
       Board 54
T5.1   Highlighting 58
T5.2   Recycling................. 59
T6.1   Rationale Questions 64
T6.2   Think and Say Why 64
T6.3   Share Your Reasons 65
T8.1   Group/Individual
       Questioning 80
T8.2   Responses Without
       Talking 80
T8.3   I Am Ready 81
T8.4   Please Come Back.......... 81
T8.5   Name's Up Volunteer
       Board 81
T9.1   Think About That 84
T9.2   All Talk Together 84
T9.3   Think, Pair, Share 85
T9.4   Formulate, Share, Listen,
       Create 85
T9.5   Prompts 85
T9.6   Prequestioning 86
T9.7   Please Come Back 86
T9.8   Rapid-Fire Questions 86
T9.9   Think and Say Ideas 87
T11.1 Defend Your Position 96
T11.2 Five-Minute Reviews 97
T12.1 Ask, Pause, Call 100
T12.2 Restate 101
T12.3 Pass for Now............. 101
T12.4 Consult 101
T12.5 All Together 102
T12.6 No Surprises 102
T12.7 Answer, Pair, Spotlight 103

G1.1   Effective Praise/
       Acknowledgment 106
G1.2   Think Out Loud 107
G1.3   Rationale Statements 107
G1.4   Alternating Buddies 108
G1.5   Strategic Skills 108
G1.6   Beat the Clock 108
G1.7   Assignment Questions 109
G1.8   Star Stickers 109
G1.9   Cut-Up 110
G1.10 Colored Pencils 110
G2.1   Color Coding 118
G2.2   Oral Reading Points 118
G3.1   Change the Channel 122
G3.2   Page Numbers 123
G3.3   Questions First 123
G3.4   Question/Instruction
       Repeat 123
G3.5   Listen, Write, Listen,
       Say 124
G4.1   Cooperation Keys......... 140
G4.2   Partner Board 140
G4.3   Step Out 141
G5.1   Huddle 150
G5.2   Write and Speak 150
G5.3   Signals 151
G5.4   Contribution Points 151
G5.5   Contribution Chips....... 151
G5.6   Pens in the Jar 152
I1.1   Assignment Buddies 158
I1.2   Think Out Loud 158
I2.1   Daily Checkout.......... 166
I2.2   Stop/Go Folders 167
I3.1   I Am Working/I Need
       Help Sign 176
I3.2   Ask Three Before Me 177
I3.3   The Fooler Game 177
I3.4   Emphasize Instructions.... 178
I3.5   Highlight Key Words 179
I4.1   Checking Station 184
I4.2   Write the Steps 184
F2.1   Confidence Building 214
F4.1   Formative Assessment 226
F4.2   Coded Grading 227
F4.3   Asterisk Grading......... 227
F4.4   A/B/C/Not Yet 228
F4.5   Double Grading 228

 More Preparation Time

T1.6   What Will I Do? Log....... 38
T1.7   Minimal/Advanced
       Competencies 39
T2.5   Following Instructions..... 42
T2.6   Buddy Nose (Knows)....... 43
T2.7   Behavior Bingo 43
T2.8   Yes/No Game............. 44
T2.9   Tracking Directions 44
T3.3   Participation Jigsaw 48
T3.4   Wild Card Spinner......... 48
T3.5   Participation Dots......... 49
T3.6   Mystery Motivators 50
T3.7   Participation Points 50
T4.5   Following Instructions...... 54
T4.6   Keeping the Numbers
       Low...................... 55
T4.7   Getting the Teacher's
       Attention................. 55
T4.8   Responsibility Roles........ 56
T4.9   Countoon 57
T5.3   Mnemonics............... 59
T5.4   Note Stacks.............. 60
T5.5   Memory Log.............. 61
T5.6   Study Guides (Standard).... 62
T5.7   Graphic Organizers
       (Top Down) 63
T6.4   What, Where/When, and
       Why Strategy 65
T6.5   Futures Map 67
T7.1   Positive and Negative
       Examples 68
T7.2   Strategies and Rules 71
T7.3   Corrective Feedback........ 72
T7.4   Concept Angles............ 73
T7.5   Plus, Minus, Interesting
       (PMI).................... 73
T7.6   I Question That! 74
T7.7   Know/Want to Know/
       Learned (KWL)............ 74
T7.8   Learning Logs 75
T7.9   Study Guides (Margins) 76
T7.10 Graphic Organizers
       (Sequence) 77
T7.11 Attribute Maps 78
T8.6   Heads Together 82
T8.7   Folded Corners 83
T8.8   Draw-a-Name............. 83
T9.10 Up the Numbers 87
T9.11 Corrective Feedback........ 87

T9.12 Question Challenge 88
T10.1 Buddy Notes................ 90
T10.2 Four-Fold 90
T10.3 Index Cards................. 91
T10.4 Slotted Outline 92
T10.5 LITES 92
T10.6 Note Checks................ 93
T10.7 Cooperative Notes 94
T10.8 Graphic Organizers
       (Partial) 95
T11.3 Advance Organizers 97
T11.4 Think and Write
       Questions 98
T11.5 Presentation Cues 99
T12.8 Clarification 103
T12.9 Draw-a-Name............. 104
T12.10 Counting Responses....... 104
G1.11 Split the Assignment 111
G1.12 Change the Channel 111
G1.13 Slice Back 112
G1.14 Behavior Bingo 112
G1.15 Design Your Own Assignmt 113
G1.16 Assignment Aims 113
G1.17 Completion Dots 114
G1.18 Ask for Help.............. 114
G1.19 Start/Stop Time 115
G1.20 Monitoring Seatwork...... 116
G2.3 Stop and Switch........... 119
G2.4 Self-Check and Count..... 120
G2.5 Magic Pens 121
G3.6 Key Words 124
G3.7 I Am Ready to Find
      Out..................... 126
G3.8 What Is the Main Idea?.... 126
G3.9 Mark and Say Main Idea ... 127
G3.10 Answer Experts 127
G3.11 Add It Up 128
G3.12 Step-by-Step 128
G3.13 Overlapping Circles 129
G3.14 Cause/Effect.............. 129
G3.15 Star Book Report 130
G3.16 Herringbone............. 130
G3.17 Comprehension Wheels ... 131
G3.18 Story Charts............. 132
G3.19 Know/Do Not Know 132
G3.20 Comprehension
       Outlines................. 133
G3.21 Practice Sheets/Cards 133
G3.22 Stop and Think 135
G3.23 Students Ask Questions ... 135
G3.24 Study Guides (Prompts) ... 136
G3.25 Graphic Organizers 137

G3.26 SR.I.SRV (Scanning) 138
G3.27 SQ3R Worksheets......... 139
G4.4 Team Skills 141
G4.5 Role Cards 142
G4.6 Reflection Cards 144
G4.7 Assignment Co-Op 144
G4.8 Processing 145
G4.9 Classwide Peer Tutoring ... 146
G4.10 Team-Building Exercises ... 148
G5.7 Corners 152
G5.8 Graffiti Papers 153
G5.9 Inside/Outside Circle 153
G5.10 Making a Contribution 154
G5.11 Pair Interviews............ 154
G5.12 Contribution Aims........ 155
G5.13 S.M.A.R.T.S. Review 156
I1.3 Mystery Motivators 159
I1.4 Am I Working? 159
I1.5 Make the GRADE 160
I1.6 Assignment Initials........ 160
I1.7 Assignment Banking 161
I1.8 Organization Cards 162
I1.9 Assignment Log........... 162
I1.10 Time Management
      Charts 163
I1.11 Self-Management 163
I1.12 Parent Partners............ 164
I1.13 Assignment Notebooks.... 165
I2.3 Home/School Talk........ 167
I2.4 Home/School Folders 168
I2.5 Homework Tracking
      Charts 168
I2.6 Hit the Homework Target . 169
I2.7 Homework Teams......... 170
I2.8 Self-Graphing Charts...... 172
I2.9 Assignment Contracts 172
I2.10 Fill in the Dots........... 173
I2.11 Assignment Champion
      Notebook 173
I2.12 How Do I Rate? 174
I3.6 Key Words Mean.......... 179
I3.7 Getting the Help I Need ... 181
I3.8 Map the Instructions 181
I3.9 Instruction Cards (What,
      How, When/Where, Why) 182
I3.10 Group Roles.............. 182
I3.11 Independent Work
      Buddies 183
I4.3 Checking and
      Completing.............. 185
I4.4 Proofing Skills 185

I4.5 Count Corrects and
     Errors 187
I4.6 Accuracy Aims............ 188
I4.7 Challenge the Time 188
I4.8 Check-Off List............ 188
I4.9 Partners Plus.............. 189
I5.1 Test Study Sheet 190
I5.2 TERM 191
I5.3 Study Scheduling 191
I5.4 Review Guides............ 192
I5.5 Study Checklists 193
I5.6 Active Reading............ 194
I5.7 PREPARE................ 194
I5.8 Write About 195
I5.9 Information Coding........ 195
I5.10 Map It Out 196
I5.11 Practice Sheets 197
F1.1 70/30 Splits 200
F1.2 Word Probes.............. 202
F1.3 Oral Passage Probes 204
F1.4 Comprehension Probes.... 206
F1.5 Written Expression
     Probes................... 207
F1.6 Math Probes.............. 208
F1.7 Social Skills Probes........ 210
F1.8 Content Area/Functional
     Skills Probes 212
F2.2 Test-Taking Awareness..... 215
F2.3 Knowing the Question 215
F2.4 Post-Test Checklist........ 217
F2.5 Math Problem Solving..... 217
F2.6 RIDGES 218
F2.7 PIRATES 219
F3.1 Performance Tracking
     Sheets................... 220
F3.2 Performance Conference... 221
F3.3 Performance Checkouts ... 221
F3.4 Performance Journal....... 222
F3.5 Charting 222
F3.6 Goal Setting 223
F3.7 Performance Choices...... 224
F4.6 Challenge Grading........ 229
F4.7 Contract Grading........ 230

QUICK REFERENCE GUIDE

GRADE LEVELS

GRADES K–8

T1.1 Essential Questions......... 34
T1.2 Condition Shift........... 35
T1.3 Proficiency Shift 35
T1.4 Product Shift 36
T1.5 Ticket Out the Door 36
T2.1 Get Ready 40
T2.4 I Can Say It 41
T2.5 Following Instructions...... 42
T3.1 Participation Board........ 46
T3.2 Participation Buddies....... 47
T3.3 Participation Jigsaw 48
T3.4 Wild Card Spinner......... 48
T3.6 Mystery Motivators 50
T4.1 Everybody Say 52
T4.2 Frequent Questions 53
T4.5 Following Instructions...... 54
T4.6 Keeping the Numbers
      Low..................... 55
T4.7 Getting the Teacher's
      Attention................. 55
T4.8 Responsibility Roles........ 56
T4.9 Countoon 57
T5.2 Recycling................. 59
T5.3 Mnemonics................ 59
T5.7 Graphic Organizers
      (Top Down) 63
T6.1 Rationale Questions........ 64
T6.2 Think and Say Why 64
T6.3 Share Your Reasons......... 65
T7.1 Positive and Negative
      Examples 68
T7.2 Strategies and Rules 71
T7.3 Corrective Feedback........ 72
T7.4 Concept Angles............ 73
T7.5 Plus, Minus, Interesting
      (PMI).................... 73
T7.7 Know/Want to Know/
      Learned (KWL)............ 74
T8.1 Group/Individual
      Questioning 80
T8.2 Responses Without
      Talking.................. 80
T8.3 I Am Ready................ 81
T8.4 Please Come Back......... 81
T8.6 Heads Together 82
T8.7 Folded Corners 83
T8.8 Draw-a-Name............. 83
T9.1 Think About That......... 84
T9.2 All Talk Together 84

T9.3 Think, Pair, Share 85
T9.5 Prompts................... 85
T9.6 Prequestioning............. 86
T9.7 Please Come Back......... 86
T9.8 Rapid-Fire Questions........ 86
T9.9 Think and Say Ideas 87
T9.10 Up the Numbers 87
T9.11 Corrective Feedback........ 87
T9.12 Question Challenge 88
T10.8 Graphic Organizers
      (Partial) 95
T12.1 Ask, Pause, Call 100
T12.2 Restate 101
T12.3 Pass for Now............... 101
T12.5 All Together 102
T12.7 Answer, Pair, Spotlight 103
T12.8 Clarification 103
T12.9 Draw-a-Name............... 104
T12.10 Counting Responses........ 104
G1.1 Effective Praise/
      Acknowledgment 106
G1.2 Think Out Loud 107
G1.3 Rationale Statements 107
G1.6 Beat the Clock 108
G1.12 Change the Channel 111
G1.13 Slice Back 112
G1.14 Behavior Bingo 112
G1.17 Completion DOTS 114
G1.18 Ask for Help............. 114
G1.19 Start/Stop Time 115
G1.20 Monitoring Seatwork...... 116
G2.1 Color Coding............. 118
G2.2 Oral Reading Points....... 118
G2.5 Magic Pens 121
G3.1 Change the Channel 122
G3.4 Question/Instruction
      Repeat 123
G3.8 What Is the Main Idea?.... 126
G3.20 Comprehension
      Outlines.................. 133
G3.21 Practice Sheets/Cards 133
G4.1 Cooperation Keys........ 140
G4.3 Step Out 141
G4.5 Role Cards 142
G4.8 Processing 145
G4.9 Classwide Peer Tutoring ... 146
G4.10 Team-Building Exercises ... 148
G5.3 Signals 151
G5.4 Contribution Points 151
G5.5 Contribution Chips 151
G5.6 Pens in the Jar........... 152
G5.7 Corners 152

G5.12 Contribution Aims........ 155
I1.2 Think Out Loud 158
I1.3 Mystery Motivators 159
I1.4 Am I Working? 159
I1.11 Self-Management 163
I1.12 Parent Partners........... 164
I2.2 Stop/Go Folders 167
I2.3 Home/School Talk........ 167
I2.4 Home/School Folders 168
I2.12 How Do I Rate? 174
I3.2 Ask Three Before Me 177
I3.3 The Fooler Game......... 177
I3.7 Getting the Help I Need ... 181
I4.7 Challenge the Time 188
F1.1 70/30 Splits 200
F1.7 Social Skills Probes........ 210
F1.8 Content Area/Functional
      Skills Probes 212
F4.1 Formative Assessment 226
F4.3 Asterisk Grading.......... 227

GRADES K–6

T2.2 Listening Cues............. 41
T2.3 You-Me Game 41
T2.6 Buddy Nose (Knows)....... 43
T3.5 Participation Dots......... 49
T4.4 Name's Up Listening
      Board 54
T8.5 Name's Up Volunteer
      Board 81
G1.8 Star Stickers 109
G1.9 Cut-Up.................. 110
G4.2 Partner Board............. 140
I2.10 Fill in the Dots........... 173
I3.1 I Am Working/I Need
      Help Sign 176
F1.2 Word Probes............. 202

GRADES 3–8

T1.6 What Will I Do? Log....... 38
T2.7 Behavior Bingo 43
T2.8 Yes/No Game............. 44
T2.9 Tracking Directions 44
T3.7 Participation Points 50
T4.3 On-Task Chart........... 53
T5.4 Note Stacks............. 60
T5.5 Memory Log............. 61
T7.6 I Question That!.......... 74

T7.8   Learning Logs 75
T7.9   Study Guides (Margins) 76
T7.10   Graphic Organizers
            (Sequence) 77
T7.11   Attribute Maps 78
T9.4   Formulate, Share, Listen,
            Create..................... 85
T10.4   Slotted Outline 92
T11.1   Defend Your Position....... 96
T11.2   Five-Minute Reviews 97
T11.3   Advance Organizers 97
T12.4   Consult 101
T12.6   No Surprises 102
G1.4   Alternating Buddies 108
G1.5   Strategic Skills 108
G1.10   Colored Pencils 110
G1.11   Split the Assignment 111
G1.16   Assignment Aims 113
G2.3   Stop and Switch........... 119
G2.4   Self-Check and Count..... 120
G3.2   Page Numbers 123
G3.3   Questions First............ 123
G3.5   Listen, Write, Listen,
            Say....................... 124
G3.6   Key Words 124
G3.11   Add It Up 128
G3.12   Step-by-Step 128
G3.13   Overlapping Circles 129
G3.14   Cause/Effect.............. 129
G3.15   Star Book Report 130
G3.16   Herringbone.............. 130
G3.17   Comprehension Wheels ... 131
G3.18   Story Charts.............. 132
G3.19   Know/Do Not Know 132
G3.25   Graphic Organizers 137
G4.4   Team Skills 141
G4.6   Reflection Cards 144
G4.7   Assignment Co-Op 144
G5.1   Huddle................... 150
G5.8   Graffiti Papers 153
G5.9   Inside/Outside Circle 153
G5.10   Making a Contribution 154
G5.11   Pair Interviews............ 154
I1.1   Assignment Buddies....... 158
I1.5   Make the GRADE 160
I1.6   Assignment Initials........ 160
I1.7   Assignment Banking 161
I2.1   Daily Checkout 166
I2.5   Homework Tracking
            Charts 168
I2.6   Hit the Homework
            Target.................... 169

I2.7   Homework Teams......... 170
I2.8   Self-Graphing Charts...... 172
I2.11   Assignment Champion
            Notebook 173
I3.4   Emphasize Instructions 178
I4.1   Checking Station.......... 184
I4.2   Write the Steps............ 184
I4.3   Checking and
            Completing............... 185
I4.4   Proofing Skills 185
I4.5   Count Corrects and
            Errors 187
I4.6   Accuracy Aims............ 188
I4.9   Partners Plus.............. 189
I5.3   Study Scheduling 191
I5.4   Review Guides............ 192
I5.5   Study Checklists 193
I5.6   Active Reading............ 194
I5.8   Write About 195
I5.10   Map It Out 196
I5.11   Practice Sheets 197
F1.3   Oral Passage Probes 204
F1.4   Comprehension Probes.... 206
F1.6   Math Probes 208
F2.1   Confidence Building 214
F2.2   Test-Taking Awareness..... 215
F2.3   Knowing the Question 215
F2.5   Math Problem Solving..... 217
F3.1   Performance Tracking
            Sheets.................... 220
F3.2   Performance
            Conference................ 221
F3.3   Performance Checkouts ... 221
F3.5   Charting 222
F3.6   Goal Setting 223
F4.2   Coded Grading 227
F4.5   Double Grading 228

GRADES 4–8

T1.7   Minimal/Advanced
            Competencies 39
T5.1   Highlighting............... 58
T5.6   Study Guides (Standard).... 62
T6.4   What, Where/When, and
            Why Strategy 65
T6.5   Futures Map 67
T10.1   Buddy Notes............... 90
T10.2   Four-Fold 90
T10.3   Index Cards............... 91
T10.5   LITES 92

T10.6   Note Checks............... 93
T10.7   Cooperative Notes 94
T11.4   Think and Write
            Questions 98
T11.5   Presentation Cues 99
G1.7   Assignment Questions..... 109
G1.15   Design Your Own Assignmt 113
G3.7   I Am Ready to Find Out ... 126
G3.9   Mark and Say Main Idea ... 127
G3.10   Answer Experts 127
G3.22   Stop and Think 135
G3.23   Students Ask Questions ... 135
G3.24   Study Guides (Prompts) ... 136
G3.26   SR.I.SRV (Scanning)...... 138
G3.27   SQ3R Worksheets......... 139
G5.2   Write and Speak 150
G5.13   S.M.A.R.T.S. Review 156
I1.8   Organization Cards 162
I1.9   Assignment Log........... 162
I1.10   Time Management
            Charts 163
I1.13   Assignment Notebooks.... 165
I2.9   Assignment Contracts 172
I3.5   Highlight Key Words...... 179
I3.6   Key Words Mean.......... 179
I3.8   Map the Instructions 181
I3.9   Instruction Cards (What,
            How, When/Where,
            Why) 182
I3.10   Group Roles 182
I3.11   Independent Work
            Buddies 183
I4.8   Check-Off List............ 188
I5.1   Test Study Sheet 190
I5.2   TERM.................... 191
I5.7   PREPARE................ 194
I5.9   Information Coding....... 195
F1.5   Written Expression
            Probes.................... 207
F2.4   Post-Test Checklist........ 217
F2.6   RIDGES 218
F2.7   PIRATES 219
F3.4   Performance Journal....... 222
F3.7   Performance Choices...... 224
F4.4   A/B/C/Not Yet........... 228
F4.6   Challenge Grading........ 229
F4.7   Contract Grading........ 230

INTERVENTION TYPE

Academic—All

T1.1 Essential Questions......... 34
T1.2 Condition Shift............ 35
T1.3 Proficiency Shift 35
T1.4 Product Shift 36
T1.5 Ticket Out the Door 36
T1.6 What Will I Do? Log....... 38
T1.7 Minimal/Advanced
     Competencies 39
T2.1 Get Ready 40
T2.2 Listening Cues............. 41
T2.3 You-Me Game 41
T2.4 I Can Say It 41
T2.5 Following Instructions...... 42
T2.6 Buddy Nose (Knows)....... 43
T2.7 Behavior Bingo 43
T2.8 Yes/No Game.............. 44
T2.9 Tracking Directions 44
T4.1 Everybody Say 52
T4.2 Frequent Questions 53
T5.1 Highlighting.............. 58
T5.2 Recycling................. 59
T5.3 Mnemonics............... 59
T5.4 Note Stacks............... 60
T5.5 Memory Log............... 61
T5.6 Study Guides
     (Standard)................. 62
T5.7 Graphic Organizers
     (Top Down) 63
T6.1 Rationale Questions........ 64
T6.2 Think and Say Why 64
T6.3 Share Your Reasons........ 65
T6.4 What, Where/When, and
     Why Strategy 65
T6.5 Futures Map 67
T7.1 Positive and Negative
     Examples 68
T7.2 Strategies and Rules 71
T7.4 Concept Angles........... 73
T7.5 Plus, Minus, Interesting
     (PMI).................... 73
T7.6 I Question That! 74
T7.7 Know/Want to Know/
     Learned (KWL)........... 74
T7.8 Learning Logs 75
T7.9 Study Guides (Margins) 76
T7.10 Graphic Organizers
     (Sequence) 77
T7.11 Attribute Maps 78
T8.1 Group/Individual
     Questioning 80
T8.2 Responses Without
     Talking.................. 80

T8.3 I Am Ready................ 81
T8.4 Please Come Back.......... 81
T8.5 Name's Up Volunteer
     Board 81
T8.6 Heads Together 82
T8.7 Folded Corners 83
T8.8 Draw-a-Name............. 83
T9.1 Think About That........ 84
T9.2 All Talk Together 84
T9.3 Think, Pair, Share 85
T9.4 Formulate, Share, Listen,
     Create................... 85
T9.5 Prompts................. 85
T9.6 Prequestioning........... 86
T9.7 Please Come Back......... 86
T9.8 Rapid-Fire Questions...... 86
T9.9 Think and Say Ideas 87
T10.1 Buddy Notes............. 90
T10.2 Four-Fold 90
T10.3 Index Cards............. 91
T10.4 Slotted Outline 92
T10.5 LITES 92
T10.6 Note Checks............. 93
T10.7 Cooperative Notes 94
T10.8 Graphic Organizers
     (Partial) 95
T11.1 Defend Your Position....... 96
T11.2 Five-Minute Reviews 97
T11.3 Advance Organizers........ 97
T11.4 Think and Write
     Questions 98
T11.5 Presentation Cues.......... 99
T12.1 Ask, Pause, Call 100
T12.2 Restate 101
T12.3 Pass for Now............. 101
T12.4 Consult 101
T12.5 All Together 102
T12.6 No Surprises 102
T12.7 Answer, Pair, Spotlight 103
T12.9 Draw-a-Name............ 104
G1.2 Think Out Loud 107
G1.3 Rationale Statements 107
G1.4 Alternating Buddies 108
G1.5 Strategic Skills 108
G1.7 Assignment Questions..... 109
G1.8 Star Stickers 109
G1.9 Cut-Up................. 110
G1.10 Colored Pencils 110
G1.12 Change the Channel 111
G1.13 Slice Back 112
G1.15 Design Your Own Assignmt 113
G2.4 Self-Check and Count..... 120
G2.5 Magic Pens 121
G3.1 Change the Channel 122
G3.2 Page Numbers 123
G3.3 Questions First.......... 123

G3.4 Question/Instruction
     Repeat 123
G3.5 Listen, Write, Listen, Say... 124
G3.6 Key Words 124
G3.7 I Am Ready to Find
     Out..................... 126
G3.8 What Is the Main Idea?.... 126
G3.9 Mark and Say Main Idea ... 127
G3.10 Answer Experts 127
G3.12 Step-by-Step 128
G3.13 Overlapping Circles 129
G3.14 Cause/Effect............. 129
G3.15 Star Book Report 130
G3.16 Herringbone............. 130
G3.17 Comprehension Wheels ... 131
G3.18 Story Charts............. 132
G3.19 Know/Do Not Know 132
G3.20 Comprehension
     Outlines................. 133
G3.21 Practice Sheets/Cards 133
G3.22 Stop and Think 135
G3.23 Students Ask Questions ... 135
G3.24 Study Guides (Prompts) ... 136
G3.25 Graphic Organizers 137
G3.26 SR.I.SRV (Scanning)..... 138
G3.27 SQ3R Worksheets........ 139
G4.5 Role Cards 142
G4.7 Assignment Co-Op 144
G4.9 Classwide Peer Tutoring ... 146
G5.1 Huddle.................. 150
G5.2 Write and Speak 150
G5.3 Signals 151
G5.4 Contribution Points....... 151
G5.5 Contribution Chips 151
G5.6 Pens in the Jar........... 152
G5.7 Corners 152
G5.8 Graffiti Papers 153
G5.9 Inside/Outside Circle 153
G5.10 Making a Contribution 154
G5.11 Pair Interviews........... 154
G5.13 S.M.A.R.T.S. Review 156
I1.1 Assignment Buddies....... 158
I1.2 Think Out Loud 158
I1.5 Make the GRADE 160
I3.5 Highlight Key Words...... 179
I3.6 Key Words Mean......... 179
I3.8 Map the Instructions 181
I3.9 Instruction Cards 182
I4.1 Checking Station......... 184
I4.2 Write the Steps.......... 184
I4.3 Checking and
     Completing............... 185
I4.4 Proofing Skills 185
I4.5 Count Corrects and
     Errors 187
I4.6 Accuracy Aims........... 188

I4.7   Challenge the Time 188
I4.9   Partners Plus.............. 189
I5.1   Test Study Sheet 190
I5.2   TERM 191
I5.3   Study Scheduling 191
I5.4   Review Guides............ 192
I5.5   Study Checklists 193
I5.6   Active Reading........... 194
I5.7   PREPARE................ 194
I5.8   Write About.............. 195
I5.9   Information Coding....... 195
I5.10   Map It Out 196
I5.11   Practice Sheets 197
F1.1   70/30 Splits 200
F1.2   Word Probes.............. 202
F1.3   Oral Passage Probes 204
F1.4   Comprehension Probes.... 206
F1.5   Written Expression
       Probes.................. 207
F1.6   Math Probes.............. 208
F1.7   Social Skills Probes 210
F1.8   Content Area/Functional
       Skills Probes 212
F2.1   Confidence Building 214
F2.2   Test-Taking Awareness..... 215
F2.3   Knowing the Question 215
F2.4   Post-Test Checklist 217
F2.7   PIRATES 219
F3.1   Performance Tracking
       Sheets................... 220
F3.2   Performance Conference... 221
F3.3   Performance Checkouts ... 221
F3.4   Performance Journal....... 222
F3.5   Charting 222
F3.6   Goal Setting 223
F3.7   Performance Choices...... 224
F4.1   Formative Assessment 226
F4.2   Coded Grading 227
F4.3   Asterisk Grading.......... 227
F4.4   A/B/C/Not Yet.......... 228
F4.5   Double Grading 228
F4.6   Challenge Grading........ 229
F4.7   Contract Grading......... 230

Academic—ELA
G3.11   Add It Up 128

Academic—Math
G2.3   Stop and Switch.......... 119
F2.5   Math Problem Solving..... 217
F2.6   RIDGES 218

Academic—Reading
G2.1   Color Coding............. 118
G2.2   Oral Reading Points 118
G2.3   Stop and Switch 119

Behavior—Motivation
T1.5   Ticket Out the Door 36
T2.1   Get Ready 40
T2.2   Listening Cues............. 41
T2.3   You-Me Game 41
T2.4   I Can Say It 41
T2.5   Following Instructions...... 42
T2.6   Buddy Nose (Knows)....... 43
T2.7   Behavior Bingo 43
T2.8   Yes/No Game............. 44
T2.9   Tracking Directions 44
T3.1   Participation Board........ 46
T3.2   Participation Buddies....... 47
T3.3   Participation Jigsaw 48
T3.4   Wild Card Spinner 48
T3.5   Participation Dots......... 49
T3.6   Mystery Motivators 50
T3.7   Participation Points 50
T4.3   On-Task Chart............ 53
T4.4   Name's Up Listening
       Board 54
T4.6   Keeping the Numbers
       Low..................... 55
T4.9   Countoon 57
T9.10   Up the Numbers 87
T12.10 Counting Responses....... 104
G1.6   Beat the Clock 108
G1.8   Star Stickers 109
G1.9   Cut-Up.................. 110
G1.10   Colored Pencils 110
G1.11   Split the Assignment 111
G1.14   Behavior Bingo 112
G1.16   Assignment Aims 113
G1.17   Completion Dots 114
G1.19   Start/Stop Time 115
G1.20   Monitoring Seatwork...... 116
G2.4   Self-Check and Count..... 120
G2.5   Magic Pens 121
G4.3   Step Out 141
G5.1   Huddle.................. 150
G5.4   Contribution Points....... 151
G5.5   Contribution Chips 151
G5.6   Pens in the Jar............ 152
G5.10   Making a Contribution 154
G5.12   Contribution Aims........ 155
I1.1   Assignment Buddies....... 158
I1.3   Mystery Motivators 159
I1.4   Am I Working? 159
I1.5   Make the GRADE 160
I1.6   Assignment Initials 160
I1.7   Assignment Banking 161
I1.8   Organization Cards 162
I1.9   Assignment Log.......... 162
I1.10   Time Management
       Charts 163
I1.11   Self-Management 163

I1.12   Parent Partners............ 164
I1.13   Assignment Notebooks.... 165
I2.1   Daily Checkout 166
I2.2   Stop/Go Folders 167
I2.3   Home/School Talk........ 167
I2.4   Home/School Folders 168
I2.5   Homework Tracking
       Charts 168
I2.6   Hit the Homework
       Target................... 169
I2.7   Homework Teams......... 170
I2.8   Self-Graphing Charts...... 172
I2.9   Assignment Contracts 172
I2.10   Fill in the Dots.......... 173
I2.11   Assignment Champion
       Notebook 173
I2.12   How Do I Rate? 174
I3.1   I Am Working/I Need
       Help Sign 176
I3.3   The Fooler Game.......... 177
I3.4   Emphasize Instructions.... 178
I3.11   Independent Work
       Buddies 183
I4.8   Check-Off List........... 188

Behavior—Social
T4.5   Following Instructions...... 54
T4.7   Getting the Teacher's
       Attention................. 55
T4.8   Responsibility Roles........ 56
T7.3   Corrective Feedback........ 72
T9.11   Corrective Feedback........ 87
T9.12   Question Challenge 88
T12.8   Clarification 103
G1.1   Effective Praise/
       Acknowledgment 106
G1.18   Ask for Help.............. 114
G4.2   Partner Board............. 140
G4.3   Step Out 141
G4.5   Role Cards 142
G4.6   Reflection Cards 144
G4.7   Assignment Co-Op 144
G4.8   Processing 145
G4.9   Classwide Peer Tutoring ... 146
I1.10   Time Management
       Charts 163
I3.2   Ask Three Before Me 177
I3.7   Getting the Help I Need... 181
I3.10   Group Roles.............. 182

Behavior—Social Development
G4.1   Cooperation Keys........ 140
G4.4   Team Skills 141
G4.10   Team-Building Exercises ... 148

Archer, A., & Gleason, M. (1989). *Skills for school success*. North Billerica, MA: Curriculum Associates.

Beck, R. (1976). *Precision teaching in review, 1973–1976*. Great Falls, MT: Great Falls Public Schools.

Beck, R. (1990). *Project RIDE: Responding to individual differences in education*. Longmont, CO: Sopris West.

Beck, R. (1993). *Project RIDE for preschoolers*. Longmont, CO: Sopris West.

Bellanca, J., & Fogarty, R. (1991). *Blueprints for thinking in the cooperative classroom*. Palatine, IL: IRI/Sky Light.

Bennett, B., Rolheiser-Bennett, C., & Stevahn, L. (1991). *Cooperative learning: Where heart meets mind*. Toronto, Canada: Educational Connections.

Bos, C., & Vaughn, S. (1988). *Strategies for teaching students with learning and behavior problems*. Boston: Allyn and Bacon.

Bost, L. W., & Riccomini, P. J. (2006). Effective instruction: An inconspicuous strategy for dropout prevention. *Remedial and Special Education, 27*(5), 301–311.

Buchanan, L. (1994, April). *No one is as smart as all of us*. Presentation conducted at International Council for Exceptional Children, Denver.

Carnine, D., Silbert, J., & Kame'enui, E. (1990). *Direct instruction reading* (2nd ed.). New York: Macmillian.

DeBoer, A. (1994). *Grading alternatives*. Presentation conducted at Project TIDE Training, Myrtle Beach, South Carolina.

Deshler, D., Schumaker, J., & Nagel, D. (1986). *Learning strategies curriculum: The FIRST strategy*. Lawrence, KS: University of Kansas.

Fister-Mulkey, S. L., Conrad, A.D., & Kemp, K. A. (1998). *Cool kids*. Longmont, CO: Sopris West.

Frost, T. (1987). *TERM: A test preparation strategy for mildly handicapped secondary students*. Unpublished master's thesis, Utah State University, Logan, Utah.

Gable, R., Evans, S., & Evans, W. (1993). It's not over until you examine our answer. *Teaching Exceptional Children, 25*(2), 61–62.

Gibbs, J. (1987). *Tribes: A process for social development and cooperative learning*. Santa Rosa, CA: Center Source Publications.

Greene, L., & Jones-Bamman, L. (1985). *Getting smarter.* Belmont, CA: Lake Publishers.

Hall, T. (2004). *Explicit instruction.* Retrieved September 1, 2008, from http://udl.cast.org/ncac/ ExplicitInstruction2875.cfm.

Harmin, M. (1995). *Strategies to inspire active learning: Complete handbook.* Norwood, MA: Christopher-gordon Publishers

Hart, A., 1993. *Human brain and human learning.* Upper Saddle River, NJ: Longman Publishing Group.

Howell, K. W., Fox, S. L., & Morehead, M. K. (1993). *Curriculum-based evaluation* (2nd ed.). Pacific Grove, CA: Brooks/Cole Publishing.

Hughes, C. A., Ruhl, K. L., & Peterson, S. K. (1988). Teaching self-management skills. *Teaching Exceptional Children, 20*(2), 70–72.

Jenson, W. R., Andrews, D., & Reavis, K. (1993, Fall). Intervention corner, the "yes" and "no" bag. *The BEST Times,* p. 3.

Jenson, W. R, Rhode, G., & Reavis, H. K. (1994). *The tough kid toolbox.* Longmont, CO: Sopris West.

Johnson, D. W., Johnson, R. T., & Bartlett, J. K. (1990). *Cooperative learning lesson structures.* Edina, MN: Interaction Book.

Johnson, R. T., Johnson, D. W., & Holubec, E. J. (Eds.). (1987). *Structuring cooperative learning: Lesson plans for teachers.* Edina, MN: Interaction Book.

Kagan, S. (1990). *Cooperative learning resources for teachers.* Mission Viejo, CA: Resources for Teachers.

Livingston, N. (1991, August). *Reading modifications.* Presentation at Chapter 1 Workshop, Duchesne, UT.

Lovitt, T. (1984). *Tactics for teaching.* Columbus, OH: Merrill.

Lovitt, T., Fister, S., Kemp, K., Moore, R. C., & Schroeder, B. E. (1992). *Translating research into practice (TRIP): Learning strategies.* Longmont, CO: Sopris West.

Marchand-Martella, N. E., Slocum, T. A., & Martella, R. C. (Eds.) (2004). *Introduction to direct instruction.* Boston: Allyn & Bacon.

Mastropieri, M. A., & Scruggs, T. E. (2004). *The inclusive classroom: Strategies for effective instruction.* Upper Saddle River, NJ: Prentice-Hall.

REFERENCES

McTighe, J., & Wiggins, G. (2004). *Understanding by design, professional development workbook.* Alexandria, VA: Association for Supervision and Curriculum Development.

Olympia, D., Andrews, D., Valum, L., & Jenson, W. (1993). *Homework teams: Homework management strategies for the classroom.* Longmont, CO: Sopris West.

Pidek, K. (1991). *Assignment notebooks.* Hoffman Estates, IL: Success by Design.

Rhode, G., Jenson, W. R, & Reavis, H. K. (1993). *The tough kid book: Practical classroom management strategies.* Longmont, CO: Sopris West.

Schumaker, J. B., Deshler, D. D., Alley, G. R., & Warner, M. M. (1983). *Learning strategies curriculum: LINKS strategy.* Lawrence, KS: University of Kansas.

Schumaker, J. B., Nolan, S. M., & Deshler, D. D. (1985). *Learning strategies curriculum: The error monitoring strategy.* Lawrence, KS: University of Kansas.

Silbert, J., Carnine, D., & Stein, M. (1990). *Direct instruction mathematics* (2nd ed.). Columbus, OH: Merrill.

Snyder, K. (1987). A problem solving strategy. *Academic Therapy, 23*(2), 261–263.

Sprick, R. S. (2006). *Discipline in the secondary classroom: A positive approach to behavior management* (2nd ed.). San Francisco: Jossey-Bass.

Starlin, C.M. (1989). *Curriculum based assessment.* Eugene, OR: University of Oregon.

Stiggins, R., Arter, J., Chappuis, J., & Chappuis, S. (2006). *Classroom assessment for student learning.* Portland, OR: Educational Testing Service.

Taylor, B. M., Pearson, P. D., Peterson, D. S., & Rodriguez, M. C. (2003). Reading growth in higher-poverty classrooms: The influence of teacher practices that encourage cognitive engagement in literacy learning, *Elementary School Journal, 104,* 3–28.